The Early American Table

THE
Early American Table

FOOD AND SOCIETY IN
THE NEW WORLD

Trudy Eden

Northern Illinois University Press

DeKalb

© 2008 by Northern Illinois University Press
Published by the Northern Illinois University Press, DeKalb, Illinois   60115
Manufactured in the United States using acid-free, postconsumer recycled paper
All Rights Reserved

Library of Congress Cataloging-in-Publication Data

Eden, Trudy.
The early American table:
food and society in the new world / Trudy Eden.
p.   cm.
Includes bibliographical references and index.
ISBN 978-0-87580-383-8 (clothbound : alk. paper)
1. Food habits—Social aspects—United States. 2. United States—
Social life and customs—To 1775. I. Title.
GT2853.U5E34 2008
394.1'2—dc22   2007028857

To Blakie and Hunter

Table of Contents

Preface

*E*very history book tells two stories, one the main subject of the book, the other how that book came to be. In many cases, and this book is no exception, the second story is nearly as complicated as the first. This study began with simple curiosity as to how early modern people cultivated good health. The search for the answer became progressively more complicated, and it took months to arrive at the conclusion that all sources pointed to food. To get from there to this book has taken years. Numerous people and institutions have supported my effort. You all have my sincerest thanks.

First there were papers and then a dissertation, all with financial assistance from the Department of the History of Science, Medicine, and Technology at Johns Hopkins University. Intellectual assistance came from my two main advisors, Gert Brieger and Jack P. Greene. They must have wondered more than once what I was doing and where I thought I was going. Nevertheless, they assisted me in countless ways throughout the dissertation process and after. In addition to professors Brieger and Greene, members of my dissertation committee—Jerry Bylebyl, Toby Ditz, Ron Walters, Larry Principe, and Robert Forster—furthered the process with their rigorous questions and insightful suggestions for the future direction of the project. Although not on my committee, Sidney Mintz also helped me shape this project in its early stages. In addition, Bob Kargon gave at the time and has continued to give invaluable counsel and support.

The transformation of the dissertation into this book would not have happened without the time, effort, patience, and advice of Nate Didier, Susan

Flett, Samuel Gladden, Robert Martin, Eric Sampson, Stuart Tufty, Charlotte Wells, Walter Woodward, Eric Wright, and the anonymous readers—all of whom read the manuscript at least once. Melody Herr at Northern Illinois University Press guided me gently and with great skill through the editorial process. Susan Bean, Julia Fauci, Pippa Letsky, and the rest of the staff at the Press all worked hard to make this book the best it could be.

The Virginia Historical Society, the College of Physicians of Philadelphia, the Huntington Library, and Dean Julia Wallace of the College of Social and Behavioral Sciences at the University of Northern Iowa, all provided me with financial assistance for research. Rosemary Meany and the cheerful ILS staff at the University of Northern Iowa Rod Library acquired numerous sources that I would have had to travel far to get. And I would like to thank presses for permission to use parts of my previously published essays: "'This Fatal Cake': The Ideals and Realities of Republican Virtue in Eighteenth-Century America" from *Eating in Eden: Food and American Utopias,* edited by Etta M. Madden and Martha L. Finch, 2006, used by permission of University of Nebraska Press; "The Art of Preserving: How Cooks in Early Virginia Used Nature to Control Nature," *Eighteenth-Century Life* 23 (1999): 13–23, used by permission of Duke University Press; "Food, Assimilation, and the Malleability of the Human Body in Early Virginia" from *A Centre of Wonders: The Body in Early America,* edited by Janet Moore Lindman and Michele Lise Tarter, copyright 2001 by Cornell University, used by permission of Cornell University Press.

The hardest aspect of acknowledgments is thanking those people who have lived this project with me in one way or another. Eve Dolan and Betty DeBerg listened and gave their support. Mark Eden has listened to me, supported me, and read and discussed the manuscript for years. This book would not be in existence were it not for him. Dhirendra Vajpeyi gave invaluable moral support and professional advice when I most needed it. Finally, this volume is dedicated to Hunter and Blakie Eden. They were young, innocent, and totally helpless when they got sucked into the vortex known as "mom's book." Nevertheless they wholeheartedly helped from beginning to end.

THE EARLY AMERICAN TABLE

*I*n May 1607 over one hundred English colonists founded Jamestown in the tidewater region of Virginia. Trusting accounts of America that depicted a fruitful land where food of all kinds grew naturally or with little effort, the Virginia Company of London had supplied limited provisions for the colonists in the belief that they would soon harvest the bounty of the New World. Yet, during the colony's first year, hunger plagued the settlement and controversies over food resulted in the dismissal of at least one leader. When John Smith took charge of Jamestown in 1608, the English were facing starvation. A former mercenary soldier whose adventures had already taken him across Europe, Smith knew the secret to survival in an inhospitable land— imitate the natives. He instructed the colonists to forage in the forest and, risking his own life, managed to obtain a supply of maize from local Indians. If he had expected gratitude in return for his efforts, however, he was disappointed. The English colonists told Smith flatly that they would not eat "savage trash."[1]

Why did these starving Englishmen turn down food? Was there something particular about wild foods or Indian maize that rendered them unacceptable? What did the colonists expect to happen if they ate these foods? What did they really mean by "savage trash"? The answers lie in the colonists' ideas concerning food, the human body, and human society. Even in the face of extreme hunger, food security for these Englishmen was a matter as much of quality as of quantity because, they believed, food shaped their personal identity and prescribed their status in society.

In 1607 English people considered themselves part of an organic world in which identity depended on the environment, and food was the most important element of that environment. Food molded and defined individual identity when the body used nutrients for growth and regeneration. The process was never neutral because the qualities, or characteristics, of foods were translated into corresponding physical, mental, moral, and spiritual qualities of the eater. Together, these qualities fell under the rubric "health." It followed that savage foods produced savage people, and coarse foods produced coarse people. Refined foods, in contrast, produced refined, virtuous people.

Virtue, in the early modern period, meant excellent health in every sense. In English society a person's virtue (or lack thereof) was arguably his or her single most important trait. Virtue distinguished a gentleman from a laborer, a leader from a follower. Because a properly fed person—one who had food security—was virtuous and because the presence or absence of virtue determined one's social status, food played a significant role in the maintenance of the English social hierarchy. For colonists creating a new society in a world lacking most of the traditional status markers, therefore, specific foods were crucial to the construction of the social order.

The Jamestown colonists told John Smith that they would not eat "savage trash" because they feared a regular diet of native foods could very possibly transform them into a lower class of human beings. The perception of food scarcity was not merely an issue of quantity. Quality mattered as well—and quality to the English meant, at the very least, English food. Within that category there existed numerous other qualitative distinctions, which at a more secure time would have swayed their food choices. At that moment, however, their choices were limited.

Evidence of this philosophy about food, personal health, and social status, appearing throughout seventeenth-century colonial records, suggests why English immigrants to North America endeavored to reestablish English foods and food habits. Colonists cleared forests and created fields where they planted English seeds and pastured English livestock. By the end of the century, many colonists and foreign observers believed that, on the whole, British Americans ate better than their social counterparts in England, though they did not enjoy the refined diet that their nutritional philosophy required for virtue.

In this era of colonial prosperity, however, conceptions of the natural world were changing. The older model featuring a malleable body gave way to a new model, which compared the body to a machine that to a large extent withstood environmental influences. More durable and mechanical, this body had different requirements for virtue. Its proper diet—known as a "middling diet"—consisted of foods that were neither refined nor coarse. Because most colonial Americans considered their own diets "middling," they concluded they were a virtuous people.

For many British Americans in the middle of the eighteenth century, scarcity such as that experienced by the first generation of Jamestown colonists was a thing of the past, yet concerns about food security had not disappeared. Americans living in a land of overabundance believed it was possible to sacrifice virtue by overconsuming refined foods and, in fact, pointed to evidence of such corruption. Consequently, moderation, a custom involving both the quantity and the quality of foods eaten, gained new emphasis as a hallmark of virtue.

This study illustrates how British Americans' beliefs about food security influenced their perception of themselves and their place in their local communities as well as in the British empire. In their opinion, both the quantity and the quality of the food they ate affected their health, personal characteristics, and social status. Despite a changing nutritional philosophy and an increasing abundance and variety of foods, food security remained as important to individual and social identity in 1776 as it was in 1607.

PART ONE

The Individual Golden Mean

CHAPTER

ONE

In the spring of 1650, fifteen Englishmen and three Englishwomen made the conscious decision to become cannibals. They refused, however, to eat flesh of the opposite sex. According to the personal account of Henry Norwood, they came to their decision in the following way. The previous September they and over three hundred passengers and crew left London on the ship *Virginia Merchant* bound for Virginia. In early November, a storm forced the *Merchant* onto breeches off Cape Hatteras. No sooner did the crew successfully dislodge the ship than another violent storm arose, which broke all but one of the ship's masts. When the storm passed, the crippled *Merchant* floundered off the mainland until another strong gale blew up and rammed the *Merchant* hour after hour. When the sea finally calmed, on 12 November 1650, neither captain, crew, nor passengers knew where they were. With one mast remaining, they proceeded weakly. A great but gentle wind pushed them, they thought, west toward Virginia. In fact, it sent them east. In such a compromised state, they could do nothing but go.[1]

Several weeks later, with their water gone and most of their food either eaten or spoiled, each survivor received only 1.6 ounces of ship's biscuit per day from the remaining supplies. They resorted to eating rats and scraping barrels for crumbs and sawdust. Finally, a westerly wind batted them back toward North America, and fifty-six days after leaving Cape Hatteras they came to an island somewhere off the North American coast. After staying overnight, the captain and passengers abandoned Norwood and his seventeen companions with some ship's biscuits and a few guns for shooting fowl. According to Norwood, the group left behind then built huts, one for the women and a larger one for the men. While winter continued they gathered oysters and killed geese and ducks. When the weather turned warmer a couple of months later, however, the water fowl migrated, the spring rains flooded the oyster beds, and the survivors were left with no hope.[2]

It was not long before one of the women died. Norwood, as leader of their group, visited the remaining two women who were themselves at death's door. "[Convert] her dead carcase into food," he told them. He did not mean for the women to get up and cook their companion for the group to share as carefully as they had their ducks, geese, oysters, and ship's biscuits. He meant that the two of them alone should eat their hut mate. They did. When the men died (there were eventually four), Norwood followed the same practice. Only men ate the dead men. Finally the thirteen survivors were rescued by Virginia colonists.[3]

That the group contemplated eating and, in fact, did eat human flesh in order to survive was not the main concern. Accounts of survivors who ate their dead companions were not new to English readers. It was a practice called the law of the sea. Their main concern was the origin of their food. They made distinctions on the basis of sex even in the case of extreme want. Food security to them not only meant quantity, it meant quality. Clearly Norwood and his companions thought very differently about food than we do today.

Early modern Europeans believed that their identity depended on what they ate. In their world (lacking even a glimmer of genetics), differences between humans depended completely on heat and moisture, and the major sources of these were the foods people ate and the climate in which they lived. Heat and moisture determined sex, appearance, intelligence, character, morality, and all other aspects of human nature. Heat and moisture levels were unstable and fluctuated constantly, however, so a change in diet meant a change in person. The degree of change depended on how greatly the new diet differed from the old. The only limit on this human plasticity was the fact of their humanity. This, at least, was guaranteed by the Bible, which affirmed the fixity of the species and assured anxious believers that an impenetrable barrier separated humanity from the rest of the animal kingdom.[4]

The belief in the malleability of human nature and its dependence on food was widely accepted in seventeenth-century England. After 1500, numerous authors published dietaries and other texts that educated their readers on human nature and the influences working on it. The dietaries stressed the importance of food and the fact that, although fluctuating heat and moisture levels caused corresponding changes, those levels could be controlled in order to achieve excellent health and virtue. One of these dietaries—the *Regimen Sanitatis Salerni,* an annotation of a twelfth-century didactic poem that originated at the medical school in Salerno, Italy—appears frequently in early American inventories and could have been in the cargo of the *Virginia Merchant.* It resembles numerous health texts written in English in the sixteenth and seventeenth centuries. Although these texts varied according to the personalities of their authors, much of the advice they gave was similar, in large part because their ideas came from the same ancient sources.[5]

HUMANS IN AN UNSTABLE UNIVERSE— THE FOUR HUMORS

The idea that human nature fluctuated with heat and moisture arose out of a broader metaphysical theory that the entire universe was composed of four immaterial qualities—hot and its opposite, cold; moist and its opposite, dry. These qualities combined and appeared in physical form as the four elements: earth, air, water, and fire. Each and every human was seen as a miniature reflection of the universe; as a concept this was known as the microcosm within the macrocosm. In the seventeenth century, no one illustrated this concept more beautifully than Robert Fludd. The title page of his text *The History of the Macrocosm and the Microcosm* represents the macrocosm as a circle of coiled rope being turned by time, a goat-footed winged creature carrying an hourglass. Concentric circles just inside the rope represent, in order, the fixed stars, the eight planets of the Ptolemaic universe, and the four elements and their qualities (represented by unmarked circles). Only the sun and the moon interrupt the flow of the planetary orbits. Touching five points on a black circle that symbolizes the outer limits of the macrocosm is man, the microcosm. He stands before his earthly essences (the humors), which were the theoretical organic combinations of the four elements known as choler, blood, phlegm, and melancholy. Choler (*cholera*), hot and dry, is represented by a circle of fire. Blood (*sanguis*), represented by air, was warm and moist. Water signified phlegm (*pituita*), which was cold and moist. Earth signified melancholy (*melancholia*), cold and dry.[6] The sun, moon, and planets appear again in the illustration because of their influence over human nature and the character of individual lives and life cycles. Like the macrocosm, the microcosm was changing constantly, endlessly, and unpredictably.

The elements comprised the building blocks of identity for all of nature. Therefore, the differences between things such as a rock and a tree, a tree and a frog, a frog and a human, or one human and another depended simply upon the ratio of their elements, a ratio that fluctuated greatly in organic nature. Early modern Europeans believed this process of flux to be one of transmutation: earth turned into water, fire, or air, or fire turned into earth, air, or water and so on. According to Aristotle, not only could the four elements transmute, in organisms they would definitely transmute, and when they did the organism changed as well.[7]

What caused elements to transmute? Because they were tangible forms of the qualities of heat and moisture, whatever altered heat and moisture in the universe affected the elements as well. These factors can be broadly defined as the environment. On a cosmic level (as shown by Robert Fludd), they were the sun and the moon. Globally, they were the climates and the seasons. Personally, six factors collectively known as the non-naturals—food, exercise, sleep, air, repletion (or fullness), and emotions—altered heat and moisture, and hence the elemental composition of the body. The degree of change depended on the variability of the factors. Eating foods other than the customary diet for one meal or one day would prompt fleeting, indistinguishable changes. A long-term radical dietary change was something else. In fact, it would be more appropriate to call human nature human *nurture* because of the almost complete lack of distinction between them. Nurture explained many of the differences between people as well as most of the changes undergone by each individual in his or her lifetime.[8]

As unyielding and chaotic as it sounds, this philosophy was not deterministic. Although the environment was the molding tool, humans believed they could control it to remake their physical, mental, moral, and emotional selves into any shape they wished, and as often as they wished. If, however, they found themselves, like Henry Norwood and the other *Virginia Merchant* passengers, stranded with few options, they lost most of this control.

THE UNSTABLE UNIVERSE WITHIN HUMANS— THE TEMPERAMENT

Like the outer cosmos, the inner universe was a swirl of air, water, fire, and earth. Different combinations of humors and transmutations of the elements created a myriad of human traits collectively known as the temperament, which, like the outer cosmos, could be anywhere from calm to tempestuous. The human temperament (also known as the complexion) depended on the ratio of the four humors and was the foundation of the philosophy of the humoral body. Authors who described the humors to their readers ranked blood over all other humors because of its balanced combination of heat and moisture. It nourished the body and repaired decay. Phlegm multiplied when faulty digestion occurred and then often combined with other humors and developed harmful characteristics. Choler, another corrupter of other humors, was hot, dry, light, and sharp. Found naturally in the body, it could also be extracted from the most refined elements of digested food. Finally, melancholy came from the dregs of pure blood. Although it mixed with all other humors, its combination with choler could incite internal heat so hot it generated lethally violent dispositions.[9]

As they did with the humors, early modern writers ordered the temperament types, the basic units of early modern identity, from least to most desirable. The melancholic temperament ranked lowest. Cold and dry, it fostered sadness, fear, and a slow-paced, brooding nature. Thomas Walkington, in *Optick Glasse of Humors,* thought melancholics to be either "Angel[s] of Heaven" or "Fiend[s] of Hell" because they lost themselves in "heavenly contemplation" or "cynical meditation." Many fell victim to suicide and all were "dead before their appointed time." They could be discerned by their dark complexions, sometimes described as black or earthy because of the predominance of the element of earth in their bodies. They usually had plain, thin hair. They digested poorly, had faint pulses, slept little, and were prone to fearful dreams. "To be short," wrote Levinus Lemnius, author of *The Touchstone of the Complexions*, "they are partakers of all those things that are common to beasts." Some resembled lions because they were "fierce, cruel, outrageous and terrible" and ready to kill their fellow men. Others acted like apes, mimicking without thinking. Yet others mirrored wolves because they were bloodsuckers.[10]

Choleric persons had more of the fire element than any others. Like their melancholic counterparts, they usually appeared lean in body, but often exhibited red or sallow skin, and black or auburn curly hair. They felt uncomfortable around hot things, slept little, and often dreamed of fire, conflict, or anger. Their inflammatory natures gave them the advantage of quick wits and the disadvantage of sharp voices, impatience, profligacy, boldness, inconstancy, and a propensity toward and talent for fighting.[11]

What choleric persons were, phlegmatic persons were not. Their cold and moist natures caused them to move and to learn slowly, and to lack courage. Often fat, slothful, and sleepy they digested their food poorly and dreamed of watery things or fish. They frequently were feeble, a condition that might be masked by their short thick statures. Finally, because good wit and understanding required a tempered heat, most phlegmatics were dull.[12]

Englishmen and women believed that sanguine persons most nearly approximated perfection. A sanguine complexion looked white and ruddy. Walkington described it using the royal colors of purple and scarlet. Plenty of hair, often tinted red, could accompany it. Tending toward fleshiness, the sanguine person possessed large veins and a great, full pulse. Types of this complexion loved to have fun, and they did so by laughing, singing, enjoying the music of others, drinking good wine, and eating excellent food. They could learn any science easily, seldom lost their tempers, and were gentle and amorous. They digested their foods perfectly. According to the *Regimen Sanitatis*, they were "free, not covetous but liberal." Other descriptions of this ideal temperament type linked it to royalty and even godliness.[13]

Not only did the whole person have a temperament, but body parts such as the brain, heart, liver, stomach, and genitals did as well. Physical and personality traits evidenced an organ's temperament. For example, a hot-natured brain caused a very red and hot face, fast-growing curly black hair, visible veins in the eyes, and excessive matter in the nose, ears, and eyes. A "hot-brained" person got headaches if he or she consumed hot-natured fluids or meats. Often an organ's complexion reflected a mixture of qualities. A heavy, aching head and superfluities in the nose indicated a brain distempered hot and moist, and so did head pain upon exposure to hot southern winds, strange restless dreams, and an imperfect wit. Even though authors placed everyone within only four temperaments, all health texts emphasized the individuality of each person because of the number of factors affecting the body and its parts. Authors offered the general categories to their readers only as guidelines, in order to help the readers first determine their own natures and then modify them as they wished.[14]

THE INDIVIDUAL GOLDEN MEAN

When authors of early modern health texts framed descriptions of the four temperaments in terms of physical, mental, and moral traits, they followed the theories of Hippocrates (from the fifth century B.C.), Galen (from the second century A.D.), and other early Greek and Roman thinkers. These theories were still considered valid sources of medical and scientific knowledge into the seventeenth century. These theories defined health holistically and so expansively that health encompassed all aspects of identity.

Ancient and early modern people regarded health and illness in terms of performance. One was ill if he could not get up and perform his daily tasks. This belief came from the ancient philosophy of health. Hippocrates believed health to be a "crasis" or a "regular balance of humors." Optimum health was, simply and elegantly, a perfectly adapted "movement" resulting from "breath, warmth, [digestion, . . . and] complete regimen." Furthermore, people's mental health, which included their perception, intelligence, memory, morality, and sanity, depended on the relative amounts of heat and moisture in their body as well, which was also subject to changes in daily regimen. Hippocrates wrote: "It is possible . . . to rouse intelligence or engender stupidity, by the addition or abstraction of water in proportion to the amount of heat in the body."[15]

Galen relied on Hippocrates, Aristotle, and Plato in his insistence that the nature of the soul fully depended on the state of the body. In addition, he stressed that true health existed in the whole person, not just in functions and disorders. As such, health exhibited a great latitude, which extended from perfection to the state in which a person just escaped impaired daily activity. Health depended on food, drink, and daily activities.[16]

In addition to regarding health holistically, ancient thinkers viewed health as balance. In ancient Greek philosophy, balance was the center between extremes. It was known as the golden mean. The closer to the exact center a person was, the healthier he was. Galen referred to this human golden mean as the "best constitution," one that was precisely proportioned as a whole and that possessed parts fully shaped so as to perform their designated functions to the best advantage. Physically, this perfect person represented the golden mean of all extremes in all his parts. He had a perfect internal elemental balance, exactly between cold and hot, wet and dry. One could determine the individual golden mean by observing all the traits that comprised his temperament. The person who achieved the golden mean was poised halfway between negative dichotomies such as emaciated and fat, hairy and bald, soft and hard, white and black, large- and small-veined, sluggish and alert, voluptuous and frigid. He was naturally "good-spirited, affectionate, generous and wise." He ate and drank properly, guided by flawless innate appetites. He performed "faultless mental and physical activities" and enjoyed a delicate sense of touch, exactly between hard and soft. Galen used *arete*, the Greek word for virtue, when he described this perfect person. Like Hippocrates, Galen believed a Greek statue, the *Canon of Polykleitos*, to be virtue's stone icon because the statue exemplified flawlessness in form and function and, consequently, in nature.[17]

ACHIEVING THE GOLDEN MEAN

When health text authors wrote about the temperaments, they were giving their readers a guide to achieving virtue, the individual golden mean. Their descriptions of the temperaments helped readers determine their own temperaments and their goal, which was always the sanguine temperament because this resulted from the true balance of hot and cold, wet and dry. Virtue was, quite literally for early modern Europeans, the balance of heat and moisture within the body. Virtue permeated flesh and soul and melded them together. As the above descriptions of the basic temperaments indicate, form and function were so closely connected that people believed they could detect the presence of virtue by looking at the shape and proportion of a person's arms, legs, trunk, and face, and by evaluating his or her temperament.

Although only a few people were believed to be born with the balanced temperament that fell within the golden mean and signified virtue, it was believed that other people could acquire it. In either case a person had to work at keeping the golden mean by living a lifestyle that fostered it. One needed the knowledge to detect the signs of imbalance and to determine the remedy, and most important, one needed the wherewithal to do something about that imbalance. Not everyone could afford to buy the necessary foods, to modify their exercise, or to live in areas with fresh clear air, so this philosophy in early modern England was rightly considered a wealthy man's prerogative.

Such human engineering worked through the conscious manipulation of the environmental non-naturals to influence or exchange the body's humors. Of all the non-naturals, food was the most important because the body turned it into flesh, blood, and bone, and its effects could not be quickly reversed. All foods were classified to six degrees of heat and moisture and could be grown, prepared, and consumed with great attention to their effects on the body. As for the other non-naturals, air, both indoor and outdoor, ranged from humid to dry and hot to cold. Dry air drew moisture out of the body whereas moist air suffused it. Hot air forced the cold deep within the body, which is why people from Africa were considered generally melancholic. Cold air, then, drove heat inside. Exercise heated the body and dried it through perspiration. Sleep restored the body's elemental balance that was disturbed by the day's activities. Repletion, a complex concept meaning fullness, comprised the general level of bodily moisture that could be excreted through urine, sweat, tears, semen, and menstrual blood as well as the fullness of the digestive tract. Regular evacuation kept the body balanced. Infrequent or overly frequent evacuation disrupted that balance. Finally, the emotions heated, cooled, or dried the body. For example, anger heated, sadness cooled, and tears dehydrated.[18]

The six non-naturals worked as a system in which the individual factors could function in harmony or in opposition with each other. If, for example, a person lived in a very hot dry climate, he could minimize its effects by exercising less and thereby not heating up and drying out his body even more. He could eat moist foods to counterbalance the influence of the air. To give a different example, an angry person (also known as hot-tempered) could counter this tendency by sitting still and drinking and eating cooling beverages and foods. These would not necessarily be foods with a cool temperature but, rather, foods possessing large amounts of phlegm or melancholy. Sleep would also help restore some balance. A sad person, however, considered to be leaning toward or clearly melancholy could eat warming foods and get more exercise—though only a moderate amount, lest he lose precious moisture.

Early modern dietaries characterized the humoral effects of food on the body in two ways. One way was to consider food's humoral effects as building blocks, whereby the body used the humors in foods to repair or replace worn-out body parts. The other effects of food on the body were more general and could be discerned by scrutinizing the temperament. Authorities emphasized the importance and flexibility of food in this process and always framed their advice in terms of the quality of the food; they also thought the amount of food a person ate affected his humoral balance. Hippocrates observed that the bulk of food a person ate had to be proportioned on an individual basis to his or her activity level. This ratio could be detected only by constant observation of bodily increase or decrease, and even then it was difficult. If one had to choose a single rule for eating—indeed a single rule for achieving the individual golden mean—out of the numerous suggestions formulated over the centuries of western European civilization, this would be it: that the quantity of food a person eats should match his or her activity level. From observance of this rule came virtue; from its avoidance came intellectual, spiritual, and physical degradation, even death.[19]

Evaluating Food

The humoral qualities of foods corresponded to humors within the body. For example, garlic, onions, leeks, mustard, pepper, and sweetmeats, all extremely hot and dry, promoted choler and counteracted phlegm. All "slimy" and "cleaving" meats, new cheese, fish, lamb, offal, and cucumbers produced phlegm with their very cold moisture, and thus they opposed choler. Because beef, goat, hare, boar, salt flesh, salt fish, coleworts, all legumes except white peas, coarse brown bread, thick or black wine, old cheese, old fish, and the great fish of the sea contained large amounts of melancholy, they greatly increased its presence within the body and counteracted the most valued sanguine humor. Sugar, on the other hand, was perceived as a perfect combination of heat and moisture and represented an excellent source of the sanguine humor.[20]

Early modern people determined the elemental quality of a food by its taste, that is, the action of a food on the taste buds. They differentiated five elementally hot tastes (hot, sweet, salty, bitter, and sharp) and three elementally cold tastes (rough, sour, and harsh). A sweet food like sugar refreshed the tongue and therefore had to be very much like the balanced human body, hot and moist. Once ingested, sweet foods cleansed and nourished the body. Sour foods caused the taste buds to constrict, an indication that they were cold and dry. They cooled the body but hastened aging if taken in large quantities. Salty foods dried phlegm but could disturb the stomach if taken in excess. Bitter foods offered little nourishment.[21]

In daily eating, humoral suitability was not the only dietary aspect affecting human nature. The substance or texture of a food mattered a great deal as well. Substance contributed directly to the suitability of the body's "juice," a term for chyle, the milky liquid made by the stomach from ingested foods. The liver turned chyle into blood, and the rest of the body turned it into flesh, bone, mind, and spirit. Foods could make either refined blood or gross blood depending on their textures, of which dietitians recognized three. Dense or heavy foods that the stomach digested with difficulty, such as hard cheese, beans, rice, all whole grains, unleavened bread, and pottage, fell into the gross category. Examples of light or delicate textures were poultry, wine, lettuce, and many of the aromatic herbs. They were considered refined, as in the highest quality. The third category of slimy or viscous foods, often referred to as unctuous, included butter, fish, and uncooked fruits. Often these three categories elided into two, gross and subtle, which early modern English people often interpreted in terms of freshness and delicacy. "Subtle" was the equivalent of balanced; "gross" on the other hand meant coarse and therefore unbalanced.

The textural quality of a food duplicated its characteristics in the eater. For example, lighter, fresher, more delicate foods—such as well-baked leavened bread made of pure wheat flour, fresh eggs, new milk, and soft cheeses—formed highly refined people, as did fowl of medium size and some of larger size (such as peacocks or swans), fish from stony and clear-running rivers, sweet fruits, the flesh of young animals, properly aged wine and ale, fat flesh such as bacon, and the liver and brains of poultry. On the other hand, the consumption of coarse foods such as the flesh of older animals, foods of poor quality, hard cheeses, raw herbs, chickpeas, fish from muddy waters, and all salted flesh would make a person coarse and prevent him or her from ever approximating the golden mean in appearance, wit, or ability.[22]

Digestion and Proper Eating

To a large degree the quantity and quality of foods were determined by their digestibility. Digestion took place not only in the stomach but also in the small intestine and liver, which broke foods down and combined them with blood, and in all body parts, where those foods were metabolized, a process known as assimilation. It would be hard to overestimate the importance of the digestive system, particularly the stomach, to achieving the individual golden mean. Digestion was the primary activity of corruption in the human body. Corruption arose from the oppression of nature by the self-imposed or forced misuse or abuse of the six non-naturals. Hippocrates saw the abuse as tripartite, including overwork, overindulgence, and overfeeding. Galen thought that individual occupations, poverty, excessive ambition, and slavery all oppressed human nature to different degrees. Early modern Europeans believed that physical, intellectual, and spiritual corruption—indications of a loss of the golden mean—most frequently began in the digestive tract as a result of eating too much, eating the wrong foods, or eating the right foods improperly.[23]

Sixteenth-century dietaries stated that the stomach resembled a simple cooking pot and that digestion was just a process of cooking. When the stomach received food, the body supplied heat and the stomach provided motion to "concoct" the food into chyle, which was said to resemble human milk. Belying the simplicity of the metaphor, the stomach had to be treated carefully because, if it were prevented from digesting foods well, grave problems would result. Just as a pot that is crammed full will not cook foods evenly or adequately, the dietary authors counseled, neither would a stomach. Foods would stagnate and decay. Furthermore, if one ate too much at one sitting, the pylorus at the base of the stomach might not open until all the foods had been digested. This delay induced corruption as well because the foods eaten first, having been held too long in that warm closed environment, putrefied and tainted the fresher stomach contents. Gravity assisted digestion, texts suggested, so that after eating one should stand upright for a short while, in order to allow the food to sink to the bottom of the stomach where it was believed digestion actually occurred. Of course, food would not sink so easily in a stuffed stomach. Walking could help if it were not too fast, because too much speed expelled the natural heat of the body, lowering the internal stomach temperature and retarding the already taxed digestive process. The small intestine further refined the chyle and passed it to the liver, which converted it into blood, the quality of which depended on the quantity and quality of the food eaten and the efficiency of digestion thus far. If the liver received poorly processed or faulty ingredients, it could process them only into substandard blood. Despite its poor quality, that blood traveled throughout the body through the veins and provided substandard materials for assimilation.[24]

Assimilation was the final stage of the digestive process. The body completed it in four steps using its four faculties, or agents of change, known as attraction, retention, transformation, and expulsion. First, when any body part needed rebuilding, it "attracted" from the blood the digested nutriment that most resembled itself. Second, because of the constant state of internal motion, the body "retained" the nutriment to transform it into human tissues during the lengthy third step. Finally, the body collected and expelled all useless substances.[25]

Although this understanding of digestion seems basic, ancient and early modern authorities puzzled over it. To Galen the process was neither clear-cut nor simple. First of all, what was a food and what was not? He classified a substance as a food if the body could assimilate it, which required some degree of qualitative similarity between the two. To Hippocrates food was any substance that provided being, growth, and strength. Aristotle stated that some believed proper food resembled the body while others firmly believed it differed. Proper nutrition did not require exact precision because the body would expel foods that varied too greatly and could not be assimilated. The ease with which a food assimilated and its amount of waste, called superfluities, determined a food's nutritional value. Foods with higher values could be assimilated quickly and simply, and they left little waste. Meat, which so closely resembles parts of the body, was regarded as highly nutritional. Dissimilar substances that required more time to assimilate and left greater quantities of superfluities fell into the least nutritious category. Most authorities placed vegetables there because they displayed little qualitative affinity with the human body and contained numerous superfluities.[26]

How did the body know what to assimilate and what not to? Galen thought assimilation was an "artistic process" because the body willfully and intentionally sought the nutrition it needed. He believed that an innate drive to preserve individual identity during constant bodily flux directed a person's appetite to the appropriate foods. Once found, the stomach "drank down" the foods and changed them into a form of nutriment that could be "received" by the veins. Each organ attracted the nutriment to it, "devoured" all of the useful fluids to the point of satisfaction, forced those fluids to adhere, and finally, when satisfied, assimilated them. The writer of the Hippocratic treatise "Nutriment" presented the concept as less aggressive. To him, proper nourishment varied because people, their habits, and their environments varied also. He too, however, believed that no one needed to be taught what to eat because his natural instinct guided him. Aristotle, on the other hand, stated that the ability to seek out proper nourishment was a psychic power, the presence of which defined life. He described the actual process of assimilation as an "active principle of growth, dwelling in the growing thing [that] lays hold of an acceding food which is potentially flesh and converts it into actual flesh."[27]

Philosophers also wondered what happened if the humoral quality of the nutriment differed from that of the body part using it. Would the body change? All authors agreed that it would. The process was adversarial rather than unilateral because all forms of nourishment exerted some effect upon the body even if slight. Only a diet that did not vary caused no physical alteration. If it differed in quality from the customary diet, the body changed readily or over time depending on the degree and rapidity of dietary change. To quote Galen: "whenever two bodies meet and engage over a considerable period of time in mutual conflict in relation to their alterations it is inevitable that each of them acts and is acted upon." Assimilation, then, was not a value-neutral bodily function. Rather, it resembled a negotiated and potentially hostile takeover in which the body altered and assimilated food, and the food in turn produced change within the body, mind, and soul.[28]

It is this aspect of digestive theory that employs the building block metaphor and suggests the wide latitude available for personal change. Just as a house built of brick and patched with straw is not of the same quality throughout, so too a body grown on high quality foods and then fed an inferior diet was not the same as before. However, as health texts were quick to point out, a body grown on foods of a lesser quality that then received a better diet would grow to be more balanced and would then more closely approximate the individual golden mean.

SECURITY IN AN INSECURE WORLD

Any nutritional philosophy has two parts: the food and the body that ingests it. In their elaborations early modern authors relied on two basic rules of Hippocrates. The first rule, of the quality of food, stated that like makes like, unlike makes unlike. It meant that each food had its own distinct identity, which did not disappear during digestion and that would affect the identity of the eater. If someone ate the same foods as always, he would not change. If he altered his diet, he would change. The perceived qualities of foods, therefore, transferred to the eater. A plentiful and varied diet of high quality fine foods created refined, virtuous, and talented people. A more restricted diet composed of poor quality coarse foods made the people who ate them coarse, even beastly. All foods, then, not only had the power to nourish, they had the power to shape who one was. The second Hippocratic rule, concerning quantity, held that the amount of food a person ate had to balance his activity level. Stuffing the stomach with more food than the body needed prevented complete digestion and caused physical, mental, and moral corruption. Not feeding it enough forced it to digest itself and led to an equally disastrous result. Improper eating also eroded the virtue of the eater and could lead him or her into a vicious circle of gluttony, in which excessive eating or eating the wrong foods pushed one out of the golden mean. To early modern people who followed this philosophy, complete food security meant far more than just having something digestible in one's stomach. The quality of food a person ate mattered as much as, perhaps even more than, the quantity. Alone or together, quality and quantity could maintain a person's identity or change it.

This dietary theory goes far in explaining the metaphysical universe in which Henry Norwood and his shipmates lived as they sought not only to survive but also to retain as much of their identity as possible. Food scarcity limited their choices and put pressure on the eaters to choose or compete for those food sources they deemed most valuable. Value was tightly bound to identity and virtue. The eaters' choices were not made strictly on the basis of keeping the physical body alive. Had that been the case, they would not have felt the need to make any choices at all and simply would have eaten anything that was edible.

Because food habits are often so deeply submerged in a culture, neither Norwood nor his companions might have consciously realized why they made the choices they did. The crucial issue is the consequences they thought their choices would produce. In the list Norwood gave of the foods they ate during their entire journey, most foods were standard English fare. Ducks, geese, ship's biscuits, oysters, even what they believed to be leeks, all were part of the English gastronomic lexicon. They and the effects of eating them would have been understood by this group. Despite the fact that Norwood and his group had been able to eat many foods within their normal food boundaries, they did cross over them when they ate rats and humans. The ship rats could be likened to squirrels, a foodstuff familiar to these English eaters, who could have at least roughly anticipated some of their humoral effects before they ate them and determined more after they tasted them. Furthermore, the rats were, if nothing else, products of the English climate and so would have had the basic cold and moist characteristic of all things English. So this may have been a boundary crossed without too much difficulty.

Eating a woman, though, was a different matter. The problem with eating human flesh was that the consequences were all too predictable. Dietaries stated that the most nutritional food was that which most closely resembled the human body because it could be digested with the greatest ease and turned into flesh with the least amount of waste. While under normal conditions human flesh was out of the question, for cultural reasons, it was not so for the purposes of survival. Cannibalism for survival was the custom of the sea. Norwood and his group understood this rule. Yet, even under such severe circumstances, they recognized that they still had a choice. That choice was sex. Women were thought to be colder and moister than men. This elemental difference not only explained what early modern people believed to be standard female traits, it explained why some individuals were women in the first place. Early modern men and women believed they had the same sexual organs. The heat of the male body caused those organs to descend to the exterior of the body. In other words, the penis was an extruded uterus turned inside out in the process. Testicles were external ovaries. Therefore, they believed that if the internal heat of the male body was reduced and the moisture increased, say by a diet of human female flesh, the penis and testicles would ascend back into the abdominal cavity and the male would become female. For early modern people, such an occurrence seemed entirely possible, as attested by the case of a French woman whose sex changed because of the heat she generated and the moisture she lost while chasing hogs.[29] The men and women of Norwood's group had a dietary option, hence an identity option. By choosing to eat human flesh only of their own sex, they also chose to retain their sexual identity and keep at least one distinction among them. By doing so, they maintained one of the most basic and important boundaries of their traditional social structure. How they did so is unusual but the fact that they did is not.

CONCLUSION

Galen wrote that every day a part of each and every one of us dies and our bodies must regenerate those parts anew. The nature of being human in a humoral world was to participate in the struggle to maintain physiological stability within a chaotic universe. Early modern Europeans believed they could control this stability through the manipulation of their environment, particularly their food, hence they believed they could place themselves within the golden mean.

When the customary diet is altered, the social order changes. Food has such remarkable social capabilities because of its several unique properties. First, it is eaten, digested, and turned into the body. Second, all foods exhibit organic characteristics of their own. In addition, they have sensually detectable traits such as texture, color, smell, and shape, and they grow in environments that can all be given social value. Furthermore, food has to be grown or gathered, prepared, and served, all activities that can add to or detract from social value. Food, therefore, is a perfect tool for embodying social relationships—because of all these properties, and also because everyone needs to eat and for most people eating alone is an exception rather than a rule. Food can be and is used symbolically to alter social boundaries as well as to establish or break down social bonds. The belief of early modern people that the consumption of different foods could prompt unknown changes is not uncommon. People in many different cultures and times have believed that food transforms them, that food can shift characteristics from one group to another, and seventeenth-century English people were no exception.[30]

*T*he philosophy of food security affected the social structure of early modern England. Although all English people ate many foods in common, people of higher status had more variety, adequate quantity, and better quality in their diets. Thus they were the only social group who enjoyed continual food security. They were also the only ones entitled to govern. This perception supported an unbalanced society, in which the few people at one extreme of the social spectrum—not the mean —held most of the power in society.

An excellent description of this phenomenon is a sociological analysis of England written by William Harrison and published in 1587. Harrison, a parish rector, first gave a description of all the people of Britain (meaning England, Scotland, and Wales), a group united by the fact that they lived on the same island and in the same general climate. Their common inhabitance imbued the British with constitutional similarities. They were, believed Harrison, of "good complexion, tall of stature, strong in body, white of color, and thereto of great boldness and courage in the wars." Because of their cold moist nature, Britons were courteous, sincere, and as intelligent as any people who lived in warmer climates. In addition, they were hardy and long-lived, retaining their good looks past middle age (believed to end around age sixty). Many old men lived to be eighty and some reached one hundred. A further sign of the hardy constitutions of the British was the fact that when they died their carcasses remained intact without corrupting for four or five days (in some countries decay began immediately). Britain had a northerly position on the globe, and its cold air drove the heat of the inhabitants' bodies inward, increasing the efficiency and capacity of their digestive systems and causing them to "crave a little more ample nourishment" than people from warmer regions. As a result, Britons ate more plentifully than others.[1]

FOODS THAT UNITED THE ENGLISH

Strengthening the sense of identity among the English was a common diet comprised of the same basic foods. This commonality derived from the climate and, of course, the culture. The food groups were bread, pottage, meat, fish, dairy products, and fruits and vegetables.

Bread

All English eaters at the time ate many types of bread. Wheat flour made the finest and the healthiest. Its gluten content enabled leavening, which gave it a lighter consistency than other breads. There were many places in England where wheat did not grow, and where locals who could not afford to purchase imported wheat (anyone below the level of gentry) used whatever grew best. Rye, barley, oats, peas, and (for the very desperate) beans were all ground into flour and used.

Bakers produced numerous varieties of bread with these basic flours. Manchet, made of sifted wheat flour, was white and light whether made with a sourdough starter, ale-barm, or even without leavening, in which case it had a denser texture. Sometimes butter, eggs, and milk were added to the bread, giving it the lightest consistency of all. Cheat and brown breads, made of coarser flour, were much darker and heavier, but they were still made of wheat and were well leavened. Sometimes wheat and rye were combined, and the mixture, known as maslin, formed a bread of the same name, darker and heavier than brown bread although still with some leavening capacity. Barley bread was baked in either leavened or unleavened cakes, in an oven or on the hearth under a pot covered with hot ashes. Some people preferred its sweeter taste. Its dense texture made it a useful trencher, an edible plate on which other foods were served. Depending on the amount of leavening and the style of baking, barley bread could be almost of the same quality as brown wheat bread, some believed, although darker and somewhat more sour. English cooks also used rye, wheat, barley, oats, peas, and beans to make flatbreads, which could be little more than ground grain or pulse mixed with water and cooked on a griddle or baking stone. The mixture was sometimes left overnight in what was known as a sour trough to make it lighter.[2]

Pottage

Another major food category that bound the English together as a group was pottage. As one sixteenth-century author put it: "Potage is not so moch used in al Crystendom as it is used in Englande." All members of English society ate it, and like bread, it was infinitely flexible. Its basic ingredients were two: a cereal or pulse and a liquid. Basic to all human civilizations that cook, pottage was made in a pot over a slow fire. The English ate it savory or sweet. Sweet pottages had a cereal base and often contained dried fruit and spices, of which frumenty, a wheat pottage made from the whole grain and milk, was an English classic. In areas where wheat did not grow, cooks substituted barley or oats.[3]

The English usually ate sweet pottages at breakfast or supper but not at the main meal of the day. If pottage was eaten then it was savory, although this is not to say that savory pottages were not eaten at breakfast, for they were. Cooks made a pottage with wheat, barley, or oats, but they could and often did make it with peas or lentils as well. When they desired, they added meat, bones, herbs, and vegetables such as onions, peas, or beans. With the addition of more liquid, cooks could turn pottages into stews or soups or could cook them down to become quite thick, depending on the needs and desires of the cook and the eaters. These pottages should not be considered unappetizing or dull. People of the time were familiar with a wide range of flavors and were quite aware of fine differences in taste and texture. Everyone could embellish a pottage with greens, roots, herbs, fruits, and nuts that grew wild or were cultivated in gardens, so people would not have thought they ate the same thing every day, even if they ate pottage every day.[4]

In the sixteenth century, Gervase Markham's *The English House-Wife* offered readers pottage recipes that illustrate the variability of this food. He counseled his readers that his "ordinary" pottage, made with oatmeal, could be used to feed the poor as well as the rich. His recipe is very simple and inexpensive. Find some mutton (meat of a sheep at least three years old) with good bones for flavor, cut the meat into pieces, put it into a pot with the bones and water. Add herbs and oatmeal and bring everything to a boil. Stirring often, cook the entire mixture down by a third and add salt.[5]

Markham gave his readers another recipe, this time for what he felt was an oatmeal pottage of the "best and daintiest kind." "Dainty," in sixteenth-century parlance, meant "refined." This pottage differs from the ordinary one in the quality and variety of meats used. Veal and kid are both meat of young animals and would have been more expensive than mutton. The meat is left whole and probably would have been served in larger chunks, not as bits and pieces within the pottage itself. More vegetables are used, as is verjuice, the juice of unripe grapes. These ingredients all give the basic pottage a different flavor although it costs more than the ordinary pottage.[6]

Meat

Like bread and pottage, meat-eating united English people. Foreign visitors to the upper strata of English society frequently commented on the amount of meat eaten by the English as compared to the inhabitants of other European countries. By the mid-sixteenth century, the English preferred beef to mutton. Accounts of huge banquets with haunches of beef, venison, mutton, and other prime cuts are legendary, but these banquets were not ordinary affairs. Fowl, wild and domestic game such as rabbits, coneys, and venison, and a wide variety of fish were all eaten on those occasions. Daily meals were not as extravagant. One account tells of sausages and cabbage given to children at an ordinary noon meal. The adults at the table ate pike with a sauce, blackbirds, larks, woodcocks, and partridges. Even this meal may have been more elaborate than customary, for one of the guests commented that the number of dishes made him feel as if he was at a wedding. This is not to say that the upper strata of English society ate only choice meats. All the English ate the lesser cuts of meat such as whole heads, brains, snouts, palates, tongues, hearts, kidneys, livers, lungs, stones, udders, sweetbreads, intestines, blood, fat, and marrow. Roasts, steaks, and other more desirable cuts of meat, however, appeared on the tables of only well-to-do eaters.[7]

Fish

In Tudor times, fish days made up half of the calendar year. Cod and whitefish caught off the coast of Iceland and in the North Sea were widely eaten, as were lobsters, crabs, shrimp, prawns, oysters, and mussels. Salted fishes such as herrings, salmon, eels, and sprats were a popular and less expensive alternative to fresh fish. Herrings were on the lower end of the fish hierarchy. Cooks prepared fish in numerous ways. Along with just about everything else the English cooked at this time period, they boiled, roasted, or baked fish as well. In addition, they pickled or soused fish and baked the richer, oilier types in savory pies. Regardless of the cooking method, fish was usually highly seasoned.[8]

Dairy Products

All members of English society consumed milk, buttermilk, cream, butter, and fresh and hard cheeses. On a basic level the English combined milk with a cereal grain to make pottage. They also curdled milk with ale to make a drink called posset. If one slowly heated milk, buttermilk, or whey and gently curdled it with rennet or another curdling agent such as nettles, curds resulted. This fresh cheese was eaten alone or with honey, cream, ale, or wine, depending on the desires of the eater and the available ingredients. Because curds molded or spoiled quickly they had to be eaten in short order. They could be made into tarts or fried as fritters. The highest form of fresh curd was junket, essentially curdled cream. Eaters usually mixed it with sugar and ate it with rosewater (water recondensed after the distillation of rose petals) as a dessert. If chopped herbs were added to curds, the resulting dish was spermyse.[9]

The English made and consumed hard cheeses as well. In the mid-sixteenth century, some of the nobility were still prejudiced against some dairy products. In 1561, for example, Thomas Elyot, the author of the health text *Castel of Helth,* stated that hard cheese was an enemy to the stomach. His opinion came in part from the belief that cheese was heavy and difficult to digest, an opinion that went hand in hand with the belief that the only people capable of eating cheese were laborers, who were believed to have strong stomachs. Others held the opinion as well, but they centered it on the hard aged cheeses, not the soft ones. This attitude began to dissipate during the period and had changed significantly by the end of the seventeenth century.[10]

Cream became increasingly popular among the rulers in Elizabethan England. The well-to-do used cream to make rich desserts called trifles, fools, and whitepots. A Tudor trifle was simply cream mixed with sugar, ginger, and rosewater and heated gently to form a sort of liquid junket. Fools resulted from cream thickened with eggs and then seasoned and boiled. The same ingredients could be turned into whitepots with the addition of currants. Whitepots, however, were baked in a pot or pan and resembled what today is known as custard. One of the more elegant cream dishes was known as snow. In one version, the cook added beaten egg whites, rosewater, and sugar to thick sweet cream and continued beating the mixture until it was light and frothy. She placed the foamiest part of the mixture in a colander around an apple and a rosemary branch. She cast the remaining "snow" upon the rosemary and served it with wafers. Cream was also used to make sauces for savory meat and fish dishes.[11]

Fruits and Vegetables

In 1600 all English men, women, and children ate many fruits and vegetables. Before the fifteenth century, the English believed that greens and fruit had little nutritional value, so these were not valued by the ruling classes. Commoners did eat them. Many greens such as samphire, rampion, and burdock grew wild. Following ancient tradition, peasants gathered them and cooked them in their pottage. The poor, too, planted vegetables wherever they could. At one time they grew carrots in the manure dumps outside London. A horticultural revolution began on the island in part due to the influence of Henry VIII, who had a strong desire for globe artichokes, which were rumored to promote the birth of male children. Furthermore, his wife Catherine of Aragon, who had grown up in southern Spain, brought with her an appetite for numerous vegetables, which resulted in the importation of cabbages, cauliflowers, turnips, carrots, early parsnips, peas, artichokes, and asparagus, among other vegetables. When many members of the upper classes began growing their own vegetables, they favored root vegetables, asparagus, beans, and peas. Greens grown included lettuce, purslane, corn salad, dandelions, mustard, cresses, radishes, turnips, spinach, chicory (or succory), celery, cibols (Welsh onions or shallots), chives, and scallions. Elizabethans also grew flowers and ate them raw, boiled, or preserved in sugar or vinegar. The increased desire for vegetables quickly turned into a market, and by the seventeenth century an impressive network of market gardens existed along the Thames in London.[12]

Also as a part of their horticultural revolution, the English cultivated and ate a wider array of fruits. Not only did numerous species grow in England, but there were many varieties of each species. By 1629, for example, the herbalist John Parkinson reported that fifty-seven kinds of apples, sixty-two different pears, sixty-one varieties of plums, thirty-five different cherries, and twenty-two peaches grew there. In addition, gooseberries, grapes, whortleberries, strawberries, quinces, apricots, raspberries, currants, barberries, and melons could also be found. The English imported many types of fruits, including those that grew in England only in hothouses, such as lemons and oranges. In the sixteenth century, many people, including physicians, frowned on eating fresh fruit. Its cold watery nature was believed to increase phlegm, a humoral shift that most English, who already considered themselves on the cold moist side of a perfectly balanced temperament, wanted to avoid. They solved the problem by cooking fruits—by themselves, with meats, in pies, or in sweet pottages. In addition, they candied them, made marmalades and conserves, and dried them.[13]

HOW TO RANK ENGLISH FOODS AND FOOD HABITS

In a healthy economy all members of English society ate from the above food groups. On the surface, particularly if one looks at this situation from the point of view of a modern food pyramid, the divide between the basic diets of the lower and the upper strata of English society seems small, perhaps even insignificant, because everyone ate of the same food groups and many of the same foods. Indeed, one of the more remarkable facts about the eating habits of the English is that the gentry and nobility of England ate the same foods as members of lower social ranks. Pease pottage, frumenty, sheep's heads, humbles, pigs' trotters, oysters, and herrings, for example, were classic English foods enjoyed by everyone. However, there was a great deal of variety created by the quality and preparation of the foods. Any time variety exists, it begs organization, and in early modern English society organization meant hierarchy. Foods were ranked on a scale from best to worst, most nutritional to least nutritional. This meant, of course, that the eaters of the various foods were ranked as well.[14]

Fresh foods were of a higher quality than stale, old, or salted foods. Foods from properly raised animals with healthy diets or plants raised in excellent soil and air were of a higher quality than animals kept in crowded conditions and fed industrial waste or plants grown in poor or polluted soil or other bad environmental conditions. The degree of processing of a food also determined its quality. Generally, the more processed it was, the higher its quality. Manchet flour, the finest creamy white flour, far exceeded brown flour or unbolted flour. Fresh cheeses were valued over the hard. Aged cheeses believed to be indigestible, such as cheddar, could not compare with fresh cheeses that must be eaten quickly. For beverages, dietary guidelines rated red wine as a superior drink that almost resembled blood. Beer, on the other hand, was not. When Henry VIII eliminated the monasteries, he also destroyed the vineyards that supplied the English with some of their wines. The well-to-do imported their wines from Europe in the sixteenth and early seventeenth centuries, making them more expensive and unavailable to most English people.

Similarly, the quality of a prepared food could vary widely, as the above recipes for pottage show. The "ordinary" pottage was made with mutton, a less expensive meat because it came from an older animal, along with herbs (some of which grew wild), a handful of oatmeal, and salt. Although the "best and daintiest" pottage could have been made with mutton, it could also have been made with veal or kid, both considered higher quality meats that cost more. To this pottage were added not wild or inexpensive herbs but more expensive herbs and vegetables such as lettuce, endive, cauliflower, the inner leaves of a cabbage, or onions. These details were not lost on the eaters. They noticed them, just as eaters today, for example, notice the difference between a basic fast-food hamburger with its light and lacy meat patty, skimpy soft vegetables, and tasteless bun and a chophouse burger with its eight ounces of freshly ground chuck or sirloin, quarter-inch thick red tomato slices, crisp lettuce and onions, and flavorful homemade roll.

In addition to the ingredients, cooking methods also gave the English a way to rank both foods and eaters. Pottage, in addition to the simplicity of its ingredients, required the simplest of cooking utensils—a pot and a spoon. Furthermore, the ingredients could be put in the pot and left over a slow fire for a long time without much attention. It was the perfect food for men and women who worked. In the late sixteenth century, the well-to-do began to spurn some of their savory pottages for more sophisticated dishes such as fricassees, hashes, and others known as "made dishes." They were foods that could not be prepared easily, requiring more skill, attention, pots, pans, hearth equipment, and consequently more hands and more time. Roasts on a spit had to be turned regularly, for example. One had to stand and turn it oneself over the course of several hours, leaving little time to go anywhere else, or hire a servant to do so, or install special and expensive jacks, mechanical devices that turned the meat using a variety of power sources. If a laborer could even afford to purchase the meat, he might very likely be hard-pressed—or even unable—to cook it properly.

Food consumption practices also divided the English. The nobility ate in great halls at well-set tables, where the menus were tailored to the diners. The poor, who lacked the ingredients and probably the hearth on which to cook their own food, ate whatever and wherever they could. Several levels of consumption existed between these two extremes.

The Nobility

The nobility had the most variety in their diet. They ate the freshest foods, and they had access to anything they might need to keep themselves within the golden mean. Hence, they were the most food secure of all the English. According to William Harrison, they ate their main meal of the day at about eleven in the morning. Their manchet breads were made of the best quality, bolted flour. The nobility could choose beef, mutton, veal, lamb, kid, pork, rabbit, capon, pig, deer, freshwater and saltwater fish, and both wild and domestic fowl, whenever these foods were in season. Although this variety suggests they ate extravagantly, in fact they probably did not. While everyone was allowed to taste the different dishes, it was expected that each diner would eat the dish that appealed to him the most. Following the nutritional wisdom concerning appetite, this dish would be the one needed by the body to restore its humoral balance. To eat every dish, claimed Harrison, would be "a speedy suppression of natural health." Barons, bishops, and other nobles commonly ate these foods off silver dishes. After diners from the nobleman's table had taken what they wanted, the foods were removed and given to the servants who, according to Harrison, ate "with convenient moderation." Whatever they did not eat was given to the poor. Those members of a nobleman's house who were not among the above mentioned groups and who fed in the halls ate daily rations. In those houses, about forty or sixty persons were fed each day. Drink, which consisted of imported wines or March beer (which had been aged at least a year), could similarly be drunk from silver goblets or, according to the latest fashion, in Venice glass. To prevent "idle tippling" in houses socially below the nobility but above the rank of knight or gentleman, the glasses were kept on sideboards and brought to the diners when they wished to drink.[15]

Cookery texts published in the late sixteenth and seventeenth centuries, many of which were written by the chefs of noble households, list numerous meat dishes, highlighting roasts, boils, and other recipes calling for premium cuts beyond the budgets of much of the population and certainly not fare for the impoverished. In addition, many of the meat recipes call for generous portions of spices, dried fruits, even sugar. These were expensive ingredients, but they were not put into the dishes just for ostentatious display. Each of these foods had significant humoral value. Spices were humorally unbalanced. For example, dietaries classified ginger as being hot and dry to the third degree. For a person feeling the need to balance his cold moist temperament, a dish with ginger would be just what was needed. No table of the well-to-do presented an array of foods with the same spices and consequently having the same humoral makeup. The housewife arranged an assortment of humorally diverse dishes and she or each eater chose the best dish for them on that day. Some members of the nobility even had personal physicians to make the choice for them. Each morning the physician examined his patient, determined the person's humoral balance, then instructed the cook on what to prepare and which spices and condiments to include to balance his patient's humors. This is how some recipes developed.[16]

By 1600 noble Elizabethan eaters had incorporated sugar into their diets. Although national consumption in the sixteenth century was only one pound per person per year, most of the eaters were the wealthy. During the reign of Elizabeth I the English began refining their own sugar, which lowered the price considerably and made sugar affordable to more eaters. At fine dinners, eaters ended their meal with what they referred to as the banquet. Essentially an elegant dessert bar, it was often spread in a setting different from the main dining hall. Many wealthy families built special small buildings on their estates, known as banqueting houses, to which the host and his guests would retire to enjoy this final course. They could choose to eat jellies, fruit pastes, and preserved fruits, or they might choose instead biscuits, cakes, gingerbreads, sugared spices known as comfits, or marzipan. Sugar was common to all these desserts for eaters believed it to be a superior food. Its warm moist taste indicated its well-balanced sanguine nature. Consumption of sugar would, they believed, balance them humorally. Furthermore, its taste indicated that it was highly digestible and therefore among the most nutritious of foods.[17]

Gentlemen and Merchants

The diets of gentlemen and merchants gave them a good deal of food security. Harrison believed continuity existed between this group and the nobility in the foods served but not in the degree of variety or quality. When gentle households had guests, they usually presented four, five, or six dishes, but when no guests sat at the table, these were reduced to only one, two, or three at the most. Servants in these households usually had an ordinary diet assigned them, in addition to leftovers from the master's table that were not kept back for later meals. Those dishes would most likely be venison, lamb, and foods the master liked to eat cold, such as pies. Like the nobility, gentlemen and merchants ate manchet. The exception to this general eating pattern came at feast time when the tables of the genteel and merchants mimicked those of the nobles, having all kinds of rare meats, jellies of all flavors, shapes, and tastes, marzipan, tarts, pies, wild fowl, venison, conserves, suckets (spiced root or fruit lozenges), marmalades, sugarbreads, gingerbreads, and foreign confections. Harrison observed that the foods that were the most expensive and acquired with the greatest difficulty were the most desired by the gentle and merchant classes on these occasions.[18]

Artificers and Husbandmen

In contrast to the above two groups, artificers and husbandmen flirted with the lower edge of food security. They felt the bumps of a difficult life, a rough economy, or a failed harvest when they had to forgo certain foods because of cost. According to Harrison, they ate whatever meat they could easily prepare. For everyday meals these two groups ate beef and whatever the butcher happened to be selling, usually mutton, veal, lamb, and pork. In addition, they consumed fruits, eggs, and prepared foods such as souse, brawn, bacon, fruit pies, cheeses, and butter. In addition the husbandman's daily diet throughout the year consisted at least of herrings, salt fish, veal, bacon, beef, mackerel, peas, mutton, pork, sprats, smelts, butter, and cheese.[19]

Exceptions to this rule were the feasts given by the members of this group living in London. When their companies met quarterly, they mimicked the nobility. It is hard to tell what they would have been eating because the custom was to have a potluck carry-in supper with each guest bringing one or more dishes. On these occasions, the host was responsible only for bread, which would have been brown; drink, which would have been new beer or perhaps cider; sauce (vegetables), the room, and a warm fire. Harrison thought that although artificers and husbandmen were not as well organized or as well supplied as their social betters, they were sufficiently friendly and liberal at their tables. Like their higher-ups, they were generally moderate in their eating and drinking, except the "meaner sort of husbandmen and country inhabitants," who occasionally ate and drank excessively.[20]

The Laborers and the Poor

Laborers and the poor did not enjoy food security and thus were never assured of having an adequate quantity and quality of food. Of all the categories of English foods in the late sixteenth century, dairy products (known at the time as white meats) were eaten in larger quantities by the poor than by the well-to-do. The poor drank milk, buttermilk, and whey and ate butter and cheese. One method of determining the minimum diet in a society is to look at the foods served in its institutions. Contemporary records indicate that soldiers received one quarter-pound of butter a day as part of their rations, but this custom began to change with the enclosure movement of the mid-sixteenth century, as more common land in England came to be fenced off and peasants lost the large open areas where they could graze their cows. Members of these lower economic orders of society ate a basic pottage of peas and water with some wild herbs and onions for flavoring for their main meal of the day, and even for all their meals. If they could afford to, they threw in some bones, some scraps of fat, or a smoked rind of bacon for flavoring. To make the pottage more substantial, they could have added beer or milk instead of water. If they had access to vegetables, they added carrots, turnips, or coleworts (a forerunner to the modern cabbage).[21]

Neither historians nor contemporaries agree on how much meat was eaten by people subsisting at lower economic levels in late sixteenth-century England. Certainly, the presence and amount of meat in their diets depended on the economic climate. England went through a depression during the second half of the sixteenth century, and prices rose significantly. The poor, according to one source, lived on bacon, cheese, fish, broth prepared with beans and salted meat, and whatever wild game, salt fish, or fowl they could catch. In the sixteenth century St. Bartholomew's Hospital, a charitable institution, fed its charges pork, mutton, beef ribs, salted and pickled herring, bread, and beer. The House of Correction in Suffolk in 1588 was ordered at the very least to give prisoners at every dinner and supper on flesh days eight ounces of rye bread, a pint of pottage, four ounces of meat, and a pint of beer. On fish days, prisoners were to receive at dinner and supper eight ounces of rye bread, a pint of pottage made with "milk or pease or such lyke," and a third of a pound of cheese, or one "good" herring or two "white or redd" herrings. Inmates who worked hard were rewarded with beer and bread between meals. In a proposal for outfitting a herring ship in 1615, the author calculated on feeding the sailors eight ounces of cheese, four ounces of bacon, four ounces of butter, one pound of ship's biscuit, three ounces of oatmeal, and one gallon of beer per day.[22]

SOCIAL CLASS, VIRTUE, AND POWER

Although William Harrison listed four social classes, he divided his society into two large groups based on gentility, which for him was not just an inherited status but was to be achieved through the combined attributes of occupation, wealth, and lifestyle. The nobility and gentry were "those whome their race and blood or at least their vertues do make noble and knowne." Urban citizens and burgesses were ranked just under nobility and gentry because of their occupations and their degree of freedom. Third were yeomen, whom Harrison classified as having land valued at forty shillings a year or who farmed for gentlemen and whose character was highly regarded by commoners. All others in English society—a numerical preponderance—occupied the second group, people who had to labor for their living. Sir Thomas Smith, a lawyer and contemporary of Harrison, called them the proletariat and stated bluntly: "These have no voice nor authority in our commonwealth and no account is made of them, but only to be ruled and not to rule others."[23]

Why was it that the social groups with the most food security were designated the rulers, and the group with the least food security the ruled? One answer is that people enjoying food security were the only ones who could achieve virtue and were, therefore, the only ones fit to rule. For example, they did not need to worry about the negative effects of phlegm-producing foods such as "slimy" and "cleaving" meats, new cheese, fish, lamb, offal, and cucumbers because they did not eat those foods every day, nor indeed at every meal. Furthermore, they could balance the cold moist properties of those foods with spices, condiments, or other foods that were hot and dry and that promoted choler and reduced phlegm. Garlic, onions, leeks, ginger, mustard, pepper, and sweetmeats are good examples. Similarly, beef, goat, hare, boar, salt flesh, salt fish, coleworts, all pulse except white peas, coarse brown bread, thick or black wine, old cheese, old fish, and the great fish of the sea, all contained large amounts of melancholy, so they greatly increased its presence within the body. To eat a diet limited to these foods, according to early modern thinking, guaranteed a melancholy disposition.

However, the rulers had no fears of eating those foods alone. Seen from another perspective, rulers should *never* have those fears. It is unknown which came first to English rulers, their power or their food security. From the viewpoint of humoral philosophy, no society would want its rulers to be without complete food security. They should, on a daily basis, be able to choose from their highly varied menus those foods that would balance their temperaments and keep them within the golden mean. Such a practice guaranteed that the rulers would be the most virtuous people in the society and consequently the best rulers.

Although food was the most important of the six non-naturals in achieving the golden mean, the others had a significant part to play in a virtuous lifestyle. To achieve virtue, a person had to monitor the amount of exercise and sleep he received on a daily basis, had to move about freely to breathe the right air, had to have a steady amount of food and beverages for a balanced state of repletion and have a life that encouraged stable emotions. Who else could do this but people who did not have to labor? Of course, the predominant form of exercise in the early modern period was labor, over which laborers had no control if they wished to survive. They could not, as the rulers could do, decide that they would not work on any particular day because their temperaments were unbalanced. If the ruled lived in areas in which the air was so wet and moist or hot and dry or foul as to distort their temperaments, too bad. They had to live with the air unless they could find another job in a more healthful climate or afford the foods that would counteract the imbalance. The rulers, on the other hand, thought nothing of traveling to another region or even another country for a change of air. When the food supply varied with the seasons and the vicissitudes of agriculture, availability and cost were both affected. The diets of the ruled fluctuated accordingly, and when their levels of repletion shifted in times of dearth, so would their temperaments. Not so with the rulers, who rode those waves successfully, keeping an even bodily keel. Finally, although the lives of the rulers were fraught with their own problems, the security of their wealth must have contributed to a sense of emotional well-being not experienced by the ruled. Perhaps this is why the balanced temperament is known as the golden mean; only the wealthy could ever hope to achieve it.

CONCLUSION

On the eve of the colonization of North America, people in England ate of the same food groups but of a greater or lesser quality and of a different variety depending on their income, social status, place of residence, and personal likes and dislikes. According to the nutritional philosophy of the time, people who ate differently were formed differently. The belief had developed to include within its parameters even the finest of details. Coarse people such as day laborers remained that way because they ate coarse foods and had limited variety and fluctuations in quantity in their diets. They lacked the food and the opportunity to achieve virtue. They were, as Thomas Smith said, unfit to rule society. The rulers did not have such limits on their diets or their social and political status. For members on all levels of English society, the argument concerning situation was circular—they were what they ate, but they also ate what they were.[24]

As severe and restrictive as it may seem, this humoral social philosophy both structured and stabilized the English and offered a sensible solution to the ever-present problem of having unstable bodies in an unstable world. If the whole society could not enjoy food security and live within reach of the golden mean, then it was better to have at least one segment that did. Members of this class would be within the golden mean and, theoretically at least, be virtuous. They could rule society well and anchor it. This belief provided a social stability of its own. It justified the existence of a ruling class and its secure and extravagant lifestyle. For a people living on a small island with a limited amount of land, the philosophy of food security resulted in a seriously unbalanced society favoring one extreme element—the wealthy—over all the others.

The New World was a different matter. The possibilities of landownership and food security offered there seemed without limit. To English eyes and minds the New World offered more land than they could ever use. Theoretically, with the widespread ownership of land came the ability of most people to control their daily lives and to obtain more easily the necessary quality and quantity of foods to be secure and to achieve the golden mean of virtue. But if large numbers of people within a society change, then so does that society, and it did not take English writers long to realize their world was changing, when they thought about the possibilities of New World colonization. Several writers from the early sixteenth century imagined a New World society that was food secure enough to dissolve the boundaries within English society and place everyone within reach of the golden mean. Thomas More called this new world Utopia.

Secure People and Societies

*A*t the beginning of the sixteenth century Thomas More created *Utopia*, a satirical critique of English society. He believed that many of the social ills of England stemmed from the lopsided English socioeconomic system, in which the eaters with the least food labored the most and those with the most food labored the least. Utopia was the fictional but not fanciful perfect society in which virtue thrived in the souls of its citizens because they all enjoyed complete food security. Later writers and explorers also employed the philosophy of food security in their praise and promotion of, or commentary about, North America. Food security was a significant factor in the English understanding of the meaning and promise of North America.

INSECURE ENGLAND

In 1516, the year that More published *Utopia*, England was experiencing an extensive and fundamental change in its system of agricultural production. It had been a country in which the small number of people who owned the majority of arable land leased out plots to tenants to produce food for themselves as well as for their landlords. While it did not ensure against harvest failures or other catastrophes ending in dearth, the system did allow thousands of families to support themselves in a modest way. On the other hand, the mere fact of landownership enabled the landlords and their households to enjoy the benefits of food security. Thomas More did not approve of the older system for precisely that reason. He believed it allowed too many men to remain idle, which led them to corruption and eventual poverty.

He approved of the enclosure movement even less. Wool production began to increase in England in the fifteenth century, and because of the high profits from selling raw wool, landowners decreased the amount of land used communally for crop production and increased the size of their private enclosed sheep pastures. This shift ejected tenants from their tenancies and deprived them and others of the use of the commons. Plant and animal production faltered. The change disturbed the diets of English laborers and poor. According to More, the "sheep that were wont to be so meek and so tame and such small eaters, now, as I hear say, become so great devourers and so wild, that they eat up and swallow the very men themselves. They consume, destroy, and devour whole fields, houses, and cities."[1]

Without a home or any place to practice the agricultural skills they had spent a lifetime learning, displaced husbandmen, "poor, silly, wretched souls, men, women, husbands, wives, fatherless children, widows, woeful mothers, with their young babes, and their whole household, small in substance and much in number . . . trudge[d]" to the towns. After they sold what few belongings they owned, they had no choice but to steal in order to survive, and adding to their misery, Henry VIII punished thievery severely. One contemporary source estimated that he hanged over seven thousand thieves during his reign. He dissolved the remaining private armies retained by noblemen, and after his conversion to Protestantism, abolished the monasteries that employed numerous servants. Purposeless soldiers and unemployed servants joined displaced peasants, first in the unrewarding search for wage labor and later in begging, poaching, and stealing. To make matters worse, from More's viewpoint, the landowners who profited from enclosure became even more idle, and in that idleness they took to sumptuous eating, thereby becoming food insecure themselves. The consequences of such behavior could only be corruption and vice. The landowners, like their sheep, became devourers. Unlike the sheep, however, they destroyed themselves as well as others and threatened the future of the entire country.[2]

REGULATED, SECURE UTOPIA

More saw his England as one of extremes, in which both the rulers and the ruled succumbed to vice as a result of food insecurity, because either they ate too little and labored too much or they ate too much and labored too little. He believed that the social body, like the human body, required moderation, the golden mean of neither too much nor too little, in order to survive, if not thrive. Most people in the early modern period spent the majority of their time and effort acquiring food. If a society wished to have universal food security, it must regulate the amount of labor its citizens expended and the quality and quantity of food they received. More's Utopia, situated somewhere in the New World, does just that.

Utopians start with the soil. Although they are not warmongers, Utopians do consider the seizure of uncultivated land to be the supremely just cause of war. To refuse to "nourish and relieve . . . void and vacant" ground contradicts the laws of nature. Hence, all Utopians learn the arts of husbandry from an early age and practice them expertly and regularly throughout their lives. First, everyone participates in large-scale agricultural production, and because of the physical toll extracted by agricultural labor, they cultivate for two-year periods at regular intervals. Second, all urban houses have sizable garden plots that Utopians use to their fullest potential, planting them with every kind of fruit, vegetable, and flower. Utopians derive a great amount of pleasure from their gardens.[3]

The key problem in any utopia is how to strike a balance between the true needs of a society and the amount of labor expended to supply those needs—an expansion of the philosophy of food security to all material needs. A society in which the workers receive a disproportionately small amount of material goods for their labor is not a healthy one. Any true utopia must provide an abundant and stable supply of high quality food for all. In addition it must assure an equal distribution of labor among its citizens.[4]

More's Utopian system easily maintains a balance. No one works more than six hours a day. Everyone receives whatever material goods and food he needs, unlike in England where huge inequities existed in what people actually ate and the labor they expended for it. Utopians maintain a system of free mutual exchange between the city and the country. Citizens from either location can simply acquire from the other whatever they need whenever they need it. As a result, urban Utopians always have a plentiful supply of "not only all sorts of herbs and the fruits of trees, with bread, but also fish and all manner of four-footed beasts and wild fowl." Their common diet unites free Utopians, but unlike in England, variations in quality and quantity do not divide them. Everyone consistently eats the same high quality and wide variety of foods. A network of markets connects Utopians, as does their order of food distribution. Hospital stewards have priority in choosing foods when the markets open in the morning. Utopians divide the remaining food equally among groups of thirty households each, known as syphogranties. There are a few exceptions: out of respect, they defer to the prince, the bishop, the leaders of the syphogranties, ambassadors, and strangers.[5]

Most of More's Utopians dine communally at the hall in their syphogranty. Individual families within the household can eat privately, but common meals require less labor and fewer resources to feed the same number of people. A "brazen trumpet" calls everyone to their meals where they receive enough to eat. Although gluttony was one of the seven deadly sins in 1516, More eliminated it in Utopia. An incredulous European traveler asks a resident of Utopia: "Howbeit, no man is prohibited or forbid, after the halls be served, to fetch home meat out of the market to his own house?" He receives the reply: "For they know that no man will do it without a cause reasonable. For though no man be prohibited to dine at home, yet no man doth it willingly because it is counted a point of small honesty. And also it were a folly to take the pain to dress a bad dinner at home, when they may be welcome to good and fine fare so nigh at the hall." In this detail, More relies on the rule of the golden mean—that anyone who eats the right foods in the proper quantities and qualities will attain virtue. Utopian authorities regulate the labor and food supply of all their residents. They can easily guide their citizens to virtue. Once each citizen achieves his personal golden mean, no controls are needed because, they believe, every virtuous person possesses a flawless appetite.[6]

From a visitor's point of view, the Utopian system appears to be perfect, an excellent example of a food secure polity. It seems to be a completely egalitarian society. Visitors, however, do not usually go into private spaces such as the slaughterhouses and kitchens, to see who does the heavy labor of food preparation. In Utopia, it is slaves, not free citizens, who hunt and slaughter all animals, domestic and wild, "for they permit not free citizens to accustom themselves to the killing of beasts." In the dining halls, slaves perform "all vile service, all slavery and drudgery, with all laboursome toil and base business." The presence of a group of bonded laborers who works continually can be seen as a chink of darkness in the bright Utopian system, but More justified the practice by explaining the nature of the slaves themselves. Utopians enslave neither prisoners of other countries' wars nor the children of slaves. Rather, they purchase most of their slaves from the pools of criminals condemned to death in other countries. Of their own citizens, they enslave only those who commit heinous offenses. They treat these men most harshly, believing that they "deserved greater punishment, because they being so godly brought up to virtue in so excellent a commonwealth, could not for all that be refrained from misdoing." The modern term for such men is "incorrigible." The Utopian social system is perfected to the point where men no longer need to steal in order to eat. Therefore, theft does not occur in Utopia. Adultery and religious zealotry do, however. The latter arises out of the sin of pride, a "hell hound [that] creepeth into men's hearts and plucketh them back from entering the right path of life, and is so deeply rooted in men's breasts, that she cannot be plucked out."[7]

Neither human nature nor human society, according to More, could be fully perfected. Individuals and human groups would always be plagued by certain fallibilities. Even with these shortcomings, however, an egalitarian commonwealth such as Utopia served and rewarded its citizens in a way that England could not and did not. Utopia, after all, did not exist in Europe, which had been cultivated for millennia and had entrenched systems of maldistributed landownership and soil that needed constant maintenance. Utopia lay somewhere in the New World, perceived to have no private landownership and more than ample available land.

NATURALLY SECURE NORTH AMERICA

Less than a century after the first publication of *Utopia,* English explorers, investors, promoters, visitors, and residents of North America remembered that promise and incorporated it into their visions of and prospects for the new societies they hoped to create there. The continent's assets, they wrote, included a mild climate and an abundant, if not luxuriant, natural food supply. It had fertile virgin soil in which plants grew prodigiously, and it possessed a multitude of wild fauna and flora. All of these qualities promised that the people living there would enjoy the golden mean of food security without the extensive regulations of Utopia.[8]

Not coincidentally, the kinds of foods that writers noted in the New World held an elevated status among the English in the early seventeenth century. These foods held a previously unachievable promise of virtue for anyone who did not consume them regularly in the Old World, which would have been a large proportion of the English population, many of whom experienced famine in the late sixteenth century. During the first half of the seventeenth century, England's economy was depressed, food prices were high, and some foods were scarce. The common laborer's diet consisted of bread, beef, cheese, and beer. Stories of the New World's multitude of foods, available to anyone for little or no labor, must have been very enticing to those people caught in the economics of the times or on the lower levels of the English social hierarchy.[9]

The Soil

Many writers believed that the soil was literally and figuratively the foundation of a nutritionally secure society in North America. For example, a mathematician who visited Virginia in the late sixteenth century, Thomas Hariot, wrote in his description of the colony, *A Briefe and True Report of the New Found Land of Virginia*: "The ground [the natives] never fatten with mucke, dounge or any other thing." Furthermore, the natives' only preparation of the soil consisted of breaking up the top few inches to lift up the weeds, grass, and "old stubbes of corne stalkes with their rootes." Both native men and women worked the ground, the men with wooden tools similar to a hoe and the women with "short peckers or parers," which they used while sitting. After letting the refuse dry for a few days, they gathered it into piles and burned it. Planting corn consisted of the simple process of poking holes in the soil a yard apart and planting four seeds in every hole. They then sowed beans, *macócqwer* (pumpkins, melons, and gourds), and *Planta solis* (sunflowers) in the spaces between the corn. Such intensive cultivation must have been scarcely believable to English readers, whose small island soil had been cultivated for centuries and needed its fertility constantly replenished through the labor-intensive practice of manure spreading. Not only did the natural qualities of the soil perform the "labor" of fertilization and plowing, they enabled many more plants to grow in the same amount of space than did English soil. According to Hariot: "an English Acre conteining fourtie pearches in length, and foure in breadth, doeth there yeeld in croppe or ofcome of corne, beanes and peaze, at the least two hundred London bushelles: besides the *Macócqwer, Melden,* and *Planta Solis.* When as in England fourtie bushelles of our wheate yielded out of such an acre is thought to be much."[10]

Maize and Other Crops

The productivity described by Hariot came from the combination of the soil and the New World wonder crop maize, known as "Turkey wheat" or "Indian corne," which contemporary accounts claimed practically planted itself and could be closely sown, saving a good deal more of the planter's labor. Maize's increase impressed Hariot the most: "It is a graine of marvelous great increase; of a thousand, fifteene hundred and some two thousand fold." Hariot understood that he was comparing apples and oranges, or rather, English wheat and Turkey wheat. He did not have actual yields for English wheat grown in this same soil because the seeds he brought with him had grown musty and absorbed saltwater during the transatlantic voyage. He assured his readers that they could expect the same kind of maize yields, because his trials of the other English staples of barley, oats, and peas had been similarly successful. *A Briefe and True Report* counseled prospective colonists that they could choose whether to plant English wheat or Turkey wheat, but the latter clearly impressed Hariot. He considered it an excellent food, because in addition to its ease of cultivation and high yields, he believed it made a sweet white flour for making bread or "pappe," could be brewed for ale, or could be parched or boiled whole.[11]

Hariot was not the only Englishman to be overwhelmed by the incredible combination of fertile soil and productive maize. Years later, John Smith reported that each maize kernel he planted in Virginia returned anywhere from six hundred to fifteen hundred grains. Similar reports came from New England. Francis Higginson, the first minister of Salem, Massachusetts, reported that for every English wheat seed they planted in the "fat blacke Earth," they received "thirtie, fortie, fiftie, sixtie" in return and that many men expected to improve that to one hundred in 1629 and to two hundred grains in the future. Maize in New England outranked wheat. Higginson believed his sources, who claimed that 13 gallons of corn seed, when planted, would yield 52 hogsheads, each holding 7 bushels, for a total of 364 bushels. Under the modern British imperial system in which a bushel holds about 8 gallons, each gallon of maize seed planted would have provided the planter with 224 gallons of maize. Higginson estimated that an investment of six shillings eight pence for the seed yielded 327 pounds sterling.[12]

Furthermore, the planting was so simple and required such easy labor that even a child of five "may by setting corne one month be able to get their own maintenance abundantly." European readers must have been scarcely able to believe the "briefe and true report" that "one man may prepare and husband so much grounde (having once borne corne before) with lesse than foure and twentie houres labour, as shall yeelde him victual in a large proportion for a twelve moneth, if hee have nothing else, but that which the same ground will yeelde, and of that kinde onelie which I have before spoken of: the saide ground being also but of five and twentie yards square." As if that were not amazing enough, if a man needed, he could harvest two maize crops yearly on the same 625 square yards.[13]

The motifs in early narratives of other types of cultivated produce echoed those of maize. North American soil produced a magnificent abundance of high quality foods for very little effort. English seeds grew "with incredible usurie," and persons with little to no skill in gardening or farming could have great success with them. To grow fruit trees, one just needed to plant the stock and then sleep while they grew to perfection. An early pamphlet, published in England in 1629, quoted a Mrs. Peirce as saying that she had lived in Virginia for the previous twenty years and that she had had a three- or four-acre garden at Jamestown from which she gathered in one year one hundred bushels of "excellent" figs. Furthermore, she claimed that she kept such a good house in Virginia that it would take three to four hundred pounds a year to do the same in London. Of New England, wrote Higginson, "everything that is heere eyther sowne or planteth prospereth far better than in old England." William Wood, another early New Englander, judged the soil more conservatively, however. He wrote that few people who had actually planted the ground found it to be barren, perhaps because they used fish as a fertilizer. Corn grew very well without the fish, but it increased yields. Even so, Wood concluded, the land of New England was "better ground than the forests of England, or woodland ground, or heathy plains." And, of course, there was very much more of it.[14]

Livestock

Livestock also flourished with a minimum of care in North America. In a letter from Virginia dated 1634, colonist Thomas Yong told his correspondent that the country "aboundeth with very great plentie" and that the tables of "ordinary planters of the better sort" contained pork, kid, chicken, young turkey, geese, "Caponettes," and seasonal fowl, as well as milk, cheese, and butter. After admiring the lush grass that grew in the fertile soil, a New England colonist exclaimed: "It is scarce to be beleeved how our Kine and Goats, Horses and Hogges doe thrive and prosper here and like well of this Countrey." Much later in the century, in 1682, Englishman Thomas Ashe, who accompanied the first Huguenot settlers to Carolina and stayed there for two years, reported that in six or seven years hogs, cows, and sheep increased from a "destitute" number to many thousand head. This growth required little to no effort on the part of their owners because nature provided their year-round fodder. Cows grazed on "the sweet Leaves growing on the Trees and Bushes, or on the wholesome Herbage growing underneath." Hogs surfeited on fruits in the summer, particularly peaches, and on roots and nuts in the winter. Sheep grazed so well that they produced excellent wool and the ewes frequently bore two or three lambs at a time. Similarly, a Swedish settler living in the mid-Atlantic region in the early eighteenth century recalled of his childhood that the countryside was abundant with fat cattle and cows that gave three to four times more milk than at the time of his telling.[15]

Wild Nuts and Fruit

Commentators believed that the natural fertility of the soil supported a wide array of wild North American plants and animals as well. Many of the numerous species were eaten in England also, or they resembled species that were eaten there. Their ready availability sparked two comments. First, they grew without human assistance, so they required less labor than cultivated foods. Second, they grew so prolifically that even the labor required to gather or hunt them was reduced. Both factors enhanced food security because they reduced the labor needed to acquire food.

North America offered, for only the labor of gathering, many wild foods prized by the English. Many of these foods grew in England only with intensive cultivation and at great expense. Even the most sparing of writers often used words such as "full," "multitudes," "numerous," or "abundant" to describe the amounts of available wild fruits. Hariot reported the presence in Virginia of strawberries, mulberries, "applecrabs," hurtleberries (huckleberries), and two kinds of grapes, all of which were familiar to English readers. John Smith's account added cherries and *rawcomenes,* which he believed to be a type of gooseberry. In addition, he told of maracocks, fruits he considered wholesome and similar to lemons. By 1650, writers included barberries and cranberries among the wild fruits available in the Chesapeake. No one told more dramatically of American abundance than Edward Williams when he described the fruit trees as being "so delectable an aspect, that the melancholyest eye in the World cannot look upon it without contentment." In regards to strawberries, he wrote: "No shrubs choake up your passage [in the woods], and in its season your foot can hardly direct it selfe where it will not be died in the bloud of large and delicious Strawberries."[16]

Nuts ranked high on the list of native products that were valued by the early writers, among them chestnuts of a quality equal to those grown in France, Spain, Germany, and Italy. Other native species of nuts included walnuts and several varieties of acorns. Over the seventeenth century, visitors to and residents of New England, New Amsterdam, and Pennsylvania gave similar assessments.[17]

Wild Game and Fish

Writers divided the world of edible wild animals into fish, flesh, and fowl. To Hariot the hares, squirrels, and deer were the wild mammals that seemed the most similar to those eaten in England. John Smith presented a larger list of beasts, and although he did not explicitly state that Englishmen or natives ate them all, he did include them within a larger discussion of food. Another source mentioned deer, raccoons, hares, conies, beavers, squirrels, and bears as "delightful nourishment." As with the wild plants, the mammals could be found in great numbers. Moose, whose flesh was likened to beef in tastiness and whose hide made sturdy clothes, lived in great quantities just forty miles northeast of Massachusetts Bay. Carolina had "such infinite Herds" of deer "that the whole Country seems but one continued Park." The large numbers rewarded the hunter. It was reported that one hunting Indian could take one hundred or even two hundred head in just one year. Similar reports came from up and down the eastern seaboard.[18]

North American fish, both freshwater and saltwater, greatly impressed the English. Thomas Hariot and his men ate trout, porpoise, herrings, mullet, plaice, oldwives, and rays. They noted plenty of crabs, oysters, mussels, scallops, periwinkles, crayfish, and tortoises. Smith added seals, turbot, salmon, sole, conyfish, rockfish, eels, lamprey, catfish, shad, and three varieties of perch. As late as 1650, reports of the abundance of fish included one that claimed five thousand fish could be taken at one draught at Cape Charles near the entrance to the Chesapeake Bay. Of all the Chesapeake species, none caused more excitement than the sturgeon. Almost every report praised its size, taste, and superabundance. In the summer numerous sturgeon filled the rivers, and reports claimed that fishermen might not even need to use fishing equipment because these fish simply jumped right into the boat. At spawning time the salmon could be caught as easily. In New England a plethora of saltwater fish enabled fishermen to catch great numbers with far less effort than their English counterparts. After returning to England, John Smith reiterated the philosophy of food security when he wrote: "If a man worke but three dayes in seaven, he may get more then hee can spend, unlesse he will be excessive. Now that Carpenter, Mason, Gardiner, Taylor, Smith, Sailer, Forgers, or what other, may they not make this a pretty recreation though they fish but an houre in a day, to take more then they eate in a week: or if they will not eate it, because there is so much better choise; yet sell it, or change it, with the fisher men, or marchants, for any thing they want."[19]

Although Smith did not stay to colonize the area, others who did stay affirmed the natural wealth of fish. Typical are comments such as Francis Higginson's note in a letter that his wife had just informed him local fishermen had caught sixteen hundred bass at one draught, a quantity seldom caught in England. The abundance spanned freshwater as well as saltwater fish and included oysters, some of which were up to ten inches wide.[20]

The bounty of fish did not even compare to the great populations of fowl that reportedly flew over North America. Three years after he arrived in New England, William Hammond wrote of a flock of pigeons so great it took two hours to fly overhead. For one writer, the types of fowl varied so much that he found it "too tedious" to mention every kind. He did list swans, geese, brants, ducks, wigeons, and teals as the most prevalent water fowl. The land fowl consisted of eagles, hawks, vultures, cranes, crows, turkeys, partridges, pigeons, larks, redbirds, "the Baltenore bird," bluebirds, mockingbirds, and woodpeckers, although it is not clear that he considered all these varieties either edible or desirable. Another, earlier author indicated that most land fowl were palatable and included thrushes, herons, wigeons, and oxeyes. Both Hariot and Smith wrote about the wonderful array of fowl in the Chesapeake. Hariot, in particular, noted eating numerous kinds of fowl, except parrots, falcons, and Marlin hawks. Many types could be easily killed because of their extravagant numbers. A promotional piece declared that 150 could be brought down with just three charges of shot and powder. Another piece simply stated that the waterfowl covered the rivers from August to February in an abundance not to be equaled anywhere in the world. Like the sturgeon, the wild turkey—in part because of its size—received the most attention from the writers on fowl. Estimates ranged from as large as the domestic turkeys in England to what one observer believed to be twice that size, forty pounds, with fifty pounds being the maximum. Not only were these turkeys huge but, like all the foodstuffs mentioned so far, the sources indicated that they were acquired effortlessly.[21]

Water

In addition to a sumptuous food supply, many parts of North America offered plentiful potable water in streams and from underground supplies. New England settlers in particular commented on the quality of their water and the fact that they did not have to make ale or beer in order to have a wholesome drink. Those colonists who lacked ready access to a spring or river could most likely find water by digging a well. Around Massachusetts Bay, landholders needed only to dig their wells three feet deep to find water. William Wood judged it markedly different from the water of England. The former was "not so sharpe" as the latter "but of a fatter substance, and of a more jetty color." Many colonists thought it beneficial and the best water in the world. Wood wrote: "Those that drinke it be as healthfull, fresh, and lustie, as they that drinke beere."[22]

Lest readers should miss the point about the perceived benefits of life in a New World that promised food security for everyone, several authors and others offered the example of the natives and explained their individual and group virtue.

Thomas Hariot's Briefe and True Report

An excellent example is the 1590 Theodore de Bry edition of Thomas Hariot's *Briefe and True Report,* which echoes the contemporary health texts in its description of a stunningly healthy and long-lived native people who, despite their cultural backwardness, achieved the golden mean of food security. They surpassed the English "in many things, as in Sober feedinge and dexterity of witte." Like the Utopians, they had achieved the state of virtue in which they could control their appetites. Hariot lamented that the English did not follow the natives' example and cease their sumptuous dining and their culinary quest for new dishes to satisfy their insatiable appetites.[23]

The engravings that accompany Hariot's text depict natives as finely proportioned, considered the exterior mark of inner virtue. To underscore this virtuosity, the figures hold classical poses reminiscent of ancient Greek sculpture in general and of the *Canon of Polykleitos,* the marble symbol of virtue, in particular. Later observers affirmed Hariot's observation, using words such as "full and strong limbed," "crafty, proper, clean-jointed," and "tall and straight." John Smith, in his *General History of Virginia, New England and the Somer Isles* noted that the "Indians differ in stature but they are generally tall and straight of a comely proportion." In addition, he observed them to be "strong, of an able body and full of agility," hardy, crafty, "quicke of apprehension and very ingenious."[24]

Thomas Morton's New English Canaan

One of the most thorough explanations of the complex relationship between the natives and their food, including the influence of the climate on both, is by Thomas Morton, an early Massachusetts colonist. Disgraced by the Pilgrim community at Plymouth Plantation for what they regarded as misbehavior, Morton wrote a defense of his actions entitled *New English Canaan.* He began his work with a humoral geography lesson on the most and least habitable parts of the earth: "The wise Creator of the universal Globe hath placed a golden mean betwixt two extremes: I mean the temperate Zones, betwixt the hot and cold."[25] With this first sentence, Morton placed dividing lines around the planet that hovered on either side of the forty-five-degree latitude. These lines mapped heat and moisture.

Morton did not invent these zones. Rather, he relayed the general understanding of early seventeenth-century European cosmography. In doing so, he accomplished far more than merely giving his readers an idea of what part of the Atlantic Ocean was bounded by New England, and where this land lay in relation to Old England. Morton's dividing lines set off New England as the geographical golden mean, a location that promised to foster health and virtue. The species living there could reach the highest state of existence possible because they were not subject to the extremes of heat, cold, dryness, and moisture that produced plants and animals of similar elemental balance and that created physiological, psychological, and spiritual imperfection in humans further up the food chain. These geographical boundaries, then, separated people according to their natural capabilities as well as their achievements. The boundaries enabled early modern Europeans to characterize peoples all over the world and rank them accordingly without ever having met them. As Morton observed: "the Creatures that participate of heat and cold in a mean, are best and wholesomest."[26]

According to Morton, finding the golden mean was really very simple. The distance between the North Pole and the Equator is ninety degrees. Half of that is forty-five degrees. Because he believed that one should stay slightly to the southern side of forty-five degrees "for the benefit of heat," Morton calculated the North American geographical golden mean to be the area between forty and forty-five degrees. New England, with Massachusetts in its middle, lay clearly within these lines. Because of the colony's felicitous location, according to Morton, it was the "best and the wholesomest." Being thus so, it produced vegetation and creatures of the same quality, including humans.[27]

In pointing out that New England and Old England lay on different latitudinal lines, Morton divided the inhabitants of those two regions into two different categories based on their physiology. The categories were not equivalent. Anyone living within the golden mean would have a superior capacity to anyone living outside it. Morton made great use of this presumption in the first part of his book in which he compared the states of humankind—both native and English—in America. He described the two kinds of people he observed when he landed in New England in 1622 as Christians and infidels. The latter, he claimed, descended from the Trojans. They possessed more "humanity" than the former, signifying they were more noble and virtuous. For example, they shared their mats, blankets, and food with anyone who chanced their way. Furthermore, if one were given a "bisket cake," he would break it into as many pieces as there were persons present and share it, a trait Morton believed signified the ideal society described by Plato in *The Republic*. Their physical appearance revealed their virtue. "To give their character in a word," said Morton, "they are as proper men and women for feature and limbs as can be found, for flesh and bloud as active." They possessed an "ingenious and very subtle" wit. They had an "admirable perfection in the use of their senses" because they could see further than any Englishman and smell more acutely.[28]

Morton commented on the observations of other English people that the Amerindians lived poorly. On the contrary, he claimed, they led a happy and free life because they did not suffer the cares of so many Christians. They possessed plenty of food and clothing, particularly in comparison to the poor of England. Had the English poor lived as well as the Amerindians, Morton conjectured, the jails and gallows of England would be less used. The Indians did not live too excessively, a sign, to Morton and others of his time, of virtue derived from food security. Fashionable clothing did not tempt them. "Dishes of plate with variety of sauces to procure appetite" proved unnecessary because the natives had "good stomachs" because of the "medicinable qualities of the [wild] sweet herbs" that perfumed the air.[29]

When Morton asserted that the Indians in New England exhibited far more humanity than the Christians, he meant they were virtuous. The Christians —who practiced deception, thievery, and murder—had lost their humanity because their extreme behaviors had turned them into beasts, evidenced by the following actions. The Plymouth planters lured natives to a feast and then stabbed them with their own knives, earning them the name of *wotawquenange,* meaning stabbers, or cutthroats. They defaced the Passonagessit monument of a sachem's dead mother by stealing the bearskins that draped it. Furthermore, these "brethren" stole corn from the Indians. When the Indians sought justice, the English hesitated to punish the felon with the death sentence mandated by English law and instead considered a deceptive plot to avoid that punishment. They also directed their treachery at other Englishmen. For example, although dismayed at the arrival of one of their financial backers, Thomas Weston, and his non-separatist group, they first showed them hospitality. In a short time, however, they defamed Weston, imprisoned him, and confiscated his ship and supplies. Later, these Plymouth men led Weston's crew to remote Wessaguscus and abandoned them without food.[30]

Thomas Morton characterized the native temperament by evaluating such physiological traits as complexion and body build, intelligence or lack of it, industry or indolence, appetite, and heightened sensitivity. As virtuous people, the natives formed a virtuous society. The civility of a people (particularly their commitment to the well-being of all members of the group as opposed to the individual), their generosity, sense of fairness, and honesty all served as boundary markers between the superior and the inferior, between the natives and the English, and between the food secure and the food insecure. In Morton's opinion, the Indians exhibited all the traits of a superior race and therefore were a virtuous people. The English, he believed, were far from it.

CONCLUSION

Central to the perception of North America as a utopia was the belief that colonists on the whole could achieve the golden mean of food security, which most could not achieve in the mother country. In England, the nature of the soil and the unavailability of land to most people, among other factors, kept the golden mean out of reach for most inhabitants. The writers examined in this chapter held the belief that the change to a secure food system transformed societies and that North America would foster a virtuous, balanced, but still English society. Thomas More expressed this idea in his hopeful *Utopia.* Commentators showed it indirectly in their descriptions of the New World. These commentators, as well as Thomas Morton, Thomas Hariot, and John Smith, all saw North America not so much as a paradise but as a place in which everyone did or could enjoy the golden mean. However, as Morton indicated and as John Smith was to find out, the promise of a food-secure society and the reality of life in a wilderness were two entirely different things.

Insecurity and the Common Kettle

On a hot muggy day in September 1607, Edward Maria Wingfield sat alone in a pinnace moored on the James River. While the other men in the colony worked, Wingfield thought and, more than likely, paced and fumed, for he could not leave. The lesser son of a noble family, Wingfield was the only investor in the Virginia Company of London to participate actively in its first attempt to colonize Virginia. In the short space of time between April and September 1607, he had been appointed by the company to sit on the expedition's ruling council, had been elected by the other members to be president of that council, and then had been tried by it and sentenced to imprisonment on the company's pinnace until he could be transported back to England. He remained on that boat from 10 September 1607 until 10 April 1608. What crime had he committed? He had refused to share his chickens and beer with other council members.

Wingfield's plight is one example of how colonists experienced the practical application in the New World of the philosophy of food security. Wingfield may not have realized his philosophical predicament. The dreams of an America of complete food security, with the achievement of the golden mean by most, proved elusive in the early years of settlement. Colonists in the first two successful colonies, Virginia and Plymouth, learned the hard way that in fact food was not easier to catch or grow there than in England. Both groups suffered extreme food insecurity and were forced to eat different foods in different ways than they were used to eating in England. The change upset the social assumptions of each colony in different ways. In addition, it tested their belief in the individual golden mean. In the end, however, neither group abandoned the philosophy.

VIRGINIA

On 14 May 1607, the Virginia Company of London, a joint stock company, established Jamestown as its first colonial base in Virginia. The immediate purpose of this 144-man expedition was to seek and extract the raw wealth of the area and return it to England (the company was hoping to find precious metals). Inadequately prepared for life in the Virginia wilderness, by September fifty members of their group had died of disease, starvation, and native attacks. By January 1608, when a ship from England arrived with food and more colonists, only 38 of the original group were alive. With fresh supplies and a new planting season, the colonists were able to slow the death rate, but only temporarily. The winter of 1609–1610, known as the "starving time" brought more food shortages, disease, and death. Some members of the group reportedly resorted to the "custom of the sea" on land when they ate the flesh of their dead fellow colonists.

Although the "starving time" was believed to be the worst period in Jamestown's early history as a proprietary colony, until the Crown assumed responsibility and control of the colony in 1624, colonists struggled with their food supply and the cohesion of their society. The records of the Virginia Company of London report a continuing cycle that revolved from healthful abundance to starvation, disease, and death, and then back to abundance. Colonists sent numerous urgent requests to London for food. The Virginia Company responded to their pleas for food with shipments of English provisions, seeds, livestock, and more colonists to perform agricultural labor. In the beginning the company supplies for the colony were scanty. After a decade of receiving desperate pleas for more English food, the company began to equip the new colonists with what it thought was a year's supply of meal, to see them through the first year. Yet still, complaints of starvation did not cease.[1]

How could such starvation occur in the center of what even conservative commentators believed to be a cornucopia? For one thing, life in the wilderness posed numerous difficulties for the English colonists. Living off the wild was not as easy as early tracts had indicated. Food did not just fall into one's hands, jump into one's boat, or appear at one's doorstep. Hunting and fishing in the New World were not the leisurely activities they were in England. Both required more time, different skills, and considerable effort. Although the rivers held many fish, they were difficult to catch with nets because of the logs and trees lying on the river bottoms. There was always the possibility of being captured by natives, as John Smith was captured while he was foraging for food near Jamestown. The colonists lacked the practical experience to live off nature. They succumbed to New World diseases or suffered from Old World diseases brought with them or developed from the unsanitary conditions on the transatlantic ships. They were lazy, lacked discipline, and may have had different ideas about labor. They may well have suffered from the psychological effects of starvation, such as anorexia and indifference.[2]

The philosophy of food security also played an important role. The scarcity of traditional English foods forced colonists to make choices about what they were going to eat. Two issues surfaced. One issue was how to divide food in general—and English food supplied by the company in particular—among the group. Would everyone get an equal portion, a practice known as the common kettle? Or would those with higher social and political status, the rulers, get first choice and more food, as was the English custom? Because food habits supported their social structure, this question was crucial. Imposition of the common kettle could implode the structure and lead to chaos. However, a policy of rations that were unequal in quality or quantity could incite unrest, if not full-scale insurrection, not to mention the possibility that such a policy might lead to massive starvation.

The second issue concerned the humoral qualities of the flora and fauna of Virginia and the changes that might be caused by their ingestion. Illness was one possibility, with death an unlikely second. Another possibility was the identity change that was sure to follow such a drastic dietary change as the one faced by Henry Norwood and his group. In the colonists' case, the possible change was not so much one from male to female but, rather, from English to native. Given their uncertainty concerning the effects of consuming native foods, colonists had to decide whether to put the native foods in the common kettle or to relegate them to a designated social group.

The Common Kettle in Jamestown

The plight of Edward Maria Wingfield provides an excellent example of the complications of the practice of the common kettle. Like many lesser sons of noble families who did not inherit their father's title or fortune, Wingfield had to choose a profession. After a wasteful youth, he did what previous family members had done and joined the military. After serving in Ireland, he fought against Spain in the Netherlands where he was captured in 1588. Upon his release, he returned to service in Ireland and later became an investor in the Virginia Company of London.

The six other men on the council had comparable experience. Captain Christopher Newport, mariner and former privateer, headed the expedition from London to Virginia. Captain Bartholomew Gosnold, like him, also had privateering experience and had been an explorer. Before going to Virginia, Captain George Kendall had been employed by Sir Robert Cecil, the secretary of state who later became the earl of Salisbury. John Martin came from a family of status and wealth like Wingfield. He was the son of Sir Richard Martin, master of the mint and Lord Mayor of London. A survivor's survivor, John

Smith came from the yeomanry. He had served as a mercenary soldier and a privateer. He had fought against the Turks in Hungary and Transylvania where he was captured and sold into slavery in Russia. He escaped and walked back to western Europe where he once again looked for a job as a mercenary. Little is known about John Ratcliffe, alias John Sicklemore. He mastered the smallest of the three ships that took these men and the other colonists to Virginia. In the months between their arrival and Wingfield's imprisonment, Newport had returned to England, Gosnold had taken sick and died, and the council had confined George Kendall for mutiny.[3]

In England, Wingfield and Martin would have received the deferential treatment due to men of their social rank. Their eating habits would have differed markedly from those of the lower classes. Individuals and groups carved their niche in the social order with their teeth and relegated others to spaces above or below them, a trait common to humans and animals alike. These silent messages could be blatant but more often were subtle, even subconscious, and could be quite intricate. For example, in hierarchical organizations such as the military, eaters sat in messes, which were groups of men of equal rank. The different tables represented different levels of food security. The higher the rank of the eaters, the higher the quality and the greater the variety of foods appearing on their tables. According to contemporary nutritional philosophy, this meant that they, too, were closer to—if not within—the golden mean and hence more capable and virtuous than the people eating in inferior messes. The person of the highest rank of the entire group often not only received the most food (no one ever received as much as the queen in Elizabethan England), he or she also ate first.[4]

The custom of eating first did not just occur in formal organizations. Within families and social groups, the person of the highest rank had first choice of what was available. However, along with this privilege came the responsibility of providing food for others, including the obligation to feed the poor. Rich and poor, neighbor and stranger, all were entitled to the munificence of the host.[5]

Everyone within early modern English society understood that, rather than outright gifting, this arrangement was one of exchange. In return for his hospitality, the host expected "honor, loyalty, alliance, and beneficence." And the hospitality had to be up to certain cultural standards. A man's virtue in the early modern period depended on the state of his household as well as of his person, and his household and person were intricately connected. Furthermore, the standards of hospitality varied according to the social rank of the host. If he were a nobleman, his guests would expect "magnificence," what one late sixteenth-century writer defined as "a virtue that consisteth in sumptuous and great expenses." The standard of hospitality was in accord with the host's assumption of his social rank. Hosts of gentle status were expected to display more modest expense, one more appropriately defined as liberal but neither sumptuous nor ostentatious. These hosts were expected to be prudent in their largesse.[6]

This cultural practice did not mean that rich, poor, neighbor, stranger, and intimate friend were all entitled to the same food or the same treatment, however. Just as effectively as this hospitality invited the closeness of commensality and included people within a group, it divided them by reinforcing social rank and reminding all guests of the power and status of the host. In high status households in the early modern era (such as those from which Edward Wingfield and John Martin came), guests were seated according to social rank. This tradition had its roots in the medieval period when all eaters sat in a great hall, and the host with his family and special guests had their own table on a dais or in a private chamber beyond it. A separate staff served them. Within the rest of the house, screens divided lesser diners, including domestic servants, from their social superiors. These great households maintained ushers or marshals who seated guests in the proper area with others of their rank so no one would be offended by association with people exhibiting fewer social graces. For example, in the fifteenth-century household of a duke, marquis, or earl, any person allowed to sit at the "lord's board" in his private chamber had to be of a social rank at least the son of a baron. Knights might be allowed in the chamber, but they sat at a different table. Clergy sat in the hall at the marshal's table. Servants of the guests or "honest personages of the country" sat in the hall with domestics. Matching these spatial arrangements were specified numbers of companions per mess as well as specific menus, all ranked accordingly.[7]

By the early seventeenth century, some English placed limits on the definition of open hospitality, yet others did not, and conflicts arose. The custom of hospitality was taken so seriously, it was even adjudicated. In the late sixteenth century a series of suits in the Star Chamber and Privy Council involved Sir Thomas Hoby, a puritan, married to Lady Margaret Hoby. Sir Thomas gained local influence as well as a manor and political connections through the union. In a region that was predominantly Catholic, Hoby's puritan ways quickly disgruntled the local populace. One family, the Eures, tested his hospitality by bringing their hunting party, uninvited, to the manor. They not only damaged property, they humiliated the couple and insulted Lady Margaret. Sir Thomas sued them for damages and claimed, essentially, that they had violated the laws of hospitality by being rude and ungrateful guests and that this action brought shame upon the Hobys and their household. The Eures responded that in regards to the violation of codes of hospitality, they did nothing more than Hoby had already done himself with his treatment of guests in the past as well as with his behavior toward their hunting party.[8]

This lawsuit gets to the essential question of attitudes toward hospitality at the time. Should it be limited to the social milieu of the host or expanded to the needy poor? How does one define one's social universe? A mid-seventeenth-century source segmented social universe into three parts: family, strangers, and the poor. Another one characterized a householder's obligations as extending outward from him with family first, then "spiritual and other kin," neighbors, friends, strangers, and then enemies. To complicate the matter, the Renaissance trend toward civility caused a disrupture in traditional notions of hospitality because it promoted exclusivity. Particularly in urban areas, civility permitted people to choose their friends on the basis of virtue, not on physical proximity. As a result, in English society as a whole, a division developed between urban society, which adopted the newer, civil customs of exclusivity, and rural society, which retained older standards of inclusion, and a part of those traditional standards, at least in the eyes of poets, was the service of the same food to all guests. Ben Jonson, in his praise of the country house Penshurst, wrote that it was a place "Where the same beere, and bread, and self-same wine, That is his Lordships, shall also be mine." Another poet described the customs more succinctly as simply "equall freedome, equall fare," meaning that people who enjoyed the same social freedom should eat the same foods.[9]

It would be very easy to be critical of Edward Wingfield for his alleged refusal to share his chickens and beer with the remaining council members. However, these contemporary ideas about commensality and hospitality show the complexity of his situation. The expedition had been in Virginia for a little over four months. Many of the colonists had died. Those remaining understood they had a limited amount of food supplies from England, though most of them did not know just how limited. As George Percy noted in his journal on 22 June 1607, when Christopher Newport left for England: "There were never Englishmen left in a foreign country in such misery as we were in this new-discovered Virginia. . . . Our food was but a small can of barley sod in water to five men a day."[10] They could only hope that Christopher Newport would return in the twenty weeks he had planned. Transatlantic travel, however, was highly unpredictable in 1607. To add to this tension, relations with the natives were strained and the possibility of getting food from them was unreliable. Furthermore, the remaining four men of the council apparently were focused more on themselves than on their success as a colony.

Wingfield, as president, found himself in a particularly tight spot because he lacked most of the symbols of authority that his group recognized. He had no army or entourage, private or otherwise, with which to enforce his authority should the colonists not like his decisions. His family name and power may have seemed less impressive to hungry men in the forests of Virginia than in England. He did not live in a house that showed his status, nor did he have the staff and amenities with which to be openly hospitable in the manner to which he and the other council members were accustomed. He most certainly wore clothes that were common to men of his status, but John Martin and other members of the expedition who came from a similar background would have worn similar clothes. Furthermore, after months on the ship and four months in the wilderness without the benefit of numerous servants to keep them looking fresh, not to mention clean, it is doubtful that these clothes could support an authoritative image.

He did have food. According to John Smith's 1608 account of Wingfield's presidency, Newport left them with enough English provisions for thirteen or fourteen weeks. Although a plethora of sturgeon swam in the streams, and some of the company surfeited on these, they can not really be included as foodstuffs under Wingfield's control. By 10 September 1607, forty-six men had died. Smith believed that almost everyone who survived hated Wingfield for the way he had managed things. Contrary to Smith's explanation, another firsthand account, that of George Percy, mentions no misbehavior by Wingfield. He simply tells of terrible suffering and does not place blame on anyone. Nevertheless, the three-member council deposed their leader and elected the last surviving ship's captain, John Ratcliffe, president. In a later publication, Smith wrote that the colonists, by force of circumstance, found themselves free from the sins of drunkenness and gluttony; all, that is, except Wingfield. He refused to eat from the "common kettle," which every day consisted of one cup of wheat, complete with worms and bran, and a small amount of boiled barley, which would have been the poorest of the poor man's pottage. According to Smith, Wingfield appropriated for himself oatmeal, sack, oil, aqua vitae, beef, and eggs from the company's provisions. He did not limit himself to water, as apparently the other colonists had done.[11]

These accusations highlight the shifting nature of hospitality in a hierarchical humoral universe. As in the Hoby dispute, each of the parties looked differently at his social situation and that of others. Smith came from a yeoman background, in which hospitality would have included a small number of recipients, and the yeoman and his guests would have eaten the same foods and shared the same status, at least during the meal. Smith first complained not that Wingfield took larger portions from the common kettle for himself but that he refused to eat from the common kettle at all. One might think that Smith and others would be grateful because this would mean they would each get a little more for themselves. But to Smith, Wingfield declined commensal relations with the other council members. In doing so Wingfield both symbolically and literally refused to integrate himself into the group. Given their humoral philosophy, the consumption of the same foods by the same people meant that some part of each of them would be composed of the same elements, as deriving from the same source.

In addition to Wingfield's stinginess with his chickens and beer, Smith also complained that he refused to allow the council members to help themselves to a larger share of the common kettle than the other colonists. Their philosophy of food security indicated that this should be the case. In this makeshift society lacking familiar social markers and groups, Smith apparently saw their council as the ruling hierarchy with each of them of equal status. After all, they were each appointed by the king, and (except for Newport) they had sailed to Virginia on an equal footing. As rulers they were entitled to larger quantities and a greater variety of food. As equals they had voted Wingfield president, and as equals they could strip him of that title, which they did.

Wingfield's version of the events, a manuscript titled "A Discourse of Virginia," tells a different story. He acknowledged the conflict between himself and the other council members. During the summer, Wingfield wrote, John Martin proposed a larger portion of the common provisions for the council and some of their favorites who were sick. According to Wingfield, neither Martin nor the other councilors knew that there remained in their stores only two gallons each of oil, vinegar, sack, and aqua vitae. Wingfield declined their demand. He insisted that every man receive the same allowance from the common kettle, divided so that they would have enough to last until Newport's return. Not happy with his direction, the council deposed him on 10 September. The following day they held court and accused him of refusing to give John Ratcliffe a chicken, a spoonful of beer, and an inexpensive knife called a pennywhittle. According to Wingfield his council members complained of different things. Ratcliffe protested that Wingfield served him "foul corn." Smith claimed Wingfield told him that, if they were in England, he would think it scornful to have him as a companion. Martin accused him of being concerned with only his "pot, spit and oven," denying him a spoonful of beer and starving his son. He vowed revenge.[12]

Wingfield denied all their charges, stating that he faithfully gave every man his allowance as apportioned by the council itself. Indeed, after the council removed him, they did no better in managing the supplies. In response to charges that he "did banquet and riot," Wingfield stated: "I never had but one squirrel roasted, whereof I gave part to Master Ratcliff, then sick, yet was that squirrel given me. I did never heat a fleshpot but when the common pot was so used likewise." The other council members, he claimed, had not been so honorable because they ate flesh in front of others who had none. Their "spits have night and day been endangered to break their backs so laden with swans, geese, ducks, etc!—how many times their fleshpots have swelled—many hungry eyes did behold to their great longing."[13]

As if being hungry were not bad enough, these men were caught in the great contemporary conundrum of humoral hospitality, the issue concerning what should be shared with whom. At its center lay the issue of food security, and those of virtue and power. The scarcity of resources made their situation even more problematic. Wingfield chose to forgo the common kettle himself and to distribute its contents evenly among the others, an act of generosity and solidarity he claimed. Early modern hospitality divided people at the same time as it united, however. Wingfield, in declining the common kettle and eating his higher quality and more varied diet of chickens, beer, and squirrel, set himself apart and above his fellow council members and the other colonists.

Also he expected loyalty for his "hospitality." No one claimed that Wingfield should have distributed his private stock equally among all the colonists. Ratcliffe and Martin objected only to Wingfield's refusal to share it with the council. Martin's comment about Wingfield's obsession with his "pot, spit and oven" is derogatory. Who, he implied, would take an oven on what was essentially a camping expedition but someone who wished to laud his status over others by eating different foods? Ratcliffe, appointed by the king to the council, most surely believed himself to be of equal status to the other members in that context. Wingfield's offer of bad corn instead of chicken and beer signaled to everyone his refusal to accept that equal status. Even if Wingfield had indeed given Ratcliffe part of his roasted squirrel when he was ill, this might not have been considered a gesture of equality because an obligation in English society to care for the sick may have overridden normal customs. Martin, being of equal status to Wingfield in England, felt entitled to chicken and beer because of this fact alone, if not for the reasons mentioned by the other council members who protested. Wingfield's actions communicated to Martin that they no longer had equal status and that Martin was in a group with the commoners Smith and Ratcliffe.

In his defense, Wingfield ignored the fine points of dining hospitality and highlighted instead what he believed to be the big issue—meat. Considering the importance of meat to the philosophy of food security, and hence to the colonists' social structure, this focus should not come as a surprise. During this period hot foods, particularly meat, were believed to be the best examples of hospitality. Meat was the most easily assimilated food and therefore was believed to be the most nutritious. To Wingfield, his refusal to eat meat except when everyone else had meat, even though he may have eaten a different kind of meat, was within the hospitality code. Yes, it was true that he reserved his meat for himself, but only when those eating from the common kettle had meat also. If the host ate meat, then so would the guests, although they would not necessarily enjoy the same type of meat. To Wingfield this was fair because everyone ate meat, and therefore he believed he was keeping to the custom of "equal freedom, equal fare." It was a shaky argument, though, for all four men—not to mention the Virginia company partners to whom he appealed—would have understood the difference between chicken and other meat such as salted beef or flesh from animals killed in the forest. Chickens, in the early seventeenth century, represented a domestic and therefore a superior food. As a seventeenth-century author wrote about chickens: "no man I think is so foolish as to commend them to ploughmen and Besomers [laborers]." To prove the point that he truly did possess the virtue expected of his status and the others did not, Wingfield stated that even though Martin, Smith, and Ratcliffe feasted on swans, ducks, and geese, this did them little good. They showed their lack of virtue by eating the fowl in front of others who had nothing.[14]

With few resources to organize their new society, with the baggage of complicated social traditions based on plenty, and with a nutritional philosophy that ranked eaters by the foods they ate, Wingfield chose to collapse his fragile social world into two categories, ruler and ruled. His councilors believed it should have been rulers and ruled. Wingfield underscored his authority with the philosophy of food security by reserving his personal stores for himself.

He was careful, though, to use them in a manner he believed to be gracious. For Smith, Ratcliffe, and Martin, it was the wrong decision to classify them with the rest of the eaters of the common kettle, those men with less status than they, and to keep them further out on the limb of food security. To them, such behavior did not constitute an exchange of hospitality for loyalty. Rather, it vaunted arrogance, elitism, stinginess, and a misuse of power. It invited redress.

Wingfield disappeared from the historical record shortly after he returned from Virginia. Whether the members of the Virginia Company ever heard the defense he laid out so carefully in the manuscript is unknown. Judging by his quick anonymity, it is likely that if they did, the members found it unconvincing.

Attitudes toward American Food in Virginia

The distinction between wild American foods and domesticated English foods and the people who ate them was, in a way, a subset of the issue of the common kettle. If everyone ate from the common kettle, the scarcity of English provisions meant that at some point everyone would have to eat American foods. They would then have to organize their society accordingly. If (as it seems was the case at times) the rulers took English foods for themselves and designated American foods for the common kettle, which they did not share, they could retain at least some part of their food habits and the social structure they supported. This decision was easier said than done, however.

Jamestown colonists were not convinced American foods were equivalent in quality to English foods. They did not see the natives as virtuous. Their attitudes had probably not been shaped or informed by Theodore de Bry's engravings that merged the categories of "Indian" and "virtuous." John Smith was impressed by the Virginia natives' height, straight stature, comely proportions, and superb agility. He also observed that they were brown-skinned, crafty, quick of apprehension, and ingenious, although quick-tempered, malicious, and fearful. Smith's description indicates they had choleric and slightly melancholic temperaments, and these were the least desired of all temperaments. The native temperament certainly did not approximate the golden mean. The colonists did not find the native identity desirable. They associated it with the insecurity of the natives' seasonal subsistence, and with native foods, particularly maize.

John Smith commented that the natives experienced marked bodily changes as their diet altered from season to season. They ate fish, turkeys, and squirrels in March and April and switched to acorns, walnuts, and fish (with occasional beasts, crabs, oysters, tortoises, and berries) in May and early June. From June through August they ate roots, berries, fish, and green corn. Smith wrote: "It is strange to see how their bodies alter with their diet, even as the deare and wilde beastes they seeme fat and leane, strong and weak." Smith's comment refers to more than the size and weight of the natives' bodies. In his world, a lean body indicated a choleric temperament because the heat of the body burned up foods before it could extract their nourishment. A fat body, which lacked enough heat to digest foods efficiently, signified a cold and moist, or phlegmatic, temperament. In these passages Smith depicted the natives as under the stressful influence of the chaotic state of the natural world. The natives were, in Galen's words, in perpetual flux. In our words, they were food insecure at some times during the year.[15]

The colonists' perception of the native diet was one of familiarity and strangeness. Superficially, the Indian and English diet had many commonalities. Both groups relied on at least one staple grain to make basic pottages and bread (an all-inclusive term for anything ranging from a rough mixture of cornmeal and water baked in ashes to a fine, yeast-raised, white bread). Both groups ate venison and wild fowl, particularly when entertaining high-status guests or at feasts. Both groups also consumed vegetables, fruits, and fish, some varieties of which were the same on both continents or at least resembled each other, like sturgeon and oysters. Furthermore, both colonists and natives experienced seasonal variations in their diets. However, the Indians were subsistence eaters. They practiced limited horticulture when they planted maize, two kinds of beans, and squash, but for much of the year they hunted and gathered a large number of foods that comprised the bulk of their diet. When they had no food, they did not eat. When they had food, they ate heartily. This variable and limited diet was not quite what the early seventeenth-century English thought of as food secure.[16]

Despite their aversions, Jamestown colonists did hunt, fish, and eat wild nature's produce. Jamestown's survivors indicated not only that they did both but also that at certain times of the year the fowl and the fish arrived in large quantities making them quite easy to catch. The narratives suggest that the colonists may have limited their selection, however. They did not mention all kinds of game eaten regularly, but only those species as were eaten in England: turkey, sturgeon, venison, and an occasional squirrel. It did not take the Indians long to figure out which wild foods the English preferred. Most of their gifts were turkeys, some fish, and occasionally venison.[17]

Two other statements found in John Smith's writings indicate that colonists resisted eating the wild foods of the New World. Smith became president of the council shortly after Wingfield's downfall, and at one point during his presidency, when food supplies were scarce, Smith wrote that about 150 colonists had fallen into a "strange condition" in which they had to be forced to acquire and prepare their meals. He commanded everyone to forage in the forest. Some of the colonists replied that they would not eat "savage trash." Whether Smith agreed with the colonists on this point is not clear. He was a survivor, a practical man who chose life over death. He told his men that, if they could get it past their mouths, their stomachs would digest it.[18]

This may have been exactly what the colonists feared. The perception of extreme food insecurity concerns not only edibility but also sensibility. The perception is based on the unavailability of preferred foods, rather than on the lack of anything merely edible. Furthermore, when people make choices during times of scarcity, they will often avoid foods that they perceive as physically or morally "polluting." Foods associated with other ethnic groups or with other social segments of the same ethnic groups, such as the poor, are often despised and refused.[19]

One narrative, written by Thomas Studley, the provisioner for Jamestown, and Anas Todkill, a carpenter, suggests as much. To Studley and Todkill, provisions were the makings of a good pottage, items such as oatmeal, peas, barley, beef, eggs, oil, and aqua vitae, not fish, deer, nuts, and berries. Although they occasionally feasted on wild foods in the early months of their occupation, courtesy of the natives' generosity or willingness to bargain, Studley and Todkill believed that they had a sufficiency of food after a supply ship arrived and they again had a stock of English foods. When shortages occurred and the opportunity arose, the colonists would purchase pilfered ship's biscuits from the sailors of visiting vessels in exchange for "money, saxefras, furres, or love." The colonists believed that when the ships left, extreme sickness and weakness began.[20]

Such beliefs about maize were common. Many people thought maize toxic. John Gerard's popular *Herball,* first published in the sixteenth century, instructed its readers that although the "barbarous Indians" who knew no better and were "constrained to make a vertue of necessitie" ate maize and believed it a good food, it actually provided little to no nourishment and made bread as hard as sea biscuits. It was "of hard and evill" digestion and "a more convenient food for swine than for men." Nearly one hundred years later, John Parkinson's herbal stated that eating too much maize would "engender grosse blood" (and hence gross or coarse bodies) and cause itches and scabs in those who were not used to it. Diego Sarmiento de Acuña, the Spanish ambassador to the court of James I, wrote to Philip III, the king of Spain, in 1613 that the majority of the English colonists in Virginia suffered from diseases because they had only maize and a little fish to eat, and water to drink, which was "contrary to the nature of the English." Another Spanish ambassador and Sarmiento de Acuña's predecessor, Pedro de Zuñiga, confirmed what the others had suggested. He informed the Spanish king that several of the English "put among" the natives had themselves become savages. Some time later, an author of a descriptive essay about the colonies of Maryland and Virginia, John Hammond, explained the high death rates in the Chesapeake as being due to "the want of such diet as best agreed with our English natures."[21]

By 1610 after many long months of struggle, the colonists had given up and left the colony. Before they even reached the Atlantic Ocean, they met a ship carrying more supplies, more colonists, and new leadership. The Virginia Company had convinced the king to alter the leadership structure of the colony by installing a governor with strong authority. Lord de la Warr became the first governor, assisted by Sir Thomas Gates and Sir Thomas Dale.

Title page of Robert Fludd, *Utriusque cosmi* (1617–1621). In 1600 Europeans believed that the body, mind, and soul of a human being (the microcosm) were constantly challenged by the forces of the cosmos (the macrocosm). (The Huntington Library, San Marino, California)

(right) The Doryphoros, ca. 440 B.C., was modeled after Greek sculptor Polykleitos' statue known as *The Canon,* the icon of virtue, which was distinguished by its perfect proportions. (The Minneapolis Institute of Arts)

(below) John Rowley's *Orrery, The Young Gentleman's and Lady's Philosophy* (1755). In 1750 many Europeans believed the universe to be a machine with less power over their identity. (General Research Division, The New York Public Library, Astor, Lenox, and Tilden Foundations)

The GRAND ORRERY *as it was first Made by* M.ʳ Rowley.

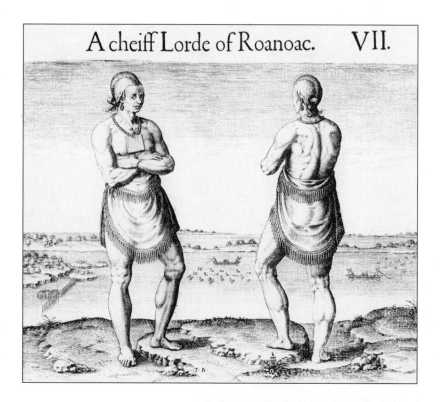

A cheiff Lorde of Roanoac. VII.

(above) A cheiff Lorde of Roanoac, in Thomas Hariot, *A Briefe and True Report of the New Found Land of Virginia* (1590). This early engraving of the American natives indicates their virtue with bodily proportions and classical poses. (Virginia Historical Society, Richmond Virginia)

(right) William Byrd II, by Hans Hyssing (ca. 1700). Colonial Americans created many images of their own idea of virtue, such as this portrait of a gentleman with a well-proportioned physique and delicate hands. (Virginia Historical Society, Richmond Virginia)

64

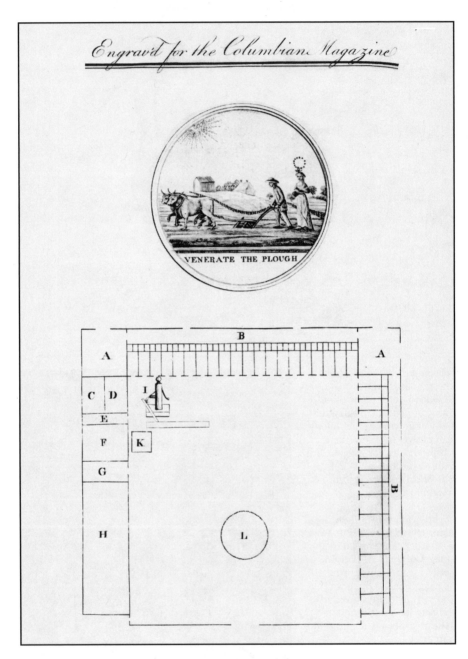

James Trenchard, "The Plan of a Farm Yard—Venerate the Plough," *Columbian Magazine* (1786). By the mid-eighteenth century, the yeoman farmer, distinguished by his land and activity, was the icon of virtue. (The Library of Congress)

Paul Revere, by John Singleton Copley (1768). The urban counterpart of the yeoman farmer, the active artisan exemplified the virtuous man in the mechanical age. (Photograph © Museum of Fine Arts, Boston)

Great Sins of DRUNKENESS and GLUTTONY set forth in proper Colours. And by Scripture sentences and pious Meditations briefly confirmed.

A DRUNKARDS PICTURE and his DOOME by Scripture

A BELLY-GOD. Phil 3. 19.
SODOMS SINN'S pride fullnefs of bread and idlenefs Ezek 16. 49

Wo unto them y are mighty to drink. The drunkard fhall come to poverty. Wine and to mingle ftrong drink Ifa 5. and be cloathed with rags pro. 23. awakeye drunkards Ioel 1. 5. wo to him that giveth his naibour fooles make a mock at fin pro 14.1. drink to make him drunk Hab 2. 13.

Be not amongft riotous eaters of flefh, the glutton fhall com to poverty pro. 23. 20. 21. They were as fed horfes Jer. 5. 8.

And fill themfelves and wax fat Deu. 31. They are inclofed in their own fat pf. 17. 10 Their eyas ftand out with fatnefs pf 73. 7. A foul eat drink. Thou foole Luk 12. 19. 20

WHy do I quaffe
Much more then nature can?
The loffe is mine:
I juftly may be tearm'd
A beaft, not man.

To drown my Reafon
In a cup of Wine,
Yea, ten fold worfe :
A monfter made at leaft.
God made me man,
I make my felf a beaft.

And muft I die?
Why furfeit I on pleafure?
Muft I needs die?
Why fwim I in delight?
Muft I needs die?
Why live I not aright?
Muft I needs die?
Why live I then in fin?
Thrice better for me
I had never been.

PRepare by dying ftill,
Left of bliffe
When time fhall be no more
Sadly thou miffe.
For in Chrifts School
This Paradox learn I ;
Who dies before he dies,
Shall never die.

If I muft die,
Then after muft begin
The life of joy or
Torment without end :
The life of torment
Purchas'd is by fin ;
Then now amend:

Why wilt thou fwear,
Curfe, luft, and lye ?
Think'ft thou on this,
That all muft die ?
            The Conclufion.
Repent therfore whilft breath doth laft
For after death repentance's paft.
And he that hopes to live for aye,
Muft leave fin, and repent each day.

London, Printed by T. C. and are to be fold by T. Croffe, in Py-corner, in Green-dragon court. 1656.

Great Sins of Drunkeness and Gluttony (1656). Virtue could be gained or lost at the table. Both the "beast" and the "belly-god" have committed the sin of gluttony, as evidenced by their disproportioned bodies. (Beinecke Rare Book and Manuscript Library, Yale University)

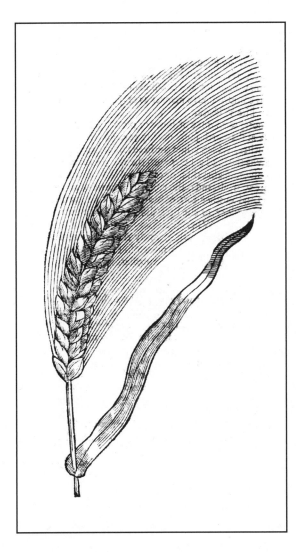

(left) *Triticum Lucidum*, Bright Eared Wheate, and (below) *Milium Indicum Maximum Maiz dictum, five Frumentum Indicum, vel Turcicum* Indian or Turkie Wheate, from John Parkinson, *Theatrum Botanicum* (1640). (The Huntington Library, San Marino, California)

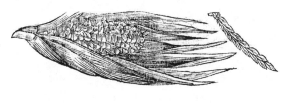

> **To make the best white broth,**
>
> To make the best white broth, whether it be with Veale, Capon, Chickins, or any other Fowle or Fish: First boile the flesh or fish by it selfe, then take the value of a quart of strong mutton broth, or fat Kidde broth, and put it into a pipkin by it selfe, and put into it a bunch of Time, Moricrome, Spinage and Endiue bound together; then when it seeths put in a pretty quantity of Beefe marrow, and the marrow of Mutton, with some whole Mace and a few bruised Cloues; then put in a pint of White-wine with a few whole slices of Ginger; after these haue boyled a while together, take blaunch't Almonds, and hauing beaten them together in a morter with some of the broth, straine them and put it in also; then in another pipkin boile Currants, Prunes, Raisins, and whole Cinamon in veriuice and Sugar, with a few sliced Dates; and boile them till the veriuice bee most part consumed, or at least come to a syrrup; then draine the fruit from the sirrup, and if you see it be high coloured; make it white with sweete creame warmed, and so mixe it with your wine broth; then take out the Capon or the other Flesh or Fish, and dish it vp drie in a dish; then powre the broth vpon it, and lay the fruite on the top of the meate, and adorne the side of the dish with very dainty sippets; first *Orenges*, *Lemmons*, and *Sugar*, and so serue it foorth to the table.

"To Make the Best White Broth," Gervase Markham, *The English House-wife* (London 1631). This recipe is an excellent example of the complexity of many of the foods eaten by high status English people in the early seventeenth century. (Special Collections Department, University of Iowa Libraries)

> *To Boil Fowls and House-Lamb.*
>
> FOWLS and House-Lamb boil in a Pot by themselves, in a good deal of Water, and if any Scum rises take it off. They will be both sweeter and whiter than if boiled in a Cloth. A little Chicken will be done in fifteen Minutes, a large Chicken in twenty Minutes, a good Fowl in Half an Hour, a little Turky or Goose in an Hour, and a large Turky in an Hour and a Half.

"To Boil Fowls and House-Lamb," Hannah Glasse, *The Art of Cookery Made Plain and Easy* (1770). This simple mid-eighteenth-century recipe is just right for the new mechanical body. (Special Collections Department, University of Iowa Libraries)

A December Dinner, in Thomas Fella, *A Book of Diverse Devices* (1622). In the early seventeenth century, complexity was found in the food, not the table setting. (Folger Shakespeare Library)

(above) The Early American Table. By the early nineteenth century, the food was simpler and the table and its accoutrements more complex. (Robert C. Lautman/Thomas Jefferson Foundation, Inc.)

(left) First Sederunt of the Ancient and Honorable Tuesday Club, Dr. Alexander Hamilton (ca. 1745). Dr. Hamilton parodied his own little dinner club's experiment with virtuous eating. (The John Work Garrett Library of The Johns Hopkins University)

The Honorable Carlo Nasifer Jole Esqr. President of the Ancient & Honorable Tuesday Club, Dr.
Alexander Hamilton (ca. 1745). (The John Work Garrett Library of The Johns Hopkins
University)

Mount Vernon. Eighteenth-century Americans embraced the ideal of the yeoman farmer—an ideal that George Washington, like many men of his era, elaborated on at his own farm, Mount Vernon. (Courtesy of the Mount Vernon Ladies' Association)

The latter two immediately created martial laws to control the excessive behavior of the colonists and to try to create some structure in their collapsed society.

Among the laws prohibiting sodomy, adultery, blasphemy, slander, and theft were statutes regulating the colonists' food consumption. One statute prohibited mariners from selling meal, oatmeal, ship's biscuit, butter, cheese, and other provisions to any "Landman" for a price higher than those prices set by the colony and fixed upon the main masts of all harboring ships. Another law forbade mariners to trade food for tools or other metal objects. Anyone, regardless of "quality or condition," who without permission from Gates killed any "Bull, Cow, Calfe, mare, Horse, Colt, Goate, Swine, Cocke, Henne, Chicken, Dogge, Turkie, or any tame Cattel, or Poultry, of what condition soever whether his owne" or belonging to another could be sentenced to death. A fourth law punished with death anyone caught robbing any garden of a root, herb, or flower or destroying any garden, robbing a vineyard or picking grapes, or stealing wheat. Two other statutes warned cooks and bakers that if they skimmed the common ingredients for their own personal gain, or in the case of bakers, if they substituted inferior ingredients or adulterated their products to increase their weight, they would lose their ears on the first offense and be sentenced to the galleys for subsequent infractions. These laws were not just idle threats. Authorities thrust a needle through the tongue of a colonist who stole two pints of oatmeal. They then chained him to a tree until he starved to death.[22]

Maize

These laws laid down the highest of penalties for the killing of *domestic* English animals, the picking of *cultivated* English vegetables and fruits, and the adulteration of English foods, but they set no price on the abundant wild—another indicator of the low regard in which colonists held the native foods they preferred not to eat. This aversion included the natives' cultivated staple, maize. From the very beginning of the Virginia Company venture, the English imported their own livestock and planted the soil with English seeds. Success came very slowly. For much of the first twenty years of the colony's existence the colonists were not nutritionally self-sufficient. Hundreds of them died. As the modern-day American myth about the country's beginnings would have it, their eventual success would not have occurred at all had it not been for maize. This might be true, but the glorification of maize has prevented scholars from analyzing the delay in its acceptance. This acceptance came very slowly, and the delay may very well have been the major source of the starvation problem in early Virginia, because in the sixteenth and seventeenth centuries, grains constituted the largest component of the diet of the English lower classes.[23]

This scholarly oversight may in part result from hindsight. The production and distribution of maize by people and its consumption by both people and animals have contributed significantly to the later economy and history of the United States. The oversight certainly also results from difficulty in interpreting the primary sources. In early modern England, and in fact still today, "corn" was a generic term for grain. The members of the Virginia Company used the term primarily to refer to wheat, barley, oats, and peas. Sometimes they wrote of "English corn" or "our corn." They also employed the term when they referred to maize, quite often with the adjectives "Indian" or "their." However, in many documents they simply wrote "corn." Because of the English definition of the term "corn" and because the writers often mentioned the specific type of grain when they meant one in particular, the term "corn" at the very least connotes multiple varieties of grain, and more than likely English grains, the most valued of which was wheat.[24]

If we conservatively reinterpret these early sources by substituting "grain" for "corn" and if we assume that the term "grain" includes all English grains and maize, we would have to conclude that the settlers did not plant or consume as much maize as has been assumed. This approach is unsatisfactory, however, because it is based on the presumption that the Virginia colonists willingly embraced maize. This may not have been the case. A more accurate approach would be to substitute the term "English grains" for "corn" except in references to the natives or where the author clearly contemplated maize, as for example is the case with the term "tribute corn."[25]

Several incidents indicate that many of the colonists did not eat or did not want to eat maize. First, from the beginning of the settlement, the intention of the company and its representatives in Virginia was to establish English plants. The company's instructions to its first group of settlers in 1607 advised them to plant their own seeds immediately, an act they successfully accomplished soon after their arrival. In the spring of the following year, the colonists cleared forests to cultivate more acres of wheat. John Smith instituted the first attempts to plant maize at that time. He met with resistance from the colonists, many of whom wished the crop would fail. This may have been because they wanted to return to England. More probably they may not have wanted to eat maize and would have preferred to see the cleared land planted with English grains. Smith had already explored more of the world, and he took a more liberal and functional approach to eating. Other Englishmen —who had probably never left their county before, much less England—did not share his attitude. The colonists neglected their maize and consumed their livestock after Smith left the colony in 1609.[26]

Lord de la Warr's first and most intense efforts were to reestablish sound agricultural practices. He ordered the colonists to plant roots and English grains, not maize. When de la Warr left the colony because of ill health and Thomas Dale replaced him, Dale also desired the colonists to devote their efforts to the cultivation of grain. To encourage them he allotted some men three acres of cleared fields for which they had to pay into the company store two and one-half barrels of "Corne," presumably English grains. He tightly regulated the consumption of English foodstuffs. No control of maize was necessary.[27]

Gates and Dale achieved success. However, several years after their depar-
ture the colony once more fell on troubled times and sent periodic urgent requests for meal and other provisions to the Virginia Company. Colonists accused Samuel Argall, the colony leader from 1617 to 1619, of appropriating
for himself the best of the colony's produce. Argall arrived at the colony during a particularly prosperous time when the common kettle seemed anything
but common. The company garden not only fed the colonists but yielded a
profit of three hundred pounds sterling and the company owned eighty cows
and eighty-eight goats. Rents in English grain and tribute maize from the natives averaged twelve hundred bushels per year. Two years later someone,
most likely not the rank-and-file colonists, had consumed everything but six
goats. Agricultural production had dwindled to practically nothing, a situation that continued as late as 1621. The Virginia Company advised the governor and council in Virginia that they were aware that the receiving colonists
took the fresh English provisions of newcomers and gave them maize as a
substitute. Believing this sudden dietary change caused illness and death, the
company commanded that the practice cease.[28]

The president of the council in 1620, George Yeardley, explicitly reiterated
many of his predecessors' general comments when he explained to the company that the provisions supplied did not allot enough wheatmeal per person. He stated that the least amount a man could live on was a bushel per
month. If they could not send the quantity of meal that was needed, he agreed
they could make up the difference in peas and oatmeal, but they would still
have to allow a pound of meal a day in addition to servings of the other English
grains. The company complained but complied with these requests. Even
though it experienced a tremendous financial drain from feeding the colonists,
the company did not pressure the council to plant more maize.[29]

In fact the Virginia Company repeatedly shipped them English seeds.
Throughout the proprietary period, the correspondence between the colony
in Virginia and the company in London show that both sides anxiously
wished to establish the cultivation of English grains, particularly wheat. Despite the declarations of some of the promotional essays, wheat may not have
been as easy to cultivate as the English had anticipated. Adaptation to the soil
and climate may have been one problem. The heavy labor involved in clear-
ing the fields and cultivating them English-style certainly took tremendous
time and energy, something that ill or inexperienced settlers may not have
been able to accomplish efficiently. Finally, the acquisition of adequate supplies of seeds presented a major obstacle, either because of the inherent quality of the seeds or their deterioration during shipment.[30]

Wheat bound the English together, and then it divided them by ranking
them into different categories depending on the quality of wheat they ate.
Maize only divided the early Jamestown colonists. To make a person eat
maize signified that his rank was equal with that of the natives—or of the
livestock to which maize may also have been fed—and put him outside the

wheat-eating group and in a state of food insecurity. In 1620 George Thorpe, a new council member, wrote to his business partner John Smith of Nibley about the struggling colony. He believed that the diseases of the settlers were of the mind rather than the body because they had had "this countrey victuall over-praised unto them in England." Six months later, Thorpe wrote to another correspondent that he was convinced the inclusion of poorly sifted maize in the bread of "the people" made it very unwholesome and was a cause of the severe diarrhea suffered by many. Thorpe's comments are interesting for his beliefs about maize and also because, in both references, he implies that he, a man of high status among the colonists, did not eat it. Rather, "the people" did. The same held true of Captain Nuce of Virginia, who expressed a desire to Sir Edwin Sandys in England that English grains would begin to prosper there. "The people," he wrote, eat only bread and water "and such manner of meate [food] as they make of the Mayze."[31]

Although the sources indicate that throughout the proprietary period the colonists sought out the natives in order to acquire the natives' maize, how they used the acquired maize is not fully understood. Some humans ate it. Livestock more than likely did as well. Shipments of cattle, dairy cows, goats, hogs, and many types of poultry regularly arrived in Virginia from England. Early on, the colonists allowed the cattle and hogs to roam freely. When Thomas Dale took control of the community he enclosed large tracts of land for grazing, in part to protect the English community and their livestock from the natives. Even though these tracts were large, they may not have provided enough sustenance for the larger animals. Hogs, which the colonists did allow to roam the forests, may have been the only exception. The fowl and the goats also had to be fed. Maize could have provided that fodder then, as it does today.

So, many Virginia colonists did not wholeheartedly include maize into their diets. It appears that social superiors forced it upon their inferiors, showing how the colonists used foods to clarify rank. In a world lacking much of the traditional structure of English culture, maize provided some order to the chaos of the early years of the Virginia settlement.

Several questions can be asked about the behavior of the Jamestown colonists. Why was it that men who were starving would not plant maize except under threat of the severest penalty? One answer is that the communal requirement to work for the benefit of the common kettle eradicated any kind of work incentive the men may have had. Why should they work hard only to receive the same return as the man who sought every chance he could to loaf? As a result, the colonists chose to work little or not at all. But would a man refuse to work on such a principle even if he were starving? Furthermore, were not men in hierarchical England used to working for others? No one in their world received better than his superior. No one received more than the king, who did not work at all. Another question is why would these same men who, at least according to John Smith, owed their very lives to the maize fields of the Indians burn those fields before the crops were harvested?

Logic leads to the conclusion that, if they objected to cultivating maize because of the perceived inequities of communal farming, they surely would
not object to freely taking maize that resulted from someone else's labor. The
fact that gentlemen and their personal servants comprised a large percentage
of the population of early Jamestown is also believed to be a cause of the fail-
ure of the colony to support itself agriculturally. Not accustomed to field-
work, these gentlemen simply refused to do it and expected someone else to
feed them. Another explanation is that they lacked husbandmen who knew
how to cultivate. Yet, by most accounts from early America, and not just
those from Virginia, maize grew well enough. Furthermore, should expertise
be needed, the natives could have easily provided it.[32]

Each of these puzzling questions can be answered by the supposition that
the colonists did not want to eat maize. Why would anyone labor at growing
something he would not eat? Thomas Dale assigned a small garden plot to
each colonist so each could keep a garden for himself. This arrangement
seemed a solution at first because those colonists who kept gardens worked for
themselves, not others. It could also have been, though, that they could then
plant what they wanted to eat, not what someone else told them to eat. The success of individual gardens shows that colonists did have husbandry skills and
contradicts the idea that they starved because they did not know how to grow
food. Their distaste for maize solves the puzzle of why they would burn the
maize fields of the natives. At the very least it would punish the Indians. At the
most, it would prevent the colonists from having to eat it themselves.

NEW ENGLAND

Pilgrims who began to settle New England in 1620 desired to and did create a society that differed markedly from that in Virginia. They arrived as
families of middling status and not as single young men. As separatists they
hoped to create a society different from and better than the one they had left behind. Many of the New England colonists had prepared themselves for their settlement of North America. They also had the experiences of Virginia colonists as
examples of what not to do. Even so, the first year of settlement presented immense difficulties. English provisions ran low, a circumstance that forced them,
like the Virginians, to explore the natural resources of the region for sustenance.
Unlike the Virginians, however, they expressed entirely different attitudes toward
food insecurity. Rather than dispute the common kettle, they embraced it and
the American foods it contained as all being a part of the communal philosophy
they had chosen to practice even before they arrived.

The Common Kettle in Plymouth

The story of the Plymouth colonists' first year of adversity, starvation, and
success ending in a feast of thanksgiving has become a fundamental part of

the American national consciousness. It shall not be disturbed here. The Pilgrims suffered greatly during their first three months, and half of their community members were dead several months later. However, firsthand accounts such as that of William Bradford, the leader of the settlement, show that the colonists thought the demise of half their colony to be caused by exposure to cold and infectious disease resulting from so many weeks of confinement during their transatlantic voyage. Said Bradford, "but that which was most sad and lamentable was, that in two or three months' time half of their company died, especially in January and February, being the depth of winter, and wanting houses and other comforts; being infected with the scurvy and other diseases which this long voyage and their inaccommodate condition had brought upon them." The colonists still lived on the *Mayflower* for lack of adequate housing on shore, and as they fell sick they were taken to shore to hastily made dwellings so as not to infect the other passengers and crew members. Those Pilgrims who were healthy fixed meals for their companions. Some hunted wild fowl, others fished, and their activities garnered seal, cod, and geese. In early February, one of their members found a deer killed by the Indians being eaten by two wolves. Curiously, the report, found in *Mourt's Relation,* does not state whether the colonists scavenged the deer or let it lie.[33]

By mid-March the colonists began spring planting. They planted English wheat and peas as well as maize, which they had found when they first arrived in New England. The English seeds did not grow. Bradford surmised that they may have been bad. They may have been planted too late in the season or have failed for some other reason. Nevertheless, the colonists suffered no scarcity that summer. In the fall, they harvested their maize, shot numerous waterfowl, wild turkeys, and deer. Furthermore, they still had "meal," which most likely was wheatmeal. Bradford claimed they had about a peck per person per week, "or now since harvest, Indian corn to that proportion." The colonists not only felt comfortable with their food supply, they wrote to friends and families in England of their plentiful life. However, new colonists arrived who were poorly provisioned. When the ship that brought them left in early December, Bradford and his assistant inventoried their provisions and realized that even if they put everyone on half provisions they had enough for only six months. Their sense of prosperity evaporated quickly, but, remarked Bradford, "they bore it patiently under hope of supply."[34]

By the following spring, they had exhausted their provisions completely. They watched anxiously for a supply ship. The only vessel that arrived was a small shallop from another part of New England that delivered seven passengers, without food, to the suffering colony. Because of their late arrival, these folks could not plant "corn" for themselves, but the colonists at Plymouth fed them, according to Bradford, as good as any of their own. To make matters worse, another group of settlers, this time sixty "lusty men," came from England, courtesy of Thomas Weston who hoped to start his own colony in the vicinity. They, too, lacked food. Most of them stayed throughout the summer. Some who were ill stayed longer. Relief of sorts finally came when the *Bona Nova,* mastered by Captain John Huddleston, took one of the men to procure food from other ships. He got enough wheat bread to allow each colonist one fourth of a pound a day. Bradford doled this amount out daily to prevent the colonists from eating it too quickly. Between that bread and "what else they could get, they made pretty shift till [their] corn was ripe."[35]

The autumn of 1622 brought another harvest that provided some relief to the colony for a short while. It could not, however, fulfill their needs for the upcoming year. Bradford believed this was in part because they were still not familiar with how to grow "corn" and because they were too weak from lack of adequate nutrition. They just did not have the energy to tend the corn. To their good fortune, or, as Bradford would have it, due to the providence of God, an English ship arrived and sold them trade goods that they could then use to procure maize from the natives. This they did, with the help of Thomas Weston's people who volunteered the use of their small ship to carry their barter back. They accumulated nearly twenty-eight hogsheads of maize and beans, some of which they shared with Weston's group, which by the early part of 1623 had misused it and, once again, was in great need. Some people from Weston's group began to steal from the natives; others fled to the forest to scrounge for groundnuts and shellfish. Others became servants to the natives. Upon hearing of their plight, Bradford sent Miles Standish to help them out or, if need be, bring them back to Plymouth. They asked Standish to give them corn to sustain them in a voyage "to the eastward." He gave them what he had.[36]

In the spring the colonists planted more "corn." They had used all their stores and prayed every day for enough food to keep them alive until the next harvest. During the spring and summer, with their one small boat and a net they purchased, they fished nonstop, sending one group of men out immediately upon the return of another. If the trips brought nothing, the whole colony dug shellfish in the sand. Some of the men were able to kill a few deer. In the winter they had fowl and groundnuts. In mid-July yet more colonists arrived. Most of them, about sixty people, came "as part of the General." In other words, they came to share equally in the collective endeavor. In addition, some independent colonists "came as their Particular," meaning they were on their own. The colonists, with their "low condition" and "ragged apparel," appalled the new arrivals. Bradford lamented: "The best dish they could present their [newly arrived] friends with was a lobster or a piece of fish without bread or anything else but a cup of fair spring water." A drought threatened to destroy their crops, but rain, following a day of humiliation and prayer, reversed that awful possibility. As a result, the Pilgrims enjoyed "a fruitful and liberal harvest." Furthermore, in March the following year, they received their first livestock, three heifers and a bull. Thus began the beginning of the end of their food insecurity.[37]

Attitudes toward American Food in Plymouth

Settlers in the two early colonies at Jamestown and Plymouth experienced similar difficulties in acquiring enough food to satisfy their needs. Both groups found that living off the land was more difficult than they had envisioned. They experienced long periods of shortages of English provisions and had to endure hunger. However, the reactions of the two groups to these conditions differed markedly. Settlers in Jamestown competed, cheated, or prostituted themselves for English foods, while many disdained maize. In Plymouth, on the other hand, the colonists (at least among those who comprised "the General") shared equally from the common kettle and expressed thanks for whatever they had. They seem to have embraced maize readily. What accounts for this difference?

Just as, in the Roman Empire, all roads seemed to lead to Rome, in Puritan studies all roads seem to point to religion. It seems a facile answer, and perhaps it is, but only on the surface. The Plymouth colonists, like many other protestants of the time period, believed that adversity had its spiritual rewards. This belief led William Bradford to comment about his pitiful band: "The long continuance of this diet, and their labours abroad, had something abated the freshness of their former complexion; but God gave them health and strength in a good measure, and showed them by experience the truth of that word, (Deuteronomy viii.3) 'That man liveth not by bread only, but by every word that proceedeth out of the mouth of the Lord doth a man live.'"[38]

In addition, the Pilgrim belief in communalism at first eliminated or at least minimized the power of food as a social demarcator within the community itself. Like Thomas More's Utopians, the Pilgrims set up their community on the basis of equal freedom, equal fare. In their case, it was equal freedom for all, equal fare for all. When it came to food, they implemented this ideal from the very beginning. They raised food together and distributed it equally among their members. When strangers or newcomers arrived, they received as the others did. In this way, maize as well as other foods served as commensal tools, equalizing the group members and binding them together. Each person got the same quality and the same variety of food. The social stratification so evident in the larger English society and at Jamestown was dissolved.

In addition, the English in general during the seventeenth century developed an increased interest in (or perhaps a better phrase might be paranoia of) gluttony and its consequences. A pure soul could not exist in a glutted body. Even so the differences between the Puritan dietary ideals and those of other English people differed markedly. Their food habits did mark social and religious boundaries, not among themselves, but between themselves as a group and everyone else.

Plymouth settlers embraced maize as a gift from God. If it was an adversity, it would build their souls. The Pilgrim members of "the general" sought to eliminate social rank within their community. Maize was actually the perfect food with which to do this. Unlike wheat it did not come in different grades or qualities, so it could only bind the colonists together, not divide them. As long as everyone ate maize, everyone was secure. Virginians, on the other hand, employed maize to create social distinctions. Underlying both practices was the humoral philosophy that the incorporation of different foods would change a person in unknown ways.

Despite what he saw as the persuasiveness of Thomas More's *Utopia* and Plato's *Republic,* William Bradford concluded, in the early spring of 1623, that the Pilgrims' plan to create a united and peaceful society would not be achieved if they continued with their policy of the common kettle. Their paltry harvest of the previous autumn had disappointed all of them. After listening to much debate as to how to increase their yield and upon the advice of "the chiefest amongst them," Bradford reluctantly agreed to allow every man to plant crops for himself and his family. This, and this alone, was to be done "in the particular." All other aspects of their communal life were to remain the same. Each family had the use of, not the title to, a plot of land large enough to support the family. In addition, Bradford distributed "all boys and youth" to work among the families. He saw the immediate success of his decision. Everyone was industrious, even women who "took their little ones with them to set corn; which before would allege weakness and inability; whom to have compelled would have been thought great tyranny and oppression." Unfortunately, we do not know whether by "corn" Bradford meant wheat or maize.[39]

According to Bradford, their experiment failed because the colonists realized that although egalitarianism was a great idea, it just did not work in practice. A communal food system, he thought, led to "much confusion and discontent and retard[ed] much employment that would have been to their benefit and comfort." Young men complained they had to work for other men's families without any recompense. Strong men complained they needed more food and clothes than weaker men. The "aged and graver" men balked at being lowered to the level of younger, less mature men, complaining that it entailed a loss of respect. Finally, married men disliked the fact that their wives were cooking, laundering, and performing other housewifery tasks for other men. Bradford concluded that total equality within the group diminished mutual respect. Furthermore, individual enterprise did not lead to corruption. Men already were corrupt, a condition for which only God had the cure.[40]

CONCLUSION

Colonists in both Jamestown and Plymouth lacked food security, but their responses to this insecurity differed. Virginia colonists refused to rethink any part of their philosophy of food security. Although given the opportunity to redefine their standards of quality by valuing maize as an equal substitute for wheat, they declined. Faced with scarcity, some of them employed the philosophy to ensure that the rulers were the most food secure. They did not seek to reinvent themselves, their society, or their philosophy. Hence, they struggled to re-create a world they had neither the quantity nor the quality of foods to make.

The Plymouth colonists, ambitious as they were to create a new and different society from the one they had left behind, were not ambitious enough. Although willing to change their ideas about food and the structure of their society, they did not and probably could not change their ideas about themselves. They struggled to implement simultaneously the two ideas of the individual golden mean and the social golden mean in which the median group of society has food security. To achieve the social golden mean following the humoral philosophy required expensive, high quality foods and a privileged lifestyle. This was impossible without extensive Utopian-like regulations or the natural abundance that early writers had fantasized about. Young men complained they had to do more work than the elders and did not get the amounts of food they needed. They lacked food security because the quantity of food they received did not balance the labor they expended. Elders who worked less complained that their superior virtues were not respected by the others. But then, why should they, if the group had dedicated itself to a golden social mean?

One solution to this Pilgrim dilemma came decades after the demise of the Plymouth experiment in the form of a new philosophy of the body, one that conceived the body in terms of mechanics rather than humors and emphasized similarity among humans, not differences. The new philosophy redefined the requirements for virtue. Including individuals as well as their society, this philosophy created a social golden mean in which the bulk of the society enjoyed food security and consequently virtue.

PART TWO

The Social Golden Mean

CHAPTER

FIVE

I

n London in 1707 an English physician, Jeremiah Wainewright, published a health text for a new age. Titled *A Mechanical Account of the Non-Naturals*, it presented to its readers an image of the human body that might have amused Hippocrates and Galen and startled their sixteenth-century interpreters. Not so Wainewright's readers. His message was hardly new. "The Humane Body," wrote Wainewright in the introduction, "is a curious Machine," so finely crafted that it can only be of divine design. At the time, the term "machine" was a double entendre. Referring to a simple or complex device, such as a lever, a spinning wheel, or a wheelbarrow, it could also refer to a theoretical construct that had its basis either in devices or in abstract mathematical mechanics and was used to explain a system such as the universe.[1]

Wainewright employed both meanings. For him an elaborate device, the human body contained many smaller yet still complex devices, which in turn were "compos'd of Solids and Fluids" of a much simpler design and could be observed and quantified. Wainewright believed the stomach to be the most important part of the body. Replacing earlier images of the stomach as a cooking pot or a fermenter, he characterized it as a muscular crusher. "The Stomach, by the help of its Muscular Fibres, together with the Diaphragm and Muscles of the Abdomen, is enabled so to toss the Meat [food] about," he wrote. The force with which the stomach accomplished this task had been mathematically estimated to be equal to 3,720 pounds and quite effectively separated the "viscid matter" of ingested food from blood, enabling further digestion to take place.[2]

The concept of the microcosm within the macrocosm, that the human body reflected the universe, remained useful in early eighteenth-century thought. When the prevailing concept of the macrocosm changed from a universe of chaos and unpredictability to one of stability and predictability, as it did in the seventeenth century, so did the understanding of the microcosm. The same laws of motion, gravity, impulse, and reaction that governed the universe affected the mechanical body. Wainewright's description of the body, therefore, employed vivid phrases such as the "comparative Force of the Muscles be as their *Solidities* or *Gravities*," "Muscular Motion," and the "Æquilibrium between the Blood and Vessels." Underlying these phrases was a belief that the mysteries of the human body could be solved in the same way that philosophers and experimenters were solving the puzzles of the universe.[3]

THE PREDICTABLE UNIVERSE

Although historians debate the term "the Scientific Revolution" and the exact nature and extent of its character, the general changes that took place between the late sixteenth century and the early eighteenth century are not in dispute. As a result of the work of Nicolaus Copernicus, Galileo Galilei, and Isaac Newton, western Europeans stopped thinking of themselves, or at least their planet, as the center of the universe, and they started believing that their planet moved. Not only did it move, it traveled around the sun. Perhaps more unbelievable, this movement could be calculated mathematically, as could the reason the planet stayed in its orbit and did not fly off unpredictably.

Certain aspects of this process are important to the discussion of how the concept of the human body changed from humoral to mechanical. Generally, with these and other new ideas, the concept of the universe had changed. The old model—of a closed cosmos in which form shaped matter in qualitative ways enabling a hierarchical organization—gave way to an open universe comprised simply of matter and motion, devoid of any qualitative character but capable of quantification. The mechanical universe was infinite, and it was homogeneous for matter did not come in varieties or qualities. Matter was the same everywhere. This thinking led to a different and more comfortable view of the universe, whose uniformity fostered predictability. The ability to reduce the universe to numbers promoted a sense of security.

While accurate, this brief description is too neat to depict presicely the slow and erratic process of starts and stops characterizing the change from old philosophical model to new. The ideas most important to this change can be organized into three areas: mechanics, metaphysics, and chemistry. Natural philosophers used all three approaches either individually or together to explain the macrocosm.

Mechanics

During the late sixteenth and early seventeenth centuries, numerous machines were invented and employed for all manner of practical and theoretical purposes. In the late sixteenth century, for example, the German mineralogist Georgius Agricola developed pumps, hoists, and derricks. Italian military engineer Agostino Ramelli attended to milling, sawing, and lifting stones. The French engineer and physicist Salomon de Caus developed his ideas of abstract mechanics. On a broader scale, but still very much as part of the general inquiry into mechanics, the Polish astronomer Copernicus announced that the earth rotated on an axis and circulated around the sun. The microscope, more accurate telescopes, the air thermometer, both mercury and water barometers, air pumps, the slide rule, and the pendulum clock were all invented between 1575 and 1675. New machines were developed for spinning, weaving, and knitting. In addition, theoretical mechanics attracted the attention of many thinkers whose overall goal was to explain mathematically the movement and interaction of celestial and earthly bodies. This accomplishment, the mathematical explanation, would eliminate once and for all the philosophical need for angels as movers of the macrocosm, and for the soul as the mover of the microcosm.[4]

The idea of a mechanical cosmos is an old one. Galileo took it to a new height with his studies of acceleration, pendular motion, trajectories, virtual velocities, acoustical resonance, and magnetism. Isaac Newton maximized the idea with his mathematical proof of gravity. This collective accumulation of ideas resulted in the widespread belief that all physical objects were "material masses reciprocally determining each other's motions or position." This belief applied to everything from a simple machine such as a lever to something as big as the universe. Matter and motion became the focal point of metaphysical speculation.[5]

Metaphysics

Many seventeenth-century philosophers relied on ancient ideas to explain matter and motion. The view that became prominent in the seventeenth century was atomism or corpuscular theory, which described the universe as composed of tiny indivisible particles, known as corpuscles, suspended in a void. These particles had two distinguishing features: they were of different sizes and shapes, and they moved constantly. Events or processes that produced change, generation, or destruction occurred as a result of the combining and recombining of the particles. Although these particles differed in size and shape, they were all composed of the same matter. The varying combinations of their size, shape, and motion gave them each their unique identity.[6]

Chemistry

Chemical concepts, both metaphysical and mundane, also played a part in the shift of knowledge from the ancient to the early modern. While mechanists viewed the universe as quantifiable, alchemists and chemists concerned themselves with the qualities of things. Most histories of chemical ideas begin with the Swiss iconoclast Paracelsus (1493–1541). He created a dynamic chemical philosophy that emphasized function and activity and that featured powers, forces, spirits, and influences of nature. Rejecting the ancient philosophy of the four elements, Paracelsus believed that the three chemicals salt, sulfur, and mercury were found in all things. Unlike the classical four elements of earth, air, water, and fire, the Paracelsian elements differed from thing to thing. The salt in one thing was not the same as the salt in another. Neither was the mercury or the sulfur. It was this difference in the basic elements that caused differences between things.[7]

Although Paracelsus's ideas were original, there were many questions about nature they left unanswered. From the sixteenth to the seventeenth century, other thinkers added their ideas to the collective understanding. A German professor of medicine, Daniel Sennert, retained the four elements of earth, air, water, and fire but added mercury, salt, and sulfur as secondary principles that shaped taste, color, and odor, something the original four elements did not do. Sennert's theory, although conciliatory, did not advance chemical thinking. However, it may have encouraged a new idea that synthesized the four elements and the three principles. Physician Joseph DuChesne was most probably the developer of this idea in 1584. Rejecting Aristotle and embracing corpuscular theory, he postulated the existence of five elements: mercury, salt, earth, sulfur, and water. Each of these was complex and functional, meaning it showed chemical behavior and could be studied and identified. In putting forward this hypothesis, DuChesne paired the theoretical with the practical. In the seventeenth century, the Flemish chemist, physiologist, and physician Jean Baptiste Van Helmont reduced the number of universal components to two—water and ferments. He believed water to be a universal element from which everything else arose. Ferments, an idea based on his observation of fermentative processes, fashioned water into individual things, giving them each their own unique properties. Chemical actions arose with the ferments, especially when the process involved fire.[8]

THE PREDICTABLE UNIVERSE IN HUMANS

Living in a world that lacked specific disciplines such as chemistry, physics, or biology, many of the philosophers and scientists in the seventeenth century easily transferred ideas from one realm to another. Thinkers from Galileo to René Descartes, William Harvey, and Isaac Newton applied their theories of the macrocosm to the microcosm. The human body, machine or no machine, is highly complex. While all of its parts were actually viewed with the naked eye and the relationship of the parts thoroughly understood by the beginning of the eighteenth century, many of the life processes, such as digestion, could not be observed and so remained the subject of speculation, but speculation with a mechanical bent.[9]

Biology, in general, and human physiology, in particular, simultaneously became mechanistic on both meso- and micro-levels. Some thinkers, such as the French mathematician and philosopher René Descartes, applied their mechanical views to everything from the universe to corpuscles. Generally, changes in thought played out in two ways. First, the new ideas eliminated ancient theories concerning the identity of all things (forms and qualities) and concerning what caused life and what kept it going (nature, faculties, spirits, and souls). The new ideas replaced these old theories with mechanisms. In addition, at both levels (of identity and of life force), the details of those mechanisms were either exposed or elaborated on. Descartes provides an excellent example with which to begin this section on iatromechanics (mechanics of the human body) because of his wide-ranging ideas and influence.[10]

Descartes had the advantage of being familiar with the work of Andreas Vesalius, a Flemish anatomist and surgeon often regarded as the founder of modern anatomy, whose detailed anatomical studies portrayed the body and its parts in a mechanical light. In his *Treatise of Man,* written between 1629 and 1632, Descartes declared that he wrote not about a man but about a machine. He placed his work in the realm of the hypothetical in order to protect himself from death (in 1624 the Parliament of Paris forbade anyone, under penalty of death, to teach or think any ideas that refuted Aristotle), which it did. But it also made strikingly clear his idea that physiological functions did not depend on the soul.[11]

Although Descartes invented analytical geometry, he did not measure the human body. He used a deductive rationalism to arrive at his theories. A believer in corpuscular theory, he concluded that the difference between life and death or between living entities and nonliving entities was motion. The metaphor often used to describe his view is that of a watch. Life in all its forms was like a watch wound and ticking. Death, on the other hand, could be compared to a broken watch incapable of any movement. Of course, a human body could not be wound like a watch. Its source of motion was the heat of the heart, which Descartes likened to a fire. The blood, a renewable resource manufactured by the liver from digested food, sustained this fire.[12]

At the same time Descartes was writing, English physician and anatomist William Harvey was conducting experiments on the heart and the blood in England. In the early seventeenth century, even the most educated people did not know that blood circulated throughout the body. They could not see capillaries beneath the skin, and they thought body tissues actually consumed blood rather than just taking nutrients from it. Harvey's 1628 treatise on circulation, *De Motu Cordis*, caused a major break from ancient physiology. His characterization of the process was strictly mechanical. The heart was a pump. Blood whisked through it like water rushed through a bellows.[13]

Neapolitan mathematician and physiologist Giovanni Borelli furthered the mechanical philosophy and refined it by giving it direction. He believed all living bodies were complex machines composed of smaller machines, on down to the smallest of particles. Life, to him, was the sum of all the movements of all the machines. Although elegant, this theory troubled many philosophers. They wondered what made the machines move and what regulated this moving force.[14]

Metaphysical concepts of matter and motion or, more correctly, matter *in* motion went hand in hand with the practical idea that the body was a machine. An excellent example of a synthesis of matter and motion is the work of the English chemist, physicist, and theologian Robert Boyle, who, like other natural philosophers, believed that all corpuscles were composed of universal matter. Differences among them came from their "bulk, figure, and either motion or rest." The individual characteristics of things arose when the corpuscles combined, which they did with great efficiency, making it difficult for them to disperse. The body itself, for Boyle, was "an engine not a rude heap of limbs and liquors" whose basic functions such as locomotion, digestion, and the production of milk and semen could be explained mechanically. These and other vital processes came about because of the separation and reunification of the corpuscles—in other words, matter in motion.[15]

Boyle did not believe in any immaterial force in the body. He believed it was an automaton with solid and fluid parts, what he called a "hydraulopneumatical engine." Other philosophers were deeply divided on this issue. The German physician Friedrich Hoffmann, an influential theoretician, disagreed with Boyle, defining life as the "continuous and appropriate movement of the fluid parts through the solids." He thought that animal spirits caused the movement of the soul, and "an immortal substance stemming from the decree of God himself" directed them.[16]

The natural philosophers who developed chemical ideas about the body sought to explain what were arguably the most difficult aspects of physiology, the life processes that could not be observed such as digestion and metabolism. Ancient philosophy characterized digestion as a heat-induced phenomenon, essentially cooking. Metabolism (assimilation) occurred at the direction of bodily "faculties," the agents of the soul that directed all life processes. By the seventeenth century, many philosophers sought a non-spiritual explanation for the bodily processes. To many of them, chemistry offered hope for such an explanation.[17]

Like mechanics and metaphysics, chemical thought changed gradually, in steps, through the work of several men, among them Van Helmont, who suggested that chemical ferments caused bodily processes. A ferment developed when a "seed" acted upon water. Van Helmont removed the soul as the motivating cause of the processes but replaced it with an interior force, the archaeus, that he believed resided in the stomach. The German chemist, physiologist, and anatomist Franciscus Sylvius agreed with Van Helmont that fermentation caused some bodily functions, but not all of them. He thought the others arose out of the opposition of acids and alkalis or the properties of salts. English anatomist and physician Thomas Willis refined Van Helmont's concept of ferments by describing fermentative action. To him it was simply "the intestine motion of particles," and it caused bodily functions.[18]

In the seventeenth century, chemists seemed like the ugly stepsisters in the philosophical world. They were philosophers but they were also practitioners who dirtied their hands with chemicals and soot from their furnaces. Many people believed their ideas inferior to their practice. Natural philosophers, many of them with pristinely clean hands, excelled at idea-making but lacked any experimental basis. Robert Boyle mastered both fields—the theoretical and the practical—and indicated how each could serve the other. Chemists could use corpuscular theory, because it explained many physiological aspects that chemical theories to date had not explained. On the other hand, philosophers could learn from the experiments and data of the chemists.[19]

The New Individual Golden Mean

The above ideas quickly became a part of collective knowledge. Most philosophers wrote books describing their ideas and experiments. Authors such as Jeremiah Wainewright took these theories and translated them into texts designed for a popular audience. Wainewright's text was one of the earliest such works, and it did not have a wide readership. A later text did, however. Scottish physician George Cheyne popularized the mechanical philosophy of the body in his highly successful work published in 1724, *An Essay of Health and Long Life*. This was the most widely sold health text in the eighteenth century, in both North America and England, which indicates the widespread acceptance of the new worldview. Cheyne's text utilized several of the mechanical theories, twisting them together into a life rope for ordinary people to grasp as they made their way through the strange new waters of the Enlightenment. Not only did his text ease the journey, it guided them to a world very different from the one they left behind. Animal bodies, Cheyne declared, were simply a conglomeration of pipes, through which "juices" ran. This was an enormous change in perception of the human form.[20]

The "before" image promoted by the older humoral philosophy described each body as a unique, highly sophisticated, and at times mystifying organism whose complex inner workings could be detected only by skilled and careful observance of external signs and whose functions could best be controlled through constant vigilance, application, and expert guidance. Although few of these bodies were perfect at birth, all of them could be maneuvered in that direction with or against the unpredictable forces of the universe. While each human body, according to the humoral philosophy, had the potential for perfection, this perfection could be achieved only if a person had the wealth to afford the education to understand the philosophy and to acquire the foods needed each day for his or her unique constitution. Furthermore, each person must have control over his lifestyle so as to be able to balance his non-naturals. The attitude that developed out of humoral philosophy was that only the wealthy could guide themselves toward perfection. Anyone who had to labor could not even hope to reach that state of human nature.

The mechanical philosophy of the body eliminated the uniqueness of each human body, removing the possibility of perfection, and replacing the awe, mystery, and beauty of human existence with a world of mechanistic pipes and "juices." Any old pipes would suffice, for all bodies were created the same. They differed only in age, use, and size. The mechanical view of the human body democratized it, presenting precepts that bodies were equal in ways they could never have been when evaluated humorally.

In this new body composed of solids and juices (a system of canals and fluids, as Cheyne put it in an earlier text), hydraulics provided the definition of good health. The purpose of a canal is to guide water and the things it carries to its destination. A well-constructed canal will guide the water efficiently by not slowing it down or speeding it up. Human canals, being divinely designed, were efficient enough, so the problem was essentially just a matter of their maintenance. If the liquids that flowed through the various canals slowed down or increased in speed, ill-health would be the result. Many body parts that today are known to be solid were in those days considered hollow. Although Cheyne himself did not consider the nerves to be canals, for example, many other authorities did.[21]

While Cheyne employed the standard metaphor of pipes and juices for the visible body, at the microscopic level he relied on particles. Tiny particles of all shapes and sizes composed the body's juices. The disuniting and recombining of the particles caused change, and problems could occur during the process. Larger particles bonded together with greater force than smaller particles. This force required an equal force to counteract it. Therefore, larger particles required much more force to break them apart than smaller particles. Relying on contemporary chemical theory, Cheyne singled out salts as an excellent example of this process. Salts were very hard, had plain surfaces, and "in all changes recovere[d] their Figure." As a result, when they united, they did so at numerous points, creating extremely strong bonds that, in the body, were often "durable and unalterable." Furthermore, when they got close to other similar particles, they united in clusters.[22]

Health, said Cheyne, resulted from the proper maintenance of three things: the consistency and texture of the juices, their chemical content, and the condition of the solids. If the juices should become viscid (thick and adhesive) or if they should contain oversized constituent particles, they would impede or even stop circulation. An overabundance of "sharp and acrimonious *Salts*," which would make the juices so corrosive they would "burst or wear out the Solids," would also impede circulation, in this case by creating a leak in the canal. The third condition that could interfere with proper circulation is the condition of the solids themselves. Should the solids become flabby (what Cheyne referred to as relaxed or wanting "of due *Force* and Springiness"), they would lack the ability to hasten the juices along. On the other hand, if they became too firm, they would dangerously speed up the flow of the juices.[23]

Because of its holism the humoral view of health encompassed all aspects of life and exhibited great depth. The depth allowed division into numerous states, and this division enabled ranking. Hierarchy is one of the main characteristics of the Aristotelian universe. Virtue was the highest state, and the people who reached it were superior to all others who did not. Health under the mechanical philosophy, on the other hand, lost most of its dimension. The fluids either circulated freely or they did not.

The Hippocratic requirement of balance appeared in this new mechanical philosophy in a slightly different form. It was no longer the four humors that must be balanced, but the circulating speed of the juices, which should not flow too fast or too slow. The tensile quality of the solids must be neither too soft nor too hard, and the condition of the solids affected the speed of the juices and vice versa. If both juices and solids were balanced in their own way, the body would be healthy. According to Cheyne, people could achieve this balance "observ[ing] the *golden Mean* in all their *Passions, Appetites* and *Desires.*" Today, we would say "moderation in all things." One should neither indulge nor become an ascetic.[24]

The requirement for mechanical balance is more simple than the requirement for humoral balance and, furthermore, reverses the roles of cause and effect. The humoral body required daily analysis, and then action designed to correct the numerous imbalances brought about by changes in the non-naturals. The cause was the imbalance, the effect was in changes in daily regimen. With the mechanical body, the daily regimen comes first. Find a moderate lifestyle, develop habits, and stick to them, advises Cheyne. If you do so, you will not change and you will remain healthy.

As a result of this reversal, virtue in the mechanical age could be acquired by living a moderate lifestyle. Virtue led to health but was not health itself. This concept differed greatly from the humoral understanding of virtue, which equated it with health and perfection. The difference is illustrated in a comparison of the icons of health of the two philosophies. The *Canon of Polykleitos,* the image of humoral health and perfection, is a marble statue of a man perfect in form and therefore considered perfect morally, physically, and spiritually. The *Canon* symbolized the fact that virtue was *being.* Cheyne chose a different icon for the healthy person in the mechanical age—the yeoman farmer. He signified that virtue was *doing.* The virtuous man worked a moderate amount, ate a moderate amount of foods raised in the country by healthy methods, controlled the amount of sleep he received, and balanced the other aspects of his life.[25]

ACHIEVING THE GOLDEN MEAN

Although Cheyne changed many aspects of the philosophy of health, he really just remodeled the Hippocratic philosophy. The six non-naturals remained the environmental factors that influenced a person's health. Of those six factors, food remained the most important. Digestion, still one of the most mysterious physiological processes, was the centerpiece of nutrition. The stomach remained the portal through which the outside became the inside. The all-important requirement of the personal golden mean remained. Yet, the new body did require some new guidelines, particularly in the areas of food and exercise.

Much of the older advice on the non-naturals other than food was commonsensical, and Cheyne simply transferred it from the older age to the newer one. Swamps and standing waters menaced. Too much sexual activity begat ill health. A happy man was a healthy man. However, whereas at the beginning of the colonial period shooting, riding, or being rowed in a boat gave the best exercise, now Cheyne supplanted these activities with farming. He replaced the "gross" work of the early seventeenth century, which people believed prevented intellectual growth, with yeoman's work, which he believed made honest, clever, and enterprising people. Regular active labor, fresh country air, and wholesome country fare guaranteed the proper internal motion so important to good health.[26]

Although Cheyne presented the body as streamlined, easy to manage, and all-purpose, he retained many elements of the ancient nutritional philosophy. Food remained the most influential factor over health and identity because it determined the quality of the juices. Most important, Cheyne retained the Hippocratic philosophy of food security. The personal golden mean was still the balance between quantity and quality of food and one's activity level. Quality remained important, but Cheyne reclassified many humoral high quality foods as foods to be avoided and claimed many foods disdained under the humoral system to be of the best quality. He explained his simple system with dichotomies of good and bad.

Evaluating Food

Cheyne still relied heavily on the four qualities of hot, cold, wet, and dry, but he paired them into the two easy categories of hot and dry on one hand and cold and moist on the other. He prefaced his text with the statement that he battled "the devil, the world and the flesh," so it is not hard to deduce he believed the hot and dry foods to be troublesome. He insisted that they caused problems because they sped up the circulation of the juices through the pipes to unnatural and dangerous rates.[27]

Like the human body, the plants and animals eaten also acquired a new, simplified identity. Some were healthful; others were not. Cheyne provided his readers with a means for their identification. Foods that took the longest to mature were the least healthy. If they were vegetables or fruits, their juices contained the heat of the "solar Rays," heat that would speed up the circulatory rate of the body's juices. Meat from mature animals contained the "most rank and most foetid urinous salts." Animals and vegetables that were larger in size were worse because their "Vessels" were stronger and more elastic, their parts brought together with greater force, and their "Fire . . . more intensely hot." Animal flesh and vegetables that "abound[ed] in oily, fat or glutinous Substance" eluded the digestive powers of the stomach because (according to Isaac Newton) their particles united more firmly together than any other substance besides salts. In addition, their softness and humidity relaxed and weakened the force of the stomach. Foods that had a "strong poignant aromatic and hot Taste" (all signs that they contained many salts) also fell into this category, as did fish from salt waters. In general, all these foods tasted strong, moved the body in irrepressible ways, and could ruin one's health. Red meats such as venison and beef, fruits and vegetables that required an entire growing season to mature (such as apples, grapes, squash, and watermelon), potent dark wines, and all distilled liquors fell squarely within this group.[28]

Against these enemies to health, Cheyne lined up an impressive array of beneficents. They resembled the angels of nature—white, cooling, "mild, soft and sweet," and capable of providing calming, cleansing relief. They contained less solar fire and would not speed up the juices. Their particles adhered "with less Velocity" and so could be easily broken apart, and they contained much smaller amounts of salts. Vegetables and meats that matured early, preferably in the spring, comprised this group. Their tender white flesh smothered the heat, revived the tissues of the glutton, and returned them to health. Lettuces, asparagus, parsnips, potatoes, veal, rabbit, and chicken, among others, sufficed for those whose conditions had not gotten too far out of hand.[29]

All these foods were to be eaten plain, without salt, sauces, spices, or pickling, and supplemented with water. More elaborate creations, those "made Dishes, rich Soop, high Sauces, Baking, Smoaking, Salting, and Pickling" were "Inventions of Luxury." They enticed the appetite, burdened nature, and were therefore to be avoided.[30]

There were exceptions to these categories also. The *Essay* had strong themes of natural and unnatural, spring and autumn, country and city, sea and land, and young and old. The first components of these pairs were the best. For instance, Cheyne approved of strawberries. They were red, but they matured in the spring and therefore did not absorb the heat of the summer sun. Blanched vegetables on the other hand, even though pale, were not nutritious because growers forced them to grow in an unnatural manner.[31]

Proper Eating

Although temperance was the guiding rule for all, there were some other guidelines as well. As a true believer in the mechanical philosophy and an adherent to the legacy of Isaac Newton, Cheyne was not content to leave his readers without some quantified guidelines for eating. He had considerably simplified the image of the human body, but he did not eliminate all differences, which came as a result of age, sex, nature, strength, activity level, and the country in which one lived. He gave these groups different advice. Young people who were still growing and people "of great Strength and large Stature" required more food than those who were older, weak, or slender. A man of "ordinary Stature" and good health who did not engage in heavy labor could eat eight ounces of meat and twelve ounces of bread and vegetables and drink about a pint of wine or other "generous liquor" during the course of the day. Men who were studious or sedentary should eat less. People who lived in northern climates or who labored during the day also needed more food. However, in all these cases, a low diet, one filled with the kinds of food Cheyne favored, would sustain everyone through a long and healthy life.[32]

Weights and measurements look good on paper, but as Cheyne himself fully realized, applying such guidelines could be very difficult, in part because "there is no Security from the Appetite." This vulnerability, Cheyne believed, was particularly prevalent "among the better Sort." Therefore, he recommended that people use a sort of scientific method when they sat down at the table to eat. If a person measured or weighed his food when it was convenient and then gauged it carefully with his eye, he could always in the future determine at a glance the proper amount to eat.[33]

Instead of foods being characterized as refined or coarse, as in the past, the mechanical schema grouped them according to their ease of digestion. The goal of digestion was to break apart the clusters of particles into chyle. Not surprisingly, good digestion came down to matter and force. The most efficient digestion occurred when the stomach and its "concoctive Powers" were stronger than the food eaten. If the crushing force of the stomach were greater than the force bonding the particles of the food, then it could easily break apart those particles. The smaller the particles, the finer the chyle, and "the *finer* the *Chyle* will be, the *Circulation* the more free, and the *Spirits* more lightsome; that is, the better will the Health be." All of this is to say that the closer attention a person paid to the food he put into his body, the better off he would be.[34]

THE SOCIAL GOLDEN MEAN

Cheyne simplified the philosophy of food to a point where anyone could implement it. Most important, almost anyone in America could acquire the foods he championed. Gone were the expensive spices, subtle textures, and sometimes rare and expensive foodstuffs claimed by humoral texts to refine the temperamental balance. It is not surprising that, in England, Cheyne's dispatch of the humoral qualities of both foods and people prompted frantic criticisms. Some detractors of his mechanical philosophy claimed that he ignored the temperament in providing his dietary schema. Stressing the hazard of such a foolish move, they wrote pages about the humoral qualities of foods and how they affected the body and mind, protests to the fact that Cheyne had realigned the traditional organizational scheme of the human body. Others balked at his reduced or eliminated meat portions. Many saw social danger in his advice. They pronounced him a "Leveller [who was] for destroying Order, Ranks and Property."[35]

They were on the right track. Cheyne's text reordered the requirements of health and identity in a way no previous text had, because it redefined who could achieve the personal golden mean, as well as the food needed to do this. The humoral philosophy reinforced the society within which it worked. The wealthy were the healthy. The Renaissance interpretation of humoral philosophy based on the personal golden mean resulted in an unbalanced society, because the ones who could achieve the golden mean were at one extreme of the social spectrum. The early modern mechanical adjustment corrected this problem. It honored the ancient rule by instead gilding the social mean, the middling classes. Cheyne declared the wealthy, whom he described as people of sedentary habits living on the edge of society, to be sick people who suffered because of their easy lives and excessively rich diets. The other extreme, the poor, endured ill health because of their hard lives and deficient diet. The middling classes, whom Cheyne exemplified with the yeoman farmer, did it just right. They labored neither too much nor too little. They ate moderate quantities of simple, fresh foods that they raised themselves. The type of work they did was neither trifling nor egregious. Neither beasts nor belly-gods, they stood firmly on the golden mean of food security.[36]

CONCLUSION

The metaphysical concept that people used to explain the human body changed during the seventeenth century from one of form, matter, and qualities to one of a machine, the sustaining function of which was matter in motion. This change came about slowly and erratically, combining concepts in mechanics, metaphysics, and chemistry. The importance of this shift in thinking is that the mechanical body, like the mechanical universe in which it existed, was democratized. The disposal of the ancient qualities, along with their building blocks known as the humors, changed the complexity of the body and the person who inhabited it, and this change eliminated hierarchy. Gone, or at least going, was the notion that some temperament types, such as the sanguine, were superior to others. This democratizing characteristic did not affect just the philosophy of human physiology but characterized mechanical thought in general.

As the philosophy of the mechanical body continued to develop, authors published health texts to explain it to the general populace. George Cheyne not only explained the philosophy to his readers, he offered concrete suggestions for implementing it in their daily lives. Although he retained the

Hippocratic philosophy of food security, he redefined the quality and quantity of foods and the activity level needed to achieve the golden mean. In doing this, as no author had done before him, he enabled the mean of society to be the group that could most easily achieve the golden mean. Cheyne made clear that the golden mean was still associated with virtue by creating a new icon, the yeoman farmer. As one might expect, some people had difficulty accepting his ideas, especially those who had lived their lives within the purview of the golden mean and suddenly found their status questioned. Cheyne was the first to put the social implications of the mechanical philosophy in print for a popular audience, and the idea was then available to anyone who cared to think about it. In any place where a majority of the population enjoyed a middling diet and lifestyle, the mechanical philosophy of the body promised to make a decided impact. One such place was British North America.

C H A P T E R

S I X

In 1735, eleven years after the publication of George Cheyne's *An Essay of Health and Long Life,* the Trustees of the colony of Georgia hoped to entice workers to emigrate there. The Trustees were the governing body of the colony, which was planned as a refuge for members of the lower segment of English society. They promised each person who accepted their contractual offer that, during the course of the first year there, he would receive 312 pounds of beef or pork, 104 pounds of rice, 104 pounds of Indian corn or peas, 104 pounds of flour (presumably wheat), 1 pint of strong beer per working day, 52 quarts of molasses for brewing beer, 16 pounds of cheese, 12 pounds of butter, 8 ounces of spices, 12 pounds of sugar, 4 gallons of vinegar, and 24 pounds of salt. Averaged out over the year, this diet would give one man a little less than a pound of beef or pork a day, over the amount (12 ounces) allotted by Cheyne for an average man.[1]

The Trustees expected their emigrants to work. Part of the work was to raise food for themselves. Judging by the account of Francis Moore, an Englishman who traveled to Georgia in 1735, nature assisted the laborers in their efforts. All the fruit trees "usual in England" grew there, as did others such as olives, figs, vines, and pomegranates that came from southern Europe. George Oglethorpe, the founder and promoter of the colony, wrote in 1733 that a colonist who was "equal in ability only to the fourth part of a laborer" and one who "was dieted but meanly" in London would quickly be able to raise an adequate amount of rice and grain and would have land and cattle "in some tolerable degree" to support himself.[2]

What Oglethorpe and the rest of the Trustees offered to Englishmen was the opportunity to become yeoman farmers. While this may have been an unusual and beneficial opportunity for them, an opportunity they could not have enjoyed in England, many people in the American colonies believed farming as a yeoman to be the norm. By the mid-eighteenth century, Americans and others saw themselves as a yeoman people who enjoyed the golden mean of food security.

THE AMERICAN DIET

By the early eighteenth century the scarcity and starvation experienced by the earliest colonists had long been forgotten. It has been suggested that scarcity, starvation, and other early colonial experiences thwarted English colonists' attempts to transplant their traditional foods and food habits. However, contemporary literature, from natural histories to travelers' accounts to contractual offers such as those of the Georgia Board of Trustees, all emphasize that not only did Anglo-Americans eat English foods but, on the whole, they ate much better than their social counterparts in England.[3]

The foods raised by Americans duplicated the range and variety of foods grown and eaten in Europe, particularly England. For English travelers, there were surprises, not that Americans lacked variety and quality in their food, but that they had so successfully achieved them, not only in Virginia, Carolina, and the middle colonies (particularly Pennsylvania) but up and down the coastline. These observations have been substantiated also by a comparison of British and American soldiers' uniforms from the War for Independence, which indicates that Americans were generally several inches taller than the British soldiers.[4]

Virginia

Wealthy Virginia planter Robert Beverley published a natural history of his colony, *The History and Present State of Virginia,* in 1705. Most of the wild flora he detailed had counterparts in England. Cherries, plums, persimmons, mulberries, currants, huckleberries, cranberries, raspberries, and strawberries completed his list of fruits. Of the nuts he described chestnuts, chinkapins, hazelnuts, hickory nuts, and walnuts. The extent to which the Virginians ate this uncultivated produce is unclear, however. After describing all these species, he added that, as well as wild peas, beans, vetches, squashes, maycocks, maracocks, melons, cucumbers, and lupines, they served as mast for the hogs and other wild creatures. On the other hand his statement may have been his way of underscoring his colony's abundance in that they had so much, they could both eat it themselves and also feed it to the hogs.[5]

In Beverley's view, herrings had replaced the sturgeon of the seventeenth-century texts. Herrings clogged the streams in the spring and could be caught merely by stepping on them. The shad and rockfish were also plentiful. He gave a short firsthand list of other freshwater and saltwater fish, many of which were abundant and easy to catch. Wild fowl flew in multitudes over Beverley's Chesapeake, although not quite so thickly as before. Still, he maintained, there were so many species that some had not even been given a name. Beverley claimed he could kill twenty with one shot (a far sight less than Edward Williams's fifty). Like his predecessors, Beverley praised the wild turkey for its size.[6]

Wilhelm Vogel (who may actually have been William Byrd II, another wealthy Virginia planter and brother-in-law of Robert Beverley) wrote a tract for prospective German immigrants to Virginia. It supported Beverley's assessment and went well beyond it. A substantial portion of the one-hundred-page narrative lists descriptions of the natural edible flora and fauna, complete with comments about their quality, taste, and desirability. Vogel would have constructed a convincing argument on the wide gastronomical use by Virginians of the incredible array of wild plants and animals had he not concluded his text with a small, succinct passage entitled "What One Generally Eats in Virginia." He excluded the bear hams, sea snails, opossum, and rays that he had described so beautifully in the previous pages of his exotic narrative. Rather, Virginians, like Englishmen, dined on pork, beef, mutton, veal, capon, duck, goose, and "fish and crayfish from the sea." They ate wheat bread, although some consumed bread made from a mixture of corn and rice, and drank Madeira, peach wine, quince wine, apple and pear juice, or imported or domestic beer made from persimmons, peaches, barley, or hops. Supporting the idea that most Anglo-Americans subsisted on a cultivated, high English diet was another small paragraph in the beginning of the text, which discussed the price of provisions in Virginia. It defined "provisions" as cow with calf, ox, steer, swine, sheep, wheat, rye, barley, peas, and beans.[7]

Both Beverley and Vogel maintained that the gardens of Virginia produced everything grown in English gardens to the same or higher degree of perfection. Most domestic animals compared favorably. Some, like the Virginia swine that by Beverley's time were already famous in the mother country for their hams and bacon, exceeded the quality of their English counterparts. As Beverley put it, the food the gentry in Virginia ate was as fine as that on the best tables of London.[8]

Carolina

The colonists in Carolina also ate high quality food. The 1709 observations of English naturalist John Lawson, who surveyed the region, come to the conclusion that the colonists in Carolina (which at the time included North Carolina, South Carolina, and Georgia) were able to grow and eat just about anything the gentry and nobility of England did. According to Lawson, many Carolinians had enough land for almost every man to have to himself "an entire Plantation, or rather Park" on which could be found fish, wildfowl, and venison. He believed the mildness of the climate and the richness of the soil were the cause.[9]

Carolina planters raised "fat and good beef at all times of the year," but in October and the cool months of the year they slaughtered the cattle in order to salt the meat and export it. Not only did the environment produce tasty beef, but the ample food supply increased the fertility of the cows to the point that heifers could calve at eighteen to twenty months of age and thereby quickly increase the size of a herd. Male calves made "very good and white" veal. Cows produced milk "very pleasant and rich" and in such quantities that large amounts were sold.[10]

Like cows, sheep in Lawson's Carolina multiplied easily, with most ewes having "two lambs at one weaning." Mutton from adult sheep was "(generally) exceeding Fat and of a good Relish." As in other parts of North America, hogs knew no bounds in North Carolina. They rampaged through the forests, stuffing themselves on acorns and other nuts. This gay abandon made "Flesh of an excellent Taste [in] great Quantities; so that Carolina ... [was] not inferior in this one commodity to any Colony in the hands of the English." One exception to their English diet was goats. They grew very well there, but the residents chose not to raise them because they proved "mischievous to Orchards and other Trees."[11]

While Lawson greatly admired the livestock raised in Carolina, he had much more to say about the field and garden produce. First, he discussed the grains. "Very good" wheat came with high yields of usually not less than thirtyfold and as high as sixty-six-fold for seeds sown in "Piny-Land" (the "meanest sort" of land to Carolinians). In some places the increase was one-hundred-fold. Most farmers, however, could not repeat that return regularly because, spoiled by the plethora of good soil, they did not take the time to analyze it for its productive qualities. Rye grew very well, but people generally did not grow it because it made black bread unless it was "very curiously handled." They preferred maize to rye. Maize—to Lawson the "Most useful Grain in the World"—was very nourishing, as he believed was proved by the fact that servants and slaves in Virginia, Maryland, and more northerly plantations subsisted solely on it. It "refuses no Ground, unless the barren Sands," wrote Lawson. Furthermore, it produced seven- or eight-hundred-fold. Even the stalks could be bruised and boiled for use in making beer. In addition to maize, several kinds of red and white, bearded and unbearded rice, "esteemed the best" and "yielding from eight hundred to a thousand fold" grew there and grew best in "wild Land that has never been broken up before." Finally, planters raised buckwheat and "Guinea Corn," but only to feed to hogs and poultry.[12]

Carolinians, at least the ones Lawson saw, were enthusiastic pulse growers and as astute about varieties as growers in England, who experienced a garden revolution in the seventeenth century. Everbearing "Bushel-Beans," which grew up poles and spread on watling to provide a summer arbor, had stalks the thickness of a man's thumb and produced flat white beans with a purple shape on each side that looked like an ear. Lawson reported that these "extraordinarily well relished Pulse" were eaten by themselves or with meat. Numerous other varieties thrived in the climate and soil. With some kinds they could get two crops a year.[13]

The true measure that the English settlers in North Carolina really had managed to transfer their English food habits is evidenced in the roots, "sallads," and potherbs they grew. Unlike livestock, however, not all vegetables and herbs grew in all places. The culinary herbs, medicinal herbs, and garden roots were numerous but did not compare to the "Sallads" and fruits, which included three kinds of lettuce, two varieties of spinach and fennel, numerous cresses, parsley, asparagus, cabbages, coleworts, melons of all types, cucumbers, pumpkins and other squashes, and "many other species of less Value, too tedious to name."[14]

The Middle Colonies

The middle colonies presented a different picture but still one of plenty. In 1685 in Pennsylvania, according to its founder and promoter William Penn, even "the poorest places in our Judgment produced large Crops of Garden Stuff and Grain." Pennsylvania was able to have a thirty-sixty-fold return on English grains. Wheat, barley, rye, oats, buckwheat, peas, beans, cabbages, turnips, carrots, parsnips, cauliflower, asparagus, onions, shallots, garlic, and Irish potatoes all thrived in Pennsylvania soils. The English fruits they tried to grow did well too, particularly peaches and grapes.[15]

Like Carolinians, Pennsylvanians could allow nature to feed their meat and dairy cattle until they went to market. Unlike Lawson, Penn did not wax lyrical concerning the vegetables. He praised the fish. "Mighty Whales roll upon the coast," he reported. "Sturgeon play continually in our rivers in Summer. . . . Alloes, as they call them in France, the Jews Allice, and our Ignorants, Shads, are excellent Fish and of the Bigness of our largest Carp: They are so Plentiful, that Captain Smyth's Overseer at the Skulkil, drew 600 and odd at one Draught; 300 is not wonder; 100 familiarly. They are excellent Pickled or Smokt'd, as well as boyled fresh." In addition, Pennsylvanians had within easy reach rockfish, sheepshead, drum ("'Tis so call'd from a noise it makes in its Belly, when it is taken, resembling a Drum"), herring, catfish, lampreys, eels, trout, perch, smelt, sunfish, oysters, cockles, "Cunks," crabs, mussels, and "Mannanoses." Penn took care to give his readers the prices of what he considered staples. With an English shilling worth twelve pence, beef, the primary English and American meat choice, sold at twopence a pound; pork at twopence halfpenny, and veal and mutton at threepence halfpenny. Wheat could be bought for four shillings a bushel, Indian corn for two shillings and sixpence, oats for two shillings a bushel. Oysters could be bought for the same price as oats. Six shad or rockfish sold for twelve pence.[16]

The Swedish traveler Peter Kalm, a less self-interested observer, visited Pennsylvania in the 1740s and gave a selective view of agriculture there. By that time nearly every Pennsylvanian had an orchard next to his house in which grew numerous fruits such as peaches, apples, pears, and cherries. Inhabitants planted okra and red peppers in their gardens. Asparagus grew wild and thus needed less work. Everyone planted maize for themselves and for their livestock, particularly the hogs because it fattened them easily and gave their flesh an "agreeable" flavor. Kalm also noted the presence of buckwheat, wheat, rye, and many kinds of squashes and melons.[17]

Food Preparation

It is one thing to look at the foods raised by two groups of people and quite another to conclude that they ate them in the same way. Just because Americans and English grew the same plants and animals for food does not mean they prepared these foods in the same manner. Documenting what people prepared and what they actually ate is difficult for this time period, because few people wrote about what they ate, and if they did, their descriptions are often perfunctory. Household accounts indicate what people purchased. Recipes and inventories of foods, pots, pans, and dishes suggest the types of dishes they may have prepared and served. All of these sources together make up a fuller, if not complete, picture of what English men and women living in early America actually ate. The conclusion to be drawn from these sources is that the English culinary tradition transferred readily to America and was well established among colonists of English descent by the beginning of the eighteenth century. In addition, those foods were of a middling nature, meaning that they were neither oversufficient nor undersufficient for the body. In the eighteenth century, middling foods were those considered wholesome and fresh. When cooked, the resulting dishes were honest and usually uncomplicated.

Personal recipe collections from early America are rare. Two cookery manuscripts known to have been owned and more than likely compiled by Virginia women in the late seventeenth and early eighteenth centuries are collections of recipes, and these recipes are in no way simple. Their contents are not original, a fact that makes them even more remarkable, because they indicate how widely and how rapidly recipes from printed English sources traveled, as well as how long they remained in use. The assortment of recipes shows that their owners had knowledge of a complex English culinary tradition, and the grease stains and marks on the original pages show also that these owners practiced it.

An unknown woman compiled *Martha Washington's Booke of Cookery and Booke of Sweetmeats* some time in the late seventeenth century. A small manuscript, measuring only eight inches by six inches, many of its recipes have been checked and then checked again. Although one person copied most of the original recipes, it is obvious that over the years several different cooks relied on them. Some of the recipes are the kind that would have been utilized in a wealthy household of high status. They call for expensive ingredients or ingredients that were difficult to acquire. Many other recipes, however, are not high status.[18]

The other manuscript, the Virginia manuscript, is of a newer generation. It resembles the Martha Washington heirloom in several ways. The exact date of its creation is unknown, and its originator is unidentified. Several of the same recipes appeared in British cookbooks published between 1705 and 1720; other recipes had first appeared in print during the last half of the seventeenth century. At least four different people wrote in this book, but most of the recipes were entered in the same early eighteenth-century script, and the creator left blank pages between sections for the addition of more recipes. Succeeding women used those pages for recipes, household accounts, and drawings. Some of these later additions date to the mid-nineteenth century.[19]

These cookbooks show that foods prepared in some early Chesapeake households were thoroughly English, of great variety, and of solid quality. The foods were the middling fare similar to that which George Cheyne later advocated in his *An Essay of Health and Long Life.* Many of the recipes duplicate recipes printed in cookery books in England. Across these women's tables passed fricassees, French pottages, hashes, roasts, boils, a wide assortment of pies (including "hartychoake Pie" and "lettice tarte"), and a host of puddings (made of fruit, nuts, meat, and poultry), bread, pancakes, fritters, tansies, custards, cheesecakes, creams, curds, cheeses, and pickles. Peas, carrots, cabbages, turnips, lettuce, lemons, oranges, cherries, gooseberries, barberries, and quinces comprised the ingredients of the several fruit and vegetable dishes. Together, the recipes in these two texts show the full panoply of early eighteenth-century cooking and the jigsaw pattern of foods eaten by the early Americans.

The recipes listed in these manuscripts have a complex history that historians are only just beginning to realize. During the seventeenth century, some English royal and noble households employed French chefs. By mid-century some French cookbooks appeared on the market in English translation. These included La Varenne's *The French Cook* (1653) and Massialot's *The Court and Country Cook* (1702). These texts purveyed an older, more elaborate style of cookery. Vincent La Chappelle, another French chef, built on this tradition but moved toward less complicated and certainly less fussy recipes, evident in the 1733 English translation of his French original titled *The Modern Cook.* At about this time, female authors came to the fore in the English cookbook trade and remained there for decades to come. Several cookbooks written by women sold widely in England and the American colonies. Eliza Smith wrote *The Compleat Housewife,* published in London in 1727, which in 1742 became the first cookbook to be printed in America. Hannah Glasse published *The Art of Cookery Made Plain and Easy* in 1747. Elizabeth Bradley wrote *The British Housewife,* which appeared in two volumes in 1758. These women were not French. They did not run huge kitchens in royal households. Their recipes represent a mix of old and new, but they clearly favored the more simple and straightforward recipes, a trend that may have come from the top down and suggests that some of the simplicity these women embraced came from French cooks. However, other historical research suggests that many of the recipes come out of a more modest form of British cookery. For example, many of the recipes found in Glasse's text had appeared decades before in the ubiquitous *Whole Duty of a Woman*, a modest moral primer for women first published in 1698.[20]

By the middle of the eighteenth century, the trend in cookery books was toward simpler recipes that boasted their middling status in their titles, their ingredients, and their methods. While their female compilers may have embraced the lighter, less complicated style credited to the French, they quite openly disdained things French as extravagant. The English food promoted by these women "represented values of freedom, an elected parliament, an English Church free of foreign domination, food without taint, fresh from the English soil, while food in the French manner was something quite insidious, almost . . . a contamination."[21]

Martha Bradley's pedagogical *British Housewife* provides an excellent example of the attitude purveyed by these cookbooks. In addition to stalwart English fare, the book also disseminated the philosophy of the mechanical body and the requirements for the new golden mean of food security. Bradley cooked in Bath, a spa town and social center, the same town in which George Cheyne had lived earlier. Her recipes show the influence of the cookbooks published by male chefs in the earlier part of the century and those produced by other women such as Hannah Glasse. They combine the older and newer trends, but Bradley clearly preferred the simpler dishes without elaborate sauces and garnishes. The frontispiece states as much in its admiration of the frugal housewife and experienced cook.

Bradley's text begins by emphasizing the importance of fresh provisions. In her presentation, British food consists of the following: three sources of domestic meat, the ox, the hog, and the sheep, which yield beef, veal, bacon, pork, pig, lamb, and mutton. To these can be added kid, venison, rabbit, and hare. It is hard to believe, but no previous cookbook author had stated British nutritional philosophy quite so clearly, perhaps because its nature was not quite so clear. In Bradley's prose, however, it all seems so simple. Fowl can be tame and wild, fish from fresh water or the sea. Although vegetables represent a "lower Class" of food than those of animal origin, they still possess "Great Value." Cabbage, broccoli, cauliflower, spinach, celery, lettuce, radishes and "salleting," asparagus, French beans, beans, and peas comprise the green vegetables. The English roots are carrots, parsnips, turnips, and potatoes. Fruits are apples, pears, plums, walnuts, chestnuts, filberts, melons, and cucumbers. "These are the best and principal kinds and are proper resources of a Table: So much therefore ought never to be out of the Person's Thoughts who is to provide."[22]

The emphasis here is definitely on British food rather than English food. The text united the rapidly growing British empire, which, by the time of the book's publication, had sent roots east to India as well as west to North America. If the proper British cook was always to have these fresh foods in her mind, she was to be allowed a few "foreign Articles." Anchovies and capers top the list, followed by caviar and cayenne pepper. Then come the basics of English cookery, vinegar, sugar, cinnamon, nutmeg, cloves, mace, ginger, allspice, and pepper. Bradley goes on to explain the larder and its ingredients such as pickled and salted fishes, hams, and brawn, which, she advises, are also to be kept on hand at all times. In these few pages, Bradley gives the reader the basics of modern British cookery. She also continues, as methodical, succinct, and quantifying as George Cheyne, to describe what it means to eat a middling diet.[23]

Bradley organized and synthesized British cookery into basic rules. Like Cheyne's rules for the mechanical body, Bradley's rules simplify cookery, making it easily accessible. Many earlier cookbooks do not even have tables of contents, much less any sort of synthesis of a particular technique or philosophy. Any person reading this work for the first time, whether familiar or unfamiliar with cooking, has to feel confident in the presence of Bradley's text. For example, when she explained boiling, that cornerstone of English cookery, she wrote: "To keep the water really boiling all of the time, to have the Meat clean, to know how long is required for doing the Joint or other Thing boiled, comprehends almost the whole Art and Mystery." She cut to the quick of the other major cookery methods as well. Roasting required a clean spit and a timely fire, proportioned to the food to be cooked and kept clear at the bottom by stirring the coals twice during cooking. Frying was "a coarse and greasy kind of cookery in Fashion in the country where there are great appetites and Strong Stomachs." On she went, through baking, sauces, soups, and broths, cleaning the messy panoply of her culinary history, organizing it, and presenting it to the public in clear modern prose.[24]

What Bradley did with cookery she accomplished also with the mélange of theories about the human body. Although the new mechanical philosophy had certainly influenced many people in the eighteenth-century British world, the older way of humoral thinking had not died out. She combined the two and put to shame the numerous health-text authors who spent many pages to say, as she did, that a variety of human constitutions existed and they needed different diets to keep them healthy. "Nature has provided in the same manner a great Variety of Foods: Our Business is to suit these to one another." To this purpose, the foods were heavy, lighter, and lightest: meat, fowl, and fish, in that order. The lighter they were, the more easily they were digested. Human constitutions came in four basic types: the sanguine, the bilious, the phlegmatic, and the melancholic. The perfectly healthy person found his constitution in the middle of them; yes, of course, the golden mean. If a person regularly determined the state of his constitution and managed his diet, he would never have to see a doctor. Bradley pointed out to her readers that digestibility and the amount of nourishment foods contained constituted the major differences among them. The simpler the food, the healthier it was. With a touch of nostalgia, reminiscent of the diets of commoners in the sixteenth century, she claimed: "Our Ancestors in the earliest Time lived upon the Products of the Earth and Milk, and they were much more healthful than we." Following Cheyne's lead, Bradley disposed of humors, stating simply that the stronger people should eat the stronger foods; people of "tender Constitutions" who did not exercise were to partake of the most tender meats.[25]

Unlike Cheyne, who advised many of his readers to avoid strong foods, Bradley believed that a skillful cook could transform even strong foods into tender and easily digestible dishes. For example, meat from animals that grew quickly, like birds, digested most easily, as did whiter meats and leaner meats. The flesh of animals that matured slowly such as beef cattle, the redder meats, and the fatter meats digested with more trouble. Firm flesh was the most nutritious. Furthermore, the different parts of an animal varied in their digestibility and, therefore, in the nourishment they provided. Liver, for example, proved easily digestible and consequently "most wholsome." So did stones, brains, and sweetbreads. Kidneys, hearts, fat, tongues, feet, ears, and guts, on the other hand, all taxed the digestive system unless altered through careful cookery. Beef suited active people with "great Spirits" and "good Stomachs." Bradley thought mutton the universal meat because it agreed with everyone. Veal, on the other hand, she believed to be delicate. Finally, she explained, there are "Cases in which all Flesh is bad; these require Vegetables, Puddings, and the like."[26]

THE GOLDEN MEAN?

These sources indicate that American colonists adequately met the first part of the social golden mean in that they had enough of the right kinds of foods. But what about the second requirement for food security? In order to be true icons of virtue, they must have a lifestyle in which their daily activity levels balanced the foods they ate. Did Americans enjoy such a life? Generally, Anglo-Americans believed they had a moderate lifestyle, made possible by the benevolent climate and (still) fertile soil, or by slaves. This admission prompted a concern not of an underbalance of food to labor but an overbalance that would just as easily make them food insecure and remove them from the golden mean. Many commentators blamed the climate for the overbalanced lifestyle of Americans. Others blamed slavery. In either case, the Southern colonies received much more criticism than those in the North.

Travelers' Accounts

In 1701, the Swiss adventurer Francis Louis Michel, who sought to establish an emigrant community in Virginia, described in disapproving terms the lazy agricultural practices of many Virginians. He complained that they allowed their cattle, hogs, and sheep to roam freely, unless they planted wheat, in which case they penned their animals to collect manure for fertilization. Because of this type of husbandry, farmers did not have to store hay or even build stables for their animals, although Michel sometimes noticed "half frozen and starved" cattle in the spring. In addition to the wild produce, he concluded: "It is indeed said truthfully that there is no other country, where it is possible with so few means and so easily to make an honest living and be in easy circumstances."[27]

Andrew Burnaby, vicar of Greenwich, England, toured America in 1759 and 1760 and offered another account. Using golden mean geography like Thomas Morton, Burnaby determined the forty-degree-latitude line to be the southern edge of the golden mean. He placed this line at the Susquehannah River, basically dividing the North from the South at the southern edge of Pennsylvania. He saw a clear distinction between the two regions. Having landed at York, Virginia, he first toured the South, where he confirmed the by-then very old tale of fine air, mild and serene winters, stupendous natural produce, plentiful water, and fertile soil. In spite of these assets (or rather because of them), however, Burnaby believed that Virginia had a long way to go to achieve "that degree of perfection which it is capable of." Its people had cultivated only one-tenth of their land, and what they had cultivated, they had done poorly. The colony had only one town and small villages, none of which impressed him. Although Virginians had built a lively trade, they had made little progress in the arts and sciences. Taking all of these factors into consideration, concerning the character of most Virginians, Burnaby concluded: "The climate and external appearance of the country conspire to make them indolent, easy, and good natured; extremely fond of society, and much given to convivial pleasures." Their indolence, he believed, led to other problems: "Their authority over their slaves renders them vain and imperious, and intire strangers to that elegance of sentiment, which is so peculiarly characteristic of refined and polished nations." Even worse, wrote Burnaby: "The display of a character thus constituted, will naturally be in acts of extravagance, ostentation, and a disregard of oeconomy; it is not extraordinary, therefore, that the Virginians out-run their incomes."[28]

Perhaps begrudging colonial success, later European travelers affirmed Burnaby's conclusions about the Southern colonists. Scotswoman Janet Schaw, who toured the American colonies from 1774 to 1776, saw North Carolinians as "tall and lean, with short waists and long limbs, sallow complexions and languid eyes." They had flat feet and loose joints, and they walked unevenly—not exactly iconic images of virtue. In spite of this observation, she did feel that the women were "fine." Just after the War for Independence, François-Jean de Beauvoir, the marquis of Chastellux, had a similar assessment of Virginians. The power that white Virginians had over their slaves "nourishes vanity and sloth." Beauvoir also noticed poverty in Virginia, something he saw nowhere else in the newly formed United States. Beauvoir's critique brings us full circle back to Thomas More's criticism of England. To Beauvoir, Virginia had become, like More's England, a place where the idle received most of the foods as well as other material goods and where the workers received little. Proprietors owned much of the land in Virginia. They used what they wished but let most of what they owned remain untouched, refusing to sell or give away even the smallest portion to someone else. This stinginess left no land for the poorer people, Chastellux felt, because the Virginia land was "generally not good" so that it required many acres to sustain one family adequately. Slaves were in a worse situation than the poor whites. In contrast to their masters, who had large houses with magnificent furnishings, the slaves were "ill lodged, ill clothed, and often overwhelmed with work." Their masters did, generally, treat them better than masters in the West Indies treated their slaves, but only because Virginians were a milder people and their agriculture not as profitable. Beauvoir concluded his remarks expressing the desire to discuss the virtues of the Virginians, but he made the discussion short because he could only find two. They possessed magnificence and hospitality.[29]

William Byrd II

Even the proud Virginian William Byrd II believed that the seemingly benevolent climate of the Southern colonies could make it more difficult to achieve the golden mean. In what many scholars consider to be Byrd's best prose work, *The Secret History of the Dividing Line,* he humorously employed the philosophy of food security to show the devastating effects of oversecurity on some American colonists. Even though he intended his work to be humorous, Byrd was still careful to place his own plantations within the geographical golden mean.

In 1728 Byrd was at the head of a team of Virginians and North Carolinians whose task was to establish the border between the two colonies. The colonies had definite but non-contiguous boundaries, which left between them a strip of land thirty-one miles wide that neither colony claimed. Byrd and his team had to decide which colony the people in the forgotten region belonged to. The area contained the unexplored Great Dismal Swamp, and while the surveyors went through the swamp to run the latitude line at thirty-six degrees thirty and a half minutes, Byrd made his calculations on the basis of other observations. In contrast to Norfolk, Virginia, which was a pleasantly located town of industrious and frugal people, Byrd, who did not go through the swamp himself but examined only its edges, described it as an "abandoned," "derelict," hot, "dirty place," full of mosquitoes that consumed great quantities of human blood. The air was "unfit for respiration" and the soil around the swamp was "aguish." In some parts, the ground could not even support vegetation.[30]

This climate produced a people about whom Byrd found few positive words to say. The mildness of their climate made them slothful, the reason

for their lack of punctuality. One man Byrd encountered was so lazy that neither he nor his common-law wife wore any clothes. Living in a bark-covered
hut, they did not practice any kind of agriculture, preferring instead to scav-
enge or steal food. Even those inhabitants who owned livestock could not be
said to practice animal husbandry. They simply allowed their animals to wan-
der. One consequence of this practice was their "custard complexions," which
Byrd believed resulted from their lack of milk. Byrd observed countless
"drones," or lazy, shiftless people, in this area, among whom were more men
than women. Of course, this might be expected in a climate where the air
was so warm and moist that even breathing seemed to require strenuous
physical effort. Although some of the areas around the swamp provided easy
fodder for livestock, the people paid a price for it in agues, corruption, and
"cadaverous" complexions. They also were prone to melancholy, a reference
to the fact that some earlier authorities recommended milk to cure the affliction. He found the food produced by these people to be very hard on his and
his companions' "English" stomachs, but the locals, whom Byrd would not
claim as fellow countrymen, had no problem eating it. In fact they had
hearty appetites for it. The great quantities of pork they devoured filled their
bodies with "gross humors" that contributed to their undesirable character
and caused their noses to fall off. So crude in behavior and appearance were
these people that when a local senator came to see the camp of Byrd's team,
the sentinels would not let him pass. These godless "Dismalites" did have one
talent. They could smell good liquor from thirty miles away and would make
the trip with great speed to get some, preferably for free.[31]

When the surveyors emerged from the swamp, they had affirmed with
their surveyors' tools what Byrd had already determined from his knowledge
of Hippocrates. The boundary placed most of the area in North Carolina. The
residents, much to Byrd's surprise and relief, actually wanted to be citizens of
that colony because there they "paid no tribute to either God or Caesar."[32]

Northern Colonies

Commentators generally felt that people in the Northern colonies did not
have the same unbalanced lifestyle as those in the South because the climate
required them to work harder. Andrew Burnaby thought that, although Pennsylvania had the same fertile soil as Virginia, its people had accomplished far
more in the eighty years of the colony's existence than Virginians had accomplished in twice that time. Pennsylvanians cultivated their landscape "to a
high degree of perfection," producing quantity and variety. The people, although not hospitable to strangers, were "frugal, and industrious" and "by far
the most enterprising people upon the continent." In the remaining Northern colonies, Burnaby saw the same signs of social health from a climate that
required its inhabitants to work for their sustenance but rewarded them gen-
erously for their efforts. New Jersey, he believed, had soil just like that in the

Holy Land. Not leaving their livelihood to nature, the people, both good-natured and hospitable, cultivated the soil well and had turned it into "the garden of North America." New Yorkers resembled Pennsylvanians. Boston, part of the "rich, populous, and well-cultivated" Massachusetts Bay area, had succeeded in fostering the arts and sciences, and its citizens were people of an improved character, although Puritanism had not completely vanished.[33]

CONCLUSION

By the final decades of the colonial period, had Americans become the living examples of George Cheyne's iconic yeoman farmer? No one disputed that a wide swath of Anglo-Americans had access to the proper quantities and qualities of middling British foods. Further, well over a century after the first colonists planted English crops on American soil, commentators remarked on the ease with which the colonists in the final decades of the colonial period did it.

Behind these confident words, however, lay some doubts. Some people believed that some Americans had overshot the food-security balance and were, as George Cheyne remarked, in need of security from their appetites. While insecurity is usually thought of as only a lack of food, it is the imbalance between the quantity and quality of food and one's activity level. The balance can be tipped one way by an inadequate food supply, or it can be tipped the other way by an overabundant food supply. The nagging doubts presented here were mostly those presented by foreign travelers, some of whom were quick to disparage the Americans and their perceived success. William Byrd II satirically raised the issue of insecurity, but because he limited his view to the Dismal Swamp, it is hard to tell whether he just saw an opportunity for humor or whether he really believed that the good life in Virginia, or all of America, could dangerously tip individual and social balance. While we will never know what this older Byrd believed, as a younger man a few decades earlier, he believed the environmental influence of America to be no laughing matter.

Which Golden Mean?

*S*tarting in 1709, the thirty-five-year-old William Byrd II expressed serious concerns about the degenerative effects of life in Virginia. Believing in the philosophy of food security and in the dangers of an imbalance between the quality and quantity of food he ate and his daily activities, he developed temperate food habits and a matching lifestyle that he followed for much of the rest of his life. He believed his regimen checked degeneration and fostered virtue.

As a young man in the late seventeenth century and early eighteenth century, another colonist slightly Byrd's senior, the Puritan minister Cotton Mather, held the same fears. He saw many signs of degeneration within his community, a phenomenon he called "Indianization," the adoption of Indian vices and manners. He believed Indianization might be affecting him. He worried about overeating. In addition, he thought there was something funny about the air. As a resident of Massachusetts, he knew the problem was not one of an indulgent climate, like that in the Southern colonies. Rather, he feared it was the cold moist quality of the North American air in general. He allayed his fear by conducting regular fasts.

The parallels between the two men are many. They both chronicled their efforts in diaries, Byrd in an obscure shorthand that effectively rendered his narrative secret. Both men came from prominent families. Mather was the descendant of the powerful Puritan ministers John Cotton and Increase Mather. Byrd was the only son of one of the wealthiest men in Virginia. Both men played leading roles in their colonies, built massive libraries during their lifetimes, and belonged to the Royal Society of Science in London when Isaac Newton was its leader. In addition, the two men shared a common predicament. They were caught between two worlds, one humoral, the other mechanical. As men well educated in science and as members of the Royal Society, they were philosophically at the heart of the Scientific Revolution and embraced its new mechanical, quantifiable, predictable view of the universe and of their own bodies. However, as children of the humoral age, they retained the humoral view of a highly influential cosmos. Both believed the North American environment could cause them to degenerate. They clung tenaciously to the humoral personal golden mean that linked perfection, individuality, and personal superiority to power. Living in a yeoman body, they each aspired to be the *Canon of Polykleitos*. Both found their fears allayed with food. Not able to distinguish themselves with the foods they ate, they did it by rejecting foods and controlling their appetites. They also believed their self-government would prevent any deleterious environmental effects.

This predicament created a link between the two men that was stronger than any of their other common interests or traits, stretching silently from Virginia to England and back to Massachusetts as each man sought to maintain —if not perfect—himself. Neither man knew of the bridge to the other. Both men decided to remedy the situation in which they found themselves. They both began dietary practices designed to garner virtue, which distinguished them from the crowd, practices that no one could say resulted in an inferior body, mind, or soul. The dietary practices were also the only option these men believed they had if they wished to avoid degeneration.

DEGENERATION

Degeneration was the mechanism through which western Europeans tried to understand the differences between humans. Cotton Mather and William Byrd II had enough knowledge of geography to know how radically peoples living around the world differed from themselves. Having a thorough knowledge of science and medicine and a belief in biblical monogenesis, they understood how they came to be like they were. Early modern philosophers, geographers, legal theorists, and others who wrote about the diversity of peoples and cultures in the world relied on Genesis for their assertion that all the peoples in the world came from the same ancestors. Differences, then, must have resulted from some external influences such as the constructed environment and its opposite, the natural environment, both of which were considered simultaneously influential. Several well-known texts collectively asserted opinions on this subject. First was the Bible. Second were the works of several Europeans discussing the variety of races of humankind and their common origin, and the influence of the natural environment. Among these were Samuel Purchas's *Purchas His Pilgrims,* Peter Heylyn's *Cosmographie in Four Books,* Walter Raleigh's *History of the World,* Edward Stillingfleet's *Origines*

Sacrae, Francis Bacon's *New Atlantis* and *Civil and Moral Essays,* Montaigne's *Essays,* Thomas Burnet's *The Theory of the Earth,* Leone Alberti's *Ten Books on Architecture,* Machiavelli's *Discourses on the First Ten Books of Livius* and *Florentine History,* and William Temple's *Observations Upon the United Provinces of the Netherlands,* in addition to Renaissance health texts based on Hippocrates' *Airs Waters Places.*[1]

Hippocrates clarified the influence that air exerted on character. In a passage comparing the inhabitants of Asia and Europe, he claimed that because Asia possessed a temperate climate and lay farther from cold areas than Europe, everything that grew there developed greater beauty and size. He stated: "Growth and freedom from wildness are most fostered when nothing is forcibly predominant, but equality in every respect prevails." Although Hippocrates admitted that Asia was not entirely monoclimatic, its usually spring-like moderate zones possessed excellent water, plentiful harvests, flourishing livestock, and well-nourished human inhabitants with tall and well-proportioned physiques. Although such an area offered the most pleasurable living conditions, its ultimate effect on the character of the inhabitants was not altogether desirable. Dwellers of such climates tended to be "feeble." They could not enjoy courage, industry, high spirits, or endurance. Because they lacked the ability to be independent, they never mastered themselves. Instead, they capitulated to despots. Only climates with extreme and volatile conditions produced independent, energetic, and warlike inhabitants who conquered hardships.[2]

In addition to philosophical speculation a long discursive tradition, both private and public, concerning the New World and the effects of its air on immigrants had developed in the two previous centuries of colonization. The tradition began with the Spanish explorers in the sixteenth century who commented on the differences between the fauna, including humans, of Europe and the New World. For North America, commentators fell into two camps: one, the extollers of its virtues such as Thomas Morton, who made great use of New England's place within the global golden mean; the other, claimants who insisted that its air caused English people, plants, and animals to degenerate. The more closely balanced the heat and moisture levels of the air, the closer to perfection were the creatures living within it. Such air was to be found at the forty-five-degree latitude, the global golden mean. Theoretically, all organisms from a different latitude would experience changes upon relocating to the golden mean. These changes were not just superficial, they were complete physiological changes. Because mind, body, and spirit were intertwined, physiological change prompted psychological, intellectual, and spiritual changes. The issue was not that transmutation would occur; rather, it concerned the kind and the degree of alteration. Some Anglo-Americans in the seventeenth century developed theories of the positive changes fostered by the northern colonies. Other reports told of degenerative physiological changes, which included a loss of vigor in the colder climates, a loss of wit in the hotter ones, changes of appearance, and possible savageness. Both extremes would induce a loss of Englishness and a transformation of personal identity.[3]

COTTON MATHER

By the 1690s, the English began to separate and distinguish themselves from their American-born English relatives, also known as creoles, because they believed the air of North America and the consumption of foods grown in that air caused biological differences between them. Cotton Mather was acutely conscious of this belief. He frequently wrote about creole degeneration in his sermons, diary, and books, and in doing so, he contributed his concern to those expressed by his father and grandfathers before him. Creole degeneration could occur to anyone born in North America. In describing it, Mather often relied on the biblical organic imagery of thwarted growth, as in one of his sermons published in 1696 where he commented on how many people believed that animals when transplanted from Europe to America degenerated over time. If this happens to people as well, what can we do but cry about such a sad remark? "Our Lord Jesus Christ from Heaven seems to bestow that Rebuke upon us, in Jer.2.21. *I planted thee a Noble Vine; How then art thou Turned into the Degenerate Plant of a strange vine unto me!"* Mather's use of this type of imagery has been interpreted as allegorical, and his fears to be only about an American culture that was a fearful hybrid of English and Indian cultures. However, the biological basis of degeneration was quite real to Mather, who theorized a great deal about human physiology and the relationship of the mind and soul to the body. He quite clearly did not separate the cultural or spiritual from the physical.[4]

Although he often referred to "Indianizing," the Indians per se did not represent to Mather the threatening living examples of degeneracy so much as did the colonists, and often his own parishioners. Many times in his diary Mather commented on the sins of his parishioners and the punishment about to be given them. Often these sins were ones that Mather characterized as "sins of the mouth." On 27 February 1696/1697, he decided he would tell certain people how they could control their behavior. He selected Abigail Day because of "untruths uttered in her Speeches," particularly the fact that she said "she would thank neither God nor Man" for the laudable food in the almshouse where she lived. In addition, she accused the man who ran the almshouse of sexual improprieties toward her, for which Mather believed she had no proof. He also chose Mary Dutton, who had been convicted of stealing and then lying about it. On 2 October 1697, he wrote about his uncle John Cotton whom the church dismissed because of his violations of the Seventh Commandment prohibiting adultery. On that day Mather admitted that he, himself, fasted to prevent God from punishing the nephew for the sins of the uncle. On 4 December 1697, he noted the case of "one very *criminal Adul-*

teress," Sarah Cox, whom the church excommunicated for adultery as well as for the "telling of diverse gross Lyes" to conceal it. On 2 April 1698, Abigail Day reappeared in his diary, this time because, while under censure for her last sins, she committed the crime of fornication, for which the church excommunicated her. On 20 May that same year, Mercy Marshal, whom Mather had previously rescued from possession by evil angels, received the punishment of excommunication for adultery. On 18 July 1699, Mather mentioned Edward Mills, excommunicated for debauching his landlady, gaming, spending whole nights in lewd company at the taverns, and neglecting his family. And on 29 November 1698, Mather fasted and thought about Sarah Threeneedles who murdered her "base-born Child" and suffered the death penalty.[5]

Mather's concern as a minister for the souls of the members of his community stands out clearly. However, he also worried about his own soul. He feared that God was punishing him for sins he had committed with his mouth. This punishment came in the form of a speech impediment that interfered with his ability to preach. "If my Sin do still rage, I will spend a Day in *Fasting* and *Prayer* ever[y] *Fortnight,* until I bee a Conqueror," wrote the twenty-year-old Cotton Mather in 1683. "Never, never, never, will I lay aside my combate, against my Temptations, or Corruptions." Although in Mather's mind his battle was ultimately one of the spirit, it manifested physically in "tormenting Pains" in his teeth and jaws and in his speech impediment. True to his puritan heritage, Mather accepted full responsibility for his ordeal. He believed it occurred because he sinned with his teeth and with his tongue by eating gracelessly and excessively and speaking evilly. Sins of the tongue and sins of the teeth are also sins of the mouth. One involves revelry in useless food, the other in useless words. But to Mather the words and foods that passed his teeth and crossed over his tongue were far more than superfluous. They were harbingers of his reprobation.[6]

Gluttony, one of the seven deadly sins, was a living death that, biblically, began with the bite of the forbidden apple. As a sin of quality and not of quantity, it was the first disruption of the golden mean of food security. The definition of gluttony had not changed by the seventeenth century, as is demonstrated by a broadside printed in London in 1656, which depicts two gluttons, one a "beast" and the other a "belly-god." The beast became that way through the excessive drinking of wine, an indication that he was someone who could afford to drink wine, which was imported, rather than beer. Resembling a bearlike Bacchus, he wears a ragged fur suggestive of his beastliness. His arms resemble legs, his hands are paws with long claws. Impatient with the small size of the goblet in his hand, he drinks straight from the skin flask. The poem and subtitle to the illustration tell of the fate of this foolish man. "God made me a man," he laments, "I make my self a beast. . . . Must I needs die? / why live I then in sin? / Thrice better for me / had I never been." The scriptures reaffirm the forecast of the poem. Woe awaits the "men mighty at drinking wine" (Isaiah 5:22).

While the drunkard beast agonizes over dying, the belly-god frets (or perhaps should fret) over not dying, for his fate is a living death. Rotund, he is about to eat a dish made from a small animal that looks like a rodent. It is clearly not beef, mutton, or pork, the standards of English cuisine. Grilling over the fire are frog legs, a blatant allusion to the French, and on the floor sits an uncooked carcass, perhaps that of a pig. One wonders if it will be cooked or eaten raw, or if it has been spurned for more exotic fare. The message below cuts to the quick: this is a sin from which you will die. Change now. The more subtle message is that overindulgence can only lead first to spiritual degeneration, next to physical degeneration, and then to death.[7]

English culture abounded with examples of gluttony and its evils, beyond the example of Adam and Eve. The biblical parable of Dives and Lazarus in which Dives feasts every day in front of the poor leprous Lazarus not only tells of wasteful and harmful display. It also indicates that to feed sumptuously in a world where many people are starving is a sort of negligent homicide. Similarly, in the medieval tale of *Piers Plowman,* eating is a "zero-sum game" in which "[t]he more you ate the less someone else did."[8] Gluttons reside in the third circle in Dante's *Inferno,* a place that repulses their gustatory senses. Rain, hail, and snow fall constantly, causing soil to putrefy and give off the worst of odors. The souls there look like real bodies sentenced to eternal decay with absolutely no hope of regeneration. Reptilian Cerberus, with red eyes and a greasy beard, rules the circle with constant barking from each of his three throats. A meat-feeder, he "claws the horde / Of spirits, he flays and quarters them in the rain. / The wretches, howling like dogs where they are mired / And pelted, squirm about again and again." For those men and women who could not read, some churches provided a sculptural reminder of their beastliness. In these works, pigs perform human activities. Some of the scenes show that omnivorousness leads to other negative qualities, as does a relief sculpture of anger riding a boar.[9]

Mather's Solution

Cotton Mather took full responsibility for his sin and its consequences. Because the sin was his, he believed that he could redeem himself with fasting and prayer. Once he accomplished this, he would vigilantly monitor himself to ensure that he remained pure. Despite his surfeit of youthful passion, angst, and determination, Mather, because he was a Puritan, knew he had no control over his success. This was in God's hands. So he laid out a clean, neat proposal. "Now," he wrote after presenting his part of the bargain, "Oh! Blessed Saviour; Save mee from the *horrible Pitt;* Let mee perform what I resolve, and bee accepted, and succeeded, in what I perform!" There, in three phrases, Mather encapsulated the tricky relationship between good works and regeneration that early American theologians spent thousands of words, hours, and pages attempting to explain. His formula was simple: responsibility, determination, beseeching. I am sinful. I will fight it until I die. Please? He reiterated these three points repeatedly in his diary. For example, on 12 May 1683, he wrote of the psalmist, "whose *Tongue* was his *Glory*," and then vowed not to sin. He vowed to endeavor to be *"a Perfect Man"* and to be *"Righteous"* by speaking *"cautiously, moderately, deliberately,* and by making all that come into my Company, the Partakers of some *useful Notion."*[10]

Mather sequestered himself in his study and denied himself both the food and the companionship that tempted his teeth, tongue, and mouth to take in too much food and spew forth too many words. On those days he cast himself "prostrate on my *Study-floor,* and there with my Mouth in the Dust I begg'd for my Father's Deliverance." When he first began his diary in 1681 at the age of eighteen, he conducted irregular fasts, but within a short time he was fasting every week, usually on Saturdays. He hoped that God would reward the tempering of his body and his repentance by giving him the ability to preach well the next day. Often he found that God did so, which encouraged him to continue the practice.[11]

He did not differ from other puritans and protestants in this. English men and women frequently conducted fasts as exercises in spiritual humility and atonement for their sins in general. Fasting, as perceived by those who wrote about it in the seventeenth century, provided a way to humble the body and ask for God's help in a time of affliction. Fasts could be done publicly, as had been the regular practice in England where, until the Commonwealth, almost half the days of the year were fast days. Those fasts consisted of abstaining from flesh and, perhaps, eliminating supper. As Henry Mason put it, they were a popish custom and really should be called fasting nights. Another author, Nicholas Bownde, recommended abstaining for an entire day, not just a part of it. For severe afflictions, the fast could be kept one day weekly. But abstention from food and drink for that day was not enough. A proper fast must be accompanied by prayer. Furthermore, proper prayer could not be done in conjunction with work of any kind. The protestant fast could be public or private. The private fasts such as those practiced by Mather could be done individually, by a family or household, or by a group of people. Their goal could be spiritual well-being, civil good, or the promotion of health. If one fasted for spiritual good, it could be for the bettering of one's own spirit, or the spirit of another or others. Fasting also tamed the flesh and turned such common vices as venery, drunkenness, gluttony, pride, talkativeness, and forgetfulness of God into virtues such as chastity, patience, humility, and tolerance.[12]

According to the contemporary nutritional philosophy, fasting decocted excess humors that had collected in the stomach and thereby provided the necessary physical concomitant to any kind of spiritual regeneration. As a puritan Mather stoutly believed in the godly course and the fine-tuning of life dictated by humoral philosophy. However, as a natural philosopher in an age of intense questioning, he tried to work out the mechanical details of divine control. How, he wondered, did the human soul work within the human body? Using the ideas of seventeenth-century scientists such as Jean Baptiste van Helmont, Jean Fernel, and Oswald Grembs, Mather developed a complex theory. The body, he postulated, contained a refined fluid that mediated between the body and the rational soul. He named this fluid the *nishmath-chajim.* Invisible within a living person, it was a *"plastic Spirit"* that fit the body precisely. However, it was not entirely malleable. God gave it enough shape to force the physical body to conform to it. In this role the *nishmath-chajim* regulated all physiological functions including the recovery of health after an illness or an injury. In addition to being the seat of all diseases, this plastic spirit controlled generation, marked fetuses in some physical way with the imaginary thoughts of their mothers, prevented people from consuming anything that would make them sick, and originated muscular motion. Mather not only believed that a further understanding of this astounding life force would explain ghosts, witchcraft, and possessions, he also thought that it answered many of the mysteries of physiology that were not adequately explained by the new mechanical philosophy.[13]

Mather used the Scriptures to extend his physiological theory to overeating. A scriptural metaphor for eating a meal is *"The Establishing of the Heart."* The heart, according to Mather, was simply a more colloquial word for the *nishmath-chajim.* The act of "establishing the heart"—in other words, eating— sustained the *nishmath-chajim.* In "Some Remarks on the Grand CAUSE of Sickness," Mather wrote that the soul and the body constitute one person, and the body served as the instrument of iniquity of the soul. Sin was the root of all disease. He also thought, as did most medical authorities from Hippocrates onward, that all disease could be traced to the sin of gluttony, the first incidence of which occurred with Adam and Eve. In *The Angel of Bethesda,* Mather quoted several maxims that reinforced this idea. "The *Cup* kills more than the *Canon.* Many *Dishes* will breed many diseases. Alas, when will Men Beleeve it? The Board slayse more than the *Sword.* And one may say *By Suppers and surfeits more have been killed than all the Physicians in the World have cured."* He relayed the story of a physician sent by the king of Persia to Muhammad. The physician stayed with the Muhammad some years but had no patients and finally complained of that fact. Muhammad replied he did not know what the problem was, but in his country of Arabia people ate only when they were hungry and always left the table with some appetite. The physician left the country because he knew the people would never need a doctor.[14]

Although occupying all parts of the body, the *nishmath-chajim* had a special relationship to the stomach. Seventeenth-century natural philosophers believed the stomach to be "the principal Wheel in the *Animal Oeconomy."* Of primary importance for understanding Cotton Mather's theory are the works of Paracelsus, who considered chemistry to be the basis of digestion, and J. B. Van Helmont, who, elaborating on the work of Paracelsus, believed the chemical process of fermentation to be the primary source of all life processes constituting digestion and occurring in several places in the body, not just in the stomach. Van Helmont did not believe life could be explained solely in chemical and physical terms, however. He posited that a central spiritual force residing in the stomach, which he termed the *archaeus,* controlled all of the body's functions. Mather's *nishmath-chajim* resembled the archaeus and was "above all the *Main Digester* . . . . [for] Else how could a *Stomach* that is actually *Cold,* and has in it no very *Tastable* or *Notable* Humour for this Purpose, *Digest* the very *Stones* that are taken down into it?" Mather's theory, like Van Helmont's, elevated the stomach from a fussy and rather inefficient cooking pot to the spiritual center of human existence, employing the more sophisticated process of fermentation to accomplish its task. In doing so, Mather maintained that digestion was a spiritual as well as a bodily function.[15]

Cotton Mather hoped that God would see the sincerity of his fasts and his other pious demonstrations. At the very least he desired a reprieve from further degeneration and, at best, the beginning of the long slow process of regeneration. Although by his lifetime New England Puritanism already had a strong tradition of public fast days to request help or reprieve from God, Mather was not just following a spiritual tradition when he threw himself down on the floor and laid his mouth in the dust. This demonstration was no empty ritual. He understood the interdependence of the body and soul. In his own metaphysical view, the two intersected in the stomach, the very site at which the *nishmath-chajim* controlled the biological processes and mediated between them. Fasting not only humbled and prepared one's soul to receive God's grace, it also cleansed the stomach of any corrupting matter that might lie hidden in its folds. Fasting emptied out the mouth and the rest of the digestive system as well and was, both ritually and literally, the cleansing of the house. For Mather, who also fretted about being lazy, fasting provided a way to prevent corruption by balancing his daily exercise with the food he ate (or did not eat). Without fasting, one would not be able to receive God's grace properly. Because Mather believed the decision ultimately lay in God's hands and that God looked at the individual as well as at his society, Mather worried constantly about his lack of control, particularly his lack of control over what he perceived to be the wide-scale cultural and religious decline of his community.[16]

WILLIAM BYRD II

Although William Byrd II suffered the same fear of degeneration as Cotton Mather, his personal circumstances and beliefs were different. Born in 1674, the only son of English immigrants in Virginia, he was sent away from the colony at age seven to attend school in England. Nine years later he apprenticed in business, and at age eighteen he joined the Middle Temple in London for legal training. With the exception of a brief visit to Virginia in 1696, he stayed in England until 1705, when, at the age of thirty-one, he returned to manage the estate bequeathed him by his father. He soon married a Virginia woman, Lucy Parke, and settled into the life of a planter.

Byrd is a puzzling and contradictory figure. He was among the leaders of Virginia and instrumental in the development of colonial America as a whole. He has been seen as a man who, outwardly, conformed to the details of convention demanded by eighteenth-century English society but whose spirit, inwardly, was at best wooden and at worst nonexistent. It seems he was a fragile, shallow man filled with anger, frustration, and disappointment. What puzzles historians most is his diary, which has a spare, repetitive quality that on the surface appears simple, without the philosophizing, imagination, or self-inspection of other great diaries. William Byrd II was an extensively educated man who built one of the largest libraries in colonial America, but his diary could have been written by a man of only basic education and intelligence. Superficial appearances can be deceiving, however, and this is especially true of Byrd's diary. It does not overtly indicate any fears, for it is a daily record of how Byrd controlled the factors that produced his fears. Like Cotton Mather, Byrd's metaphysical angst stemmed from his humoral belief that living in North America would cause him to degenerate. Also like Cotton Mather, Byrd ordered his eating habits to prevent his fears from becoming reality.[17]

In his diary Byrd offered glimpses of a happy life in literary tableaux vivants of himself and Lucy. They presided at a dinner table surrounded by guests, strolled through the garden, made punch together, or sat down to dissolve the tensions from an earlier spat with a glass of cider. When houseguests came, they talked, played games, drank wine, and "made merry." However, these pleasant scenes do not fully depict Byrd's early marriage. It was not an idyllic existence, Byrd conceded, but he felt that the discord resulted from the unruly behavior of those around him, particularly his wife, who in his view had a tempestuous nature. Byrd did have emotional outbursts of his own, but he believed that the other members of his "family" frequently lost their self-control, which required him to respond to them with carefully calculated reactions.[18]

Sometimes he blamed his anger on his servants or slaves, and often these outbursts were over food. His cook, Moll, absorbed a lot of his violent emotional energy. Once he had her beaten because she had not made the "shoats fat" as he desired. Another time she was whipped because she had not boiled the bacon to his liking, which caused him to have an "indifferent" dinner. Four days before that, he had "chastised" her for spoiling a good plum pudding. He scolded her severely for putting oil instead of butter on his green peas, the only food he ate for dinner that day. Yet another time, she caused him to lose his temper because she neglected to boil artichokes for his dinner. Once John, his servant or slave, invoked Byrd's anger and a threat of whipping because he gave away the sweetbreads of a hog he had killed that day.[19]

His wife, Lucy, also received the blame for his angry displays, the worst of which was on 22 May 1712. After Moll's whipping, Lucy "flew into such a passion," it "moved" Byrd, although not enough to make him retaliate. He confided to his diary that he controlled himself and said little for fear of appearing foolish. Three times he recorded that Lucy had acted incorrectly in food matters, incidents that required his reaction. Once it had to do with stewed cherries. Another time she prompted his displeasure by giving their child marrow to eat when he felt she should not have done so. The third incident occurred after Lucy had been sick. At dinner and in front of company, Byrd ate veal himself and refused to give her any. After the company left, they had a "mortal quarrel," for which Byrd, in a rare move, tried to make amends. Lucy "plagued" him a great while before she finally forgave him.[20]

Literarily, Byrd used Lucy's emotional behavior as a foil to his (nearly) perfectly balanced temperament. He depicted her as very temperamental, often volatile, and he usually contrasted her behavior to his. Often Lucy tried to start quarrels with him, but he would not allow her to provoke him. This literary construction gave him the appearance of being superior, to use a contemporary term, highly virtuous, and certainly a man in control. At the same time the construction portrayed Lucy Byrd as the "Indian," an excellent example of the effects degeneration could have on a creole who did not follow the same kind of regimen as his. He presented her as being "voluptuous," by which he meant sexually desiring, and perhaps lacking some control in this area as well, although he did not see this behavior as being as bothersome as some of her other traits. His first diary contains notations of their sexual exploits and of the satisfaction they both received.[21]

In addition to his diary, other evidence indicates Byrd's fear of degeneration. First, there is the fact that his father decided to send his only son to England to boarding school when he was only seven years old. It would have been cheaper and safer, not to mention emotionally easier, for him to pay an English tutor to come to Virginia. However, the father, like his son, was well versed in early modern science and medicine, and the physiological consequences of his son growing up in Virginia would not have escaped him.

Second, there is evidence left by Byrd himself. A decade earlier, while living in London, the younger Byrd left an array of sources that confirm his belief in the transformative ability of North America. The first is a 1697 account written by him and published by the Royal Society. In it, Byrd described a slave boy who had been born in Virginia. Until the age of three the child had looked like other black children, and then without his experiencing any illness, his skin began to turn white. Byrd observed the boy in London, and wrote: "now from the upper part of his Neck (where some of his Wool is already turn'd White) down to his Knees he is every where dappel'd with White spots, some of which are broader than the Palm of a Man's Hand, and others of a smaller Proportion. The Spots are wonderfully White, at least equal to the Skin of the fairest Lady." In addition to this complexion change, Byrd noted that the boy was "very Sprightly and Active and ha[d] more Ingenuity . . . than is common to that Generation." The account served as a written memorandum of the oral contribution given by the twenty-three-year-old

Byrd at the Royal Society's meeting of 20 July 1697, except that it omitted Byrd's verification that "no fancy had taken the Mother," meaning that she had had no unusual experiences during her pregnancy that would have affected her fetus. As the boy was in London, several other members of the Royal Society took the opportunity to observe him in the following months. At the 10 November 1697 meeting, they corroborated Byrd's report. The "Dappel'd Boy's" head, neck, and chest appeared sanguine. His feet and legs, however, remained stubbornly African and exhibited the darkest of melancholic complexions. What Byrd provided to the Royal Society was proof of environmentally induced transmutation. Because his account concerned an African who was in the process of turning white, his contribution suggested improvement, not degeneration, and the Royal Society received Byrd's contribution as such. When they discussed the case at subsequent meetings they pinpointed the air as the cause.[22]

Another action of Byrd's suggests that he was concerned about degeneration. On 24 January 1710, a few years after he had moved back to Virginia, he had his father's grave opened. In his diary he noted that he did so "to see him, but he was so wasted there was not anything to be distinguished." What could Byrd, who had probably not seen his father since 1696, have been looking for on that winter day? Did he seek some indication that his father had changed in some fundamental way, in a way as basic as that of the dappled boy?[23]

Byrd's Regimen

Standing all by itself or with Byrd's Royal Society report, this suggestion as to his motivation for digging up his dead father may seem a little far-fetched. However, when compared with the rest of the diary, Byrd's magnum opus against degeneration, it becomes a very real possibility. Byrd wrote approximately fourteen thousand entries between 6 February 1709 and his death in 1744. Just the fact that he kept such a record is impressive, but the daily activities it catalogs are even more so. He monitored the foods he ate, the amount of sleep he received, his emotional states, the physical activities in which he engaged, his sexual activities, and the weather. All categories but the last required conscious effort on Byrd's part, and it is clear from early diary passages that their control also required tremendous discipline.

William Byrd is an excellent example of a person who followed a regimen in order to achieve a higher goal. What he monitored and recorded in his diary were the six non-naturals—sleep, exercise, air, emotions, repletion, and food—that made up the tool-kit of humoral theory. His life practice shows that he believed in the interconnectedness of outside and inside worlds. He believed, for example, that control of some non-naturals could compensate for others, like the air, that could not be as easily managed. Every night Byrd received about eight hours of sleep. He rose early, sometimes at 3 or 4 a.m., but usually between 5 and 7 a.m., after having gone to bed at 10 p.m. or later.

He frequently offered excuses for tardy risings. On 2 June 1712, he did not get up at all but made it clear that he suffered from a distemper. Once, his wife's amorousness delayed him. Yet another time, he noted that although he rose later than normal, the time had not been wasted. He had been thinking.[24]

Contemporary medical thought advised that sleep drove the body's heat inward and ensured good digestion. If someone had a weak stomach and digested slowly or was phlegmatic or melancholic, he needed more sleep than someone with a hot complexion who digested vigorously. The sixteenth-century author Thomas Elyot (whose book *Castel of Helth* Byrd owned) believed that if one slept after meals or before the stomach had ingested food, one interfered with the remainder of the digestive process and risked abdominal pains. In addition, sleep returned the body to a temperate state and replaced weariness with energy, and anger or sadness with contentment. The degree of health or illness of a person, his natural complexion, age, and the time of the year, all dictated the amount of sleep he needed. Immoderate sleep brought about palsies, apoplexies, epilepsy, and sluggishness. How one slept was as important as the amount of time spent asleep. Healthy persons were to sleep on their right sides in order to assist digested food in its passage to the liver. People with weak digestions were to sleep on their stomachs, or at least with their hands on their bellies. No one was to lie on his back or sleep during the day.[25]

Byrd trained his mind and body daily. He read or wrote in several languages, usually just after waking. In addition, he wrote his diary in shorthand, an endeavor that may have also been to exercise his mind. Often after breakfast, he "danced my dance." When in Williamsburg, he sometimes went to the capitol building to perform these calisthenics, probably because his rented rooms lacked enough space. After dinner, if at his Westover plantation, he strolled about his garden and grounds, often with his wife and sometimes for hours. He also rode horses.[26]

According to contemporary popular dietaries, exercise greatly influenced temperamental balance, in part because it produced heat, which assisted digestion and improved nutrition. In addition, exercise increased the flow of spirits throughout the body, which caused the expulsion of excrements such as feces, urine, sweat, and flatus. Not all bodily movement qualified as physical exercise, only those actions that raised the level of breathing. Strenuous exercises consisted of digging in heavy soil, lifting or carrying heavy burdens, rope climbing, wrestling, running, throwing a ball, leaping, recreational dancing, tennis, shooting, bowling, and repeated javelin throwing. Walking long distances gave moderate exercise as did gestational exercises in which one moved forward in space but not of one's own efforts, such as riding a horse or in a coach, or being rowed in a boat. As with all the non-naturals, exercise had to be tailored to the individual, according to his constitution, age, gender, and level of health because it heated and dried all body parts. Byrd could gauge whether he had received enough exercise if his flesh swelled and became red, he began to sweat, and his performance became easier. The benefits of exercise became detriments if it continued after that point. Dietitians cautioned that exercise on a full stomach harmed the body, as did lack of preparation such as rubbing the skin vigorously with a linen cloth. Mental exercise in the form of study also aided health unless done to excess, in which case it caused more harm than excessive physical activity.[27] People who exercised heavily could not be thinkers in any sense of the word, and vice versa, because the body's three main functions were movement, digestion, and thought, and it could not perform all three well at the same time. Digestion claimed top priority.[28]

William Byrd interpreted repletion, or fullness, in reference to body fluids, particularly sexual fluids and food for which neither too much nor too little was good. Every day the body's internal receptacles, such as the stomach, veins, testicles, uterus, and bowels, filled with excess fluids. Most of these fluids qualified as hot and moist in character, and they accumulated within the body until it expelled them. Unevacuated, they created more heat and moisture and shifted the body's constitutional balance. Anglo-Americans commonly let blood, cupped, sweated, urinated, defecated, spat, and employed vomits and purges in order to remove these fluids and prevent the unwanted changes that could be caused by an excess of heat and moisture. The body naturally evacuated the plentiful reproductive fluids—semen, menstrual blood, and breast milk—through intercourse, menstruation, and breastfeeding. Just as the accumulation of reproductive fluids fostered the increase of heat and moisture within the body, their overexcretion caused an equally detrimental humoral shift. The overaccumulation of reproductive fluids harmed one's health in part because their retained heat hastened digestion and caused foods to burn up too quickly. On the other hand, the excretion of too many reproductive fluids reduced the precious heat and moisture needed by the body for digestion and retarded the process that gave foods time to decay.[29] Byrd recorded his sexual acts, whether performed alone, with his wife, or with other women. The *Secret Diary* shows that he had sex with his wife regularly if not frequently.

Food

Health-text authors insisted that immorality, disease, and other negative changes resulted from gluttony or surfeit, because the stomach could not effectively digest numerous foods at the same time. Some foods might remain undigested and corrupted in the warm moist interior of the stomach. Despite their putrid state, they would continue through the digestive system to the liver, where they would be turned into substandard blood that caused corruption.[30] Some authors advocated a spare diet. Others suggested a weekly fast.

Of all the entries concerning non-naturals in Byrd's diaries, no entries are more regular and more detailed than those about food and his eating habits. Byrd ate only one full meal a day, and he limited himself to one entree at that meal. At the beginning, he had some difficulty getting used to his spare regime. On the fifth day of the *Secret Diary*, for example, he noted that he had "transgressed the rule." He did so two more times the following week. All three of those times he was dining with others. For the rest of the *Secret Diary*, he admitted he violated his rule on three more occasions, when he dined with others away from home, or when he celebrated a joyous event.[31]

His diary entries show concern for the particular type of food, how the cook prepared it, how much he ate, and the time of day he ate it. Although Byrd certainly could afford to eat lavishly, the midday meal at his table was not a culinary adventure. The Byrds were not unusual in their regular consumption of such modest fare. The midday meal would more accurately be described as ethnic reinforcement because of its thoroughly English character. The people of his time valued such repetition as a bulwark against the constant change imposed by nature. Byrd ate a light breakfast and a large midday dinner. Beef, mutton, poultry, and pork, particularly bacon, made up his main course meats. He indulged rarely in tongue, tripe, or delicacies such as cod sounds (the swim bladders of cod served in a sauce). Occasionally he ate fish or eggs. Of vegetables he mentioned peas, artichokes, and asparagus, and these he referred to only rarely. This may not mean he never ate vegetables, but perhaps they were too insignificant to write about. The same may be true of bread, which he noted irregularly and usually in connection with breakfast or supper. Byrd ate raw fruits only in the spring and summer when they were ripe. He delighted in taking a walk in his garden after dinner to pick cherries from the trees and eat them on the spot. Evening suppers were small affairs for Byrd when he resided in Virginia. In fact, he often skipped supper altogether or would simply have a beverage such as cider or wine. When in Williamsburg, he often went to a coffeehouse during the evening, although he never recorded actually drinking coffee. If he did have a helping of meat or a serving of pie for supper, it was usually when he traveled or stayed as a guest in someone's home. He drank primarily wine, tea, and coffee, and occasionally punch or beer at suppertime. Once or twice he treated himself to cake.[32]

Judging by the diary entries, his main concern was meat. Although on the one hand it was considered very nutritious because it most closely resembled the human body and would be assimilated easily with little waste, many people thought it provoked bestial behavior. The negative emotions such as anger and lustfulness were thought more common in heavy meat eaters, as were other destructive forms of behavior. Therefore, although meat was believed an essential part of a decent diet, one had to take care not to eat too much and to make sure it was prepared in the proper manner.

The lengths to which Byrd went in food matters illustrate how closely he watched his regimen. He apparently planned his meals carefully, and substitutions or omissions often upset him. Shoats that were not fat, oil substituted for butter, missing artichokes or sweetbreads, all upset the balance of his meal and his constitution. So did inappropriate preparation. Byrd usually noted how his cook made his foods. He distinguished between roasted, boiled, and broiled meat. All three of these cooking techniques altered the quality, texture, and taste, hence the nutritional value of the dishes served at his table. Boiling added a great deal of moisture to a food; roasting and broiling dried it out. If Byrd believed his constitution to be leaning toward the dry, he would have eaten something boiled to add relieving moisture to his system. If he thought his constitution too moist, he would have demanded a roasted or broiled entree.

Attention to the singular components of each meal, their preparation, and their elemental relationship to other foods served at the same time and (most important) to the eater was not an unusual consideration in the early eighteenth century. By the time Byrd wrote his diary, several health texts had been published that were essentially lists of the properties of individual foods, their effects on the eater, and in some cases how they should be prepared. Each food choice had to be evaluated for the individual temperament and digestive system of the eater. Additionally, the complexion of the food source had to match the complexion of the eater in quality as well as in degree.[33]

Another striking characteristic about Byrd's food habits is their regularity. Except when he traveled, he ate basically the same foods at the same times every day. The English believed that culinary change, particularly drastic change, generated undesirable alterations in health and identity. For this reason Thomas Elyot (in his text *Castel of Helth*) and others stressed custom in eating. They believed that a sudden change in diet could be harmful and that a person would fare better if he continued to eat poor quality or insubstantial foods rather than to change his diet suddenly.

The time between meals and the order of foods eaten aided digestion. Robust persons in cold countries required less time between meals than weaker persons in hot countries. As a guide to his readers, Elyot recommended that men in England under the age of forty leave four hours between breakfast and dinner, and six hours between dinner and supper, to allow the food from one meal to be completely digested before they put more food in their stomachs. However, this rule served solely as a guideline because only the stomach could indicate when to eat. If a person felt hungry before the appointed time, he was to eat, because an empty stomach would either send harmful fumes to the brain or retain them where they would smolder and cause disease—if not death. On the other hand, if a person still felt full, he should not eat at all.[34]

Elyot gave his readers two general rules for eating. First, one should never eat too much and could keep from doing so by getting up from the table with some appetite left. Elyot regretted the daily abuse of this simple rule by the English. He believed gluttony drove their behavior, and he criticized sumptuary laws that prohibited the poor but not the rich from such excess. Authors of dietaries before George Cheyne seldom gave readers recommended amounts. However, they firmly agreed that eaters harmed themselves more by overeating than by undereating. Known as surfeit, excessive eating was, according to these texts, the primary method used by the English to oppress nature and cause corruption.[35]

Elyot's second rule also derived from his beliefs about digestion. He stressed the consumption of only one "meat dish," or entree, at any meal. Byrd apparently did not consider dishes with meat from more than one animal source a violation of Elyot's rule. For example, he ate "bacon and fowl" together and "tongue and chicken" without confessing that he had transgressed. Elyot believed this maxim to be the most important health advice he could give his readers. All entrees had their own elemental makeup and required varying "operations of Nature" and diverse temperatures of the stomach for proper digestion. However, the stomach could perform only one operation at one temperature at any given time. When a person simultaneously ate multiple dishes none were digested properly because the stomach could not operate on such a sophisticated level. It produced digestive "crudities" instead of chyle. When the liver sent crudities to the body parts, assimilation was imperfect or incomplete and corruption ensued.[36]

Indications of Success

That William Byrd believed his regimen to be a perfecting vehicle when he began it in 1709 is apparent in how he characterized himself, his life, and his relationships with his family in those early years. As he performed his daily routine, Byrd supposed himself to be even-tempered. Almost every day's entry ended with the comment, "I said my prayers and had good health, good thoughts, and good humor, thank God Almighty." In his first diary, he presented himself as a calm and cheerful person who seldom, if ever, sank into melancholy, desperation, or beastliness. Only rarely did he remark, as he did on 9 August 1710, "I was very much out of humor for nothing by reason of the weather or my constitution."

During the years of the first two diaries, 1709–1712 and 1717–1721, Byrd almost always "ate" milk for breakfast. He frequently wrote that he neglected to say his prayers but did have milk for breakfast, suggesting that he considered it an important part of his attempt to forestall degeneration. Milk drinking has a complicated history in Europe. It was considered both nutritious and dangerous, in part because of the perception of the stomach as a finicky and inefficient digester. The new mechanical model of the stomach that characterized it as a fermenter rather than a cooking pot dispelled some of this perception. Health texts recommended that milk be eaten alone, early in the morning, and well before doing any kind of exercise, which is exactly what Byrd did.[37]

Sometimes he went to great pains to have milk, as for example when he was forced to stay at a plantation because the weather prevented travel. He achieved variety by having ass's milk, cow's milk warm from the cow or prepared warm, cold, boiled, as porridge, or occasionally with rice, fruit, or tea. Such devotion to milk by someone who could afford to eat far more luxuriously may strike twenty-first-century readers as curious. But Byrd and his contemporaries lived in a world where many people, both past and present, praised milk as the perfect food. They believed it to be a white form of blood and therefore unable to corrupt inside the body. Byrd's regularity and devotion to milk suggests more than just a liking for a health-giving food. In fact, as early as 1709 he practiced what George Cheyne in 1724 popularized in an essay concerning his return to health from physical and moral corruption brought about by dissolute living. Cheyne, who may have followed the diet at approximately the same time as Byrd, regenerated himself by drinking milk, eating vegetables, and avoiding red meats. He ate only one "meat dish" per meal, and often ate only one meal a day. Following such a diet not only gave Cheyne physical relief from obesity and disease, it restored his virtue. Cheyne wrote that he had learned about the diet from a country doctor he met many years before. It is possible that Byrd learned of the diet from Cheyne in those early years. They both lived in London in the late seventeenth and early eighteenth centuries and were members of the Royal Society.[38]

Additionally, Byrd may have drunk milk every day to keep his complexion white. He wrote in *The Secret History of the Dividing Line* that the people of North Carolina had yellow complexions from a lack of milk. In 1728, he may have dropped the practice of having milk every day for breakfast and this remark may have been satirical, but twenty years earlier, it seems, his reliance on milk may not have been so lighthearted. For him, milk drinking could have been another way to forestall Indianization. After all, Indians did not drink milk.

Another sign of the success Byrd believed his Virginia regimen gave him is the lack of success he experienced a few years later, from 1717 to 1720, when he lived alone, back in London in rented rooms with only one manservant. His wife, Lucy, had died of smallpox, and their two young daughters boarded at a London school. As he had in Virginia, he continued to rise every morning, read, and drink milk for breakfast. However, the rest of his daily routine had changed considerably. He dined in the midday with friends or business associates, either in their homes or in taverns, but seldom at his rooms. He ate full suppers daily, after which he often patronized coffeehouses. Shortly after the beginning of the London diary, he began to visit bordellos in London, to pick up women in the park, and to have sex with acquaintances. His sexual encounters occurred frequently, too frequently by eighteenth-century health and morality standards. He recorded his numerous escapades in the same laconic hand evident in the hundreds of prior entries of his diary. His commentary indicated no concern about his behavior, except when he experienced episodes of gonorrheal discharge. However, he expressed anxiety through his diet. After months of frequent sexual activity, Byrd wrote on 13 December 1718 that his cousin Horsemanden walked home with him so he would not pick up a whore. The following January he began drinking ass's milk, considered second only to woman's milk in its superior quality. That same month he frequently substituted milk porridge for his suppers and continued to do so for several months. He still occasionally picked up women but instead of having sex with them, he simply took them to taverns, watched them eat, and paid them for their time, doing nothing more.[39] This spate of self-control, though promising, was short-lived; he soon resumed his old ways and continued them until he left London.

Byrd sailed back to Virginia in early 1720 and again took up the daily regimen recorded in his earliest diary. He rose early, read, ate milk for breakfast, exercised, had one "meat dish" for dinner, and walked about his plantation. Except for his wife's absence, only one activity had changed. When Byrd returned from London, he brought with him three servants, one of whom was a maid named Annie. At Westover, she regularly slept with Byrd in his room. Having misgivings about this relationship he decided to end it, but he failed in his resolve. His diet had returned to that of his first diary, sparse and not reducible, yet the formula for virtue that had worked so well before now failed him. He was no longer the man free from corruption. He was no longer the perfect patriarch who provided balance to those around him who could not achieve it for themselves. Momentarily—and it is the only moment in his diaries—he lost faith in his regimen. At this point he resorted to the methods of his contemporary Cotton Mather and prayed. Although Byrd routinely and perfunctorily in his diary asked for God's forgiveness for neglecting to say his prayers or for "committing uncleanness," on 25 May 1720 he specifically prayed for God's assistance after being with Annie.[40]

The second diary ended before Byrd successfully terminated his relationship with Annie. The record remains silent on how it actually did end, and on the fate of Annie herself. By 1739, at the beginning of the third volume of his diary, Byrd had been married to his second wife, an Englishwoman named Maria Taylor, for several years and had fathered three more children, the oldest of whom was named Annie. He had given up drinking milk; whether he did so in 1721 when it did not work for him or later is not known. In fact, he made few further diary references to drinking milk, even when he suffered from a lengthy illness. He retained the remainder of his regimen, including the restriction to one "meat dish" per day. Although his last diary entries contain the same information as those found in the first volume, they lack the hope, promise, and intensity of the first. His overconfidence in his own virtue had disappeared. The dull passages read as if Byrd adopted habit merely for habit's sake. The hope and promise of his prose had disappeared with his morning milk.

So had much of the threat of the Virginia air. Byrd's correspondence reflects this change. His letters after 1724 refer to the effects of his colony's air, but often as a source of satire rather than of seriousness. For example, Byrd wrote to a friend in England and jokingly described Maria's climate-induced transmutation that had occurred since her migration from England to Virginia. He claimed that his wife's amazing fertility (she bore four children in five years) had to be a result of the air, because she ate fish no more than once a week and rabbit only once in six months. These comments indicate that Byrd's thoughts about degeneration had changed and suggest that general scientific understanding had as well.[41]

CONCLUSION

The Old World and the New World wedged Cotton Mather and William Byrd between them. Both men were born at a time when the humoral view of the human body—that it was infinitely complex and required constant monitoring and adjustment to be virtuous—was the dominant philosophical metaphor. To be virtuous required careful personal discipline, such as that exercised by William Byrd, and its rewards were distinction and power as well as virtue. Although Byrd and Mather fussed over the lack of virtue of the people around them, and they managed their lifestyles in fear of becoming like these unvirtuous folk, as men of scientific learning their fears were of a much greater metaphysical nature. The mechanical body was rough, tough—and generic. This body did not need the incessant fine-tuning of its humoral predecessor, but it also eliminated the possibility for distinction as they understood it. Yeomen farmers were commonplace; Polykleitoses were not. The biggest fear for Cotton Mather and William Byrd was of being carried away in the great metaphysical tidal wave of mechanical philosophy, which could sweep away the impediments preventing the bulk of Anglo-Americans from being virtuous and enjoying its benefits and, in doing so, could erode the status and power of men like themselves.

A Mechanical Society

Sometime between 1745 and 1753, a Scottish physician and emigré to Annapolis, Maryland, Dr. Alexander Hamilton, declared that George Cheyne was ingenious. The declaration appeared in a satirical chronicle of a short but rambunctious history of a real men's social club to which Hamilton belonged. A child of the Newtonian age, Hamilton was making reference to the belief that God created the universe to operate according to certain rules and that God provided its motive force. Similarly, Cheyne created a new intellectual universe when he dethroned the "sedentary and studious" from their sociopolitical pedestal of food security and replaced them with yeoman farmers. Like Newton's *Principia,* Cheyne's *Essay* left many questions in its wake about Newton, Cheyne, and Hamilton's new world. What was the relationship between food and power? How could eaters stay within the social golden mean? What should they eat? And, in an age in which most men had virtue, how could they acquire distinction? The men of Hamilton's social club experimented to find out.[1]

Consideration of the social and political change that made up what some historians call two revolutions—a political one and a social one—did not start with the French and Indian War, the Stamp Act, or the Declaration of Independence. Long before these events, British American men and women were debating and forming opinions on republican ideology in their newspapers, homes, coffeehouses, and clubs, and some of the topics they discussed could be targeted for censure by church or government. As a result, sometimes they took efforts to conceal the speaker's identity, as in letters to newspapers signed pseudonymously. Sometimes, as occurred in private clubs all over America, they took efforts to put the controversial topic in a satirical and conversational form that often seemed so silly it could not be seriously contested without risking ridicule. Many American men formed such private clubs, which met for social and intellectual purposes either in coffeehouses or in homes. As they sat at tables and shared food and drink, these men, like men throughout the British empire who formed similar clubs, hoped to set a standard by which members could evaluate the temper of their larger society and the progress it had made.[2]

THE EXPERIMENT

Taking the rule that the middling diet promised virtue, and the custom that the virtuous were entitled to power, the Tuesday Club set itself up as a small democratic unit. All club members could vote on all laws and elect officers. At its first meeting in 1745 the members passed rules essential for their proper self-government. Weekly meetings were to convene on a rotating basis at each of the members' houses. Their meals were to be simple. The evening's host was to act as steward and had to provide "a gammon of bacon or any other dish of dressed vittles and not more" to the club members, along with liquor, which could not be served after 11 p.m. Club secretary Dr. Alexander Hamilton described the first meetings as idyllic affairs where the members lounged freely in chairs or at the table, smoking, drinking, and talking. At some point the gammon of bacon "appeared" on a sideboard with "some plates in a heap, knives and forks." They needed nothing so formal or feminine as a tablecloth. Anyone could get up at his leisure without disturbing others and, with no heed to table manners, cut himself a slice of bacon to enjoy with his cup and his companions. "How charming, how regular, and how much like the Simple frugality of the Golden age was this," wrote Hamilton, "and how different from that luxury and profuseness that prevails in most of our moderen Clubs, where, the whole apparatus of a formal table is Introduced."[3]

With these few laws, the Tuesday Club established their requirements for food security and for achieving the social golden mean. By limiting the amount and type of food they ate to a portion of bacon or one simple meat dish, the club also limited the labor required to prepare and acquire their meal. Because the gammon had to be divided among many attendees, no one person would take more than he needed. They dispensed with the time-consuming and work-intensive tablecloths, table manners, table settings, polite table talk, multicourse meals, and the hostesses who provided the goods and controlled the crowd. Their plan for attaining food security and for achieving the golden mean, then, was to eliminate as much labor as possible and cut back the type and amount of food to an equilibrilizing minimum. Surely, they believed, this would place and keep their fledgling society within the golden mean.

THE RESULTS

Over a number of meetings, Tuesday Club members tested their new democratic society in numerous ways. It was intended to be a controlled experiment, and they soon learned that, when it came to the human appetite, control was more difficult in real life than it seemed on paper. Nevertheless, as Hamilton saw it, they were able to formulate some useful conclusions.

Food and Power

As soon as they passed their food law, a problem arose. The spartan plan for food security rankled one of the bachelor members, Charles Cole (whom Hamilton nicknamed Nasifer Jole), an English merchant whose motto was to buy cheap and sell at a 300 percent profit. Cole showed no interest in women. He lived with numerous cats. He cooked expertly and extravagantly and, unlike any other Tuesday Club member, displayed numerous feminine attributes. He knew "as well as any husiff [housewife], how to stew a frecassé or ragout, mix, compound, boil or bake a pudding, or raise a pasty." Club members and others acknowledged his accomplishment in this area with high praise, which fed one of Jole's weaknesses, his "luxuriant Slip of vanity." According to Hamilton, although Cole remained "pritty tenacious" of most of his property (in other words, he was stingy), when it came to getting compliments about his cooking, "he would spare no expence in making a Show with such delicacies, and dainties, and any hungry fellow or abondon'd Epicure, might get a good meal out of him, as often as he pleased, by only praising his Cookery." He also had "elegant taste" in all the domestic arts, from interior decorating to cutting paper fly decoys, to gardening and arranging nosegays, and designing and cutting out patterns for his clothes.[4]

The first time Jole served as steward he openly violated the Tuesday Club's liquor law by giving the members arrack, an expensive liquor distilled from rice, sugar, and coconut juice imported from the East Indies. After "bewitching" the members with it, he ushered them into a large room with a table "Elegantly spread, the cloth and napkins nicely pinched, and perfumed Sweetly with Lavander and roses, and several elegant dishes of meat, were curiously Ranged on this Table." No one objected and everyone ate heartily. The next time Jole hosted the club, he added to the members' meal an iced cake "curiously wrap'd up in clean white paper." Hamilton believed that this cake, like the apple in Eden, was the downfall of the Tuesday Club: "this Cake, this fatal Cake," lamented Hamilton, "[c]ompleted the Catastrophe of the Clubs liberty, and, as Esau sold his birthright to Jacob, for fair words and a mess of porridge, so this unhappy Club, bartered their Liberty to Nasifer Jole Esqr, for an old Song, Rack punch, plumb pudding, four pounds of Candles, and a Iced Cake!"[5]

According to humoral theory, sugar was one of the most perfectly bal-anced foods. Its sweet warm taste suggested that its humoral balance was close to perfect. By Hamilton's reckoning, in this new mechanical world, however, it was an evil luxury to be avoided. Why should a piece of cake be the downfall of club members' liberty? Hamilton believed it loosened the restraint club members had imposed on themselves and thereby introduced corruption among the ranks. In the words of George Cheyne, it was a breach in security from the appetite, which could lead to physical and moral corruption—and according to Hamilton, to political corruption. In his little mechanical society, Hamilton was right. Club members happily voted Jole president.

In the humoral society, food security promised virtue to those who could achieve the golden mean. Sugar was a means to virtue, a symbol of both virtue itself and its handmaiden, power. In the mechanical society, food in general (and sugar in particular) was a means to power as well, not for those who ate it but for those who fed it to others. Nasifer Jole gave the iced cake and other foods to club members, enticing them to give their power to him. In this he practiced an eighteenth-century version of the Renaissance custom of exchanging food and hospitality for loyalty. The difference between the two is that the eighteenth-century followers were able to vote. Food still had tremendous power. Although it could no longer transform a person into someone else, it could be used as a tool to get other things.

Although Hamilton poked fun at the club's efforts to maintain an overly simple diet, he did not dispense with the idea that either overeating or eating excessively rich foods was the first step to physical, moral, and political cor-ruption. If he had dispensed with this idea, he would have defied two thou-sand years of accrued wisdom, not to mention the Bible. He did not lack con-temporaries who believed as he did that some traditions were worth keeping.

Benjamin Franklin in *Poor Richard's Almanac,* for example, disseminated a plethora of advice. The 1742 edition included many aphorisms. One should determine how much food the body would allow and keep constantly to that quantity. People who study a great deal have poor digestion and should eat less. Eat for necessity, not for pleasure. The amount of food must be calcu-lated in accordance with the "Quality and Condition of the Stomach, because the Stomach digests it." When the stomach perfectly digests the food, a per-son knows he has found the right amount to eat. The way to tell if the stom-ach is perfectly digesting is by asking certain questions. Are you dull and heavy after eating? If so, you have eaten too much. Are you unfit to do your work? If so, you have eaten too much. To avoid these conditions, stay away from feasts and banquets, because once you get there, it is difficult to keep yourself from eating too much. Also, get some mild exercise fifteen minutes before you sit down to your meal. If you do find yourself in that state of stuffed torpor, then fast for the next meal and "all may be well again." The benefits of a temperate diet are numerous. It steels the body against accidents, maintains vigorous senses, mitigates violent passions and affections, preserves the memory, reduces lustfulness, will help you die without pain, and will make you a virtuous and happy person.[6]

A few decades after the Tuesday Club, in 1772, a Philadelphia physician and prominent participant in the revolutionary movement, Benjamin Rush, published his thoughts on ease, eating, and virtue in *Sermons to the Rich and Studious on Temperance and Exercise*. In the very first words of his text, Rush made it clear that a strong bond existed between eating, politics, and freedom. Quoting Solomon in Proverbs, he wrote: "When thou sittest to eat with a ruler, consider diligently what is before thee. And put a knife to thy throat, if thou be a man given to appetite. Be not desirous of his dainties, for they are deceitful meat." In his advice Rush relied on the Hippocratic division of quality and quantity. He believed human appetites are so varied and variable that the best advice on what to eat was to keep it simple and have a good mix of meat and vegetables. He considered it difficult to go wrong on quality of food, because, as the Tuesday Club eventually concluded, nature guided men's appetites to eat what they should and avoid what was harmful. Variety, though, was another matter entirely. If someone did not feel "light and cheerful" after eating, then he had eaten too much: "The chief incentive to this is the variety of our dishes, which excites us to eat after the appetite is satisfied. It was for good reason that the Catholic Church specified fish days because it is impossible to eat too much fish. It is an example of nature guarding our health. Few men, I believe, ever eat to excess more than *once* of one plain dish." He also recommended eating only one hearty meal a day, in the evening. Any more than that kept a person "constantly fatigued, in concocting the immense supplies of food which are thrown into the stomach." Eventually, he believed, nature got its revenge.[7]

The Social Golden Mean

Within just a few months of the iced cake debacle, the Tuesday Club rallied, exhibiting what Hamilton called "an Instance of heroic temperance and moderation, much like that of a certain Roman General who, when foreign ambassadors came to have audience of him, was busied in boiling a turnip for his own Dinner." Some of the unmarried members other than Jole had difficulty in performing their steward's duties because they had neither wives nor cooks, nor even, in some cases, "[any]thing for Cooks to lick their fingers upon." The members believed that these bachelors had to go to much more trouble to steward a meeting than their married fellows. This extra labor meant that part of their community worked more than others, tilting the balance the club thought it had achieved between activity level and food. This imbalance eroded their food security and portended corruption. To forestall decay and restore an even keel to their fledgling community, they allowed bachelors to provide a cheese instead of a "dish of dressed vittles."[8]

Nasifer Jole suggested that cheese be removed from the list of suitable supper items, however. It never had been and never would, he claimed, be considered equal to a dish of "dressed vittles." Rather, it was usually eaten as a relish or a dessert. Jole claimed that the original cheese law was void and "repugnant" to the "liberty" of the club. The members approved the new law, and no one ever served cheese again. Once they did that, though, members found themselves once again demanding more labor from their few bachelors than they did from the married members because even acquiring a cheese was more activity than was engaged in by the married members, whose wives made all of the preparations for the club dinners. To solve this dilemma, they simply refused to allow any more new unmarried members into their club. While they lost their diversity and equality they did, apparently, retain their place within the social golden mean.[9]

However, with Jole as its leader, the club sank ever deeper into luxury, a sure sign that it was on the high road away from the golden mean. As host, Jole continued to entertain lavishly. He convinced the members to buy expensive and overpriced luxury items from him. Even worse, other members attempted to duplicate or outdo his successes. All members forgot the one-dish law. They began to meet biweekly because the effort and expense of weekly meetings taxed them physically and financially, throwing askew their goals of simplicity, temperance, and virtue. Although Hamilton lamented this chain of events, it really came as no surprise to him. Human nature succumbed easily to corruption. Men, he thought, "will be Induced to barter liberty, and every other valuable possession, for a little good belly timber, or what we call Eatables and drinkables."[10]

The Tuesday Club found that the Spartan plan was just not as simple as it appeared. The members tried to duplicate the "golden age" in creating and following the rules they believed would keep them within the golden mean. As soon as they did that they began to bicker. At the first sign of temptation (iced cake, no less), they lost any resolve they may have had. Clearly their new mechanical society, which existed in an increasingly material world, required a different approach.

Their new tack was to reconsider consumption. Was it as bad as they had thought? Was Nasifer Jole really the corrupt person he appeared to be? Yes, he consumed a great deal of food and other material goods. To serve elaborate meals Jole needed dishes, flatware, tablecloths, candlesticks, and numerous other paraphernalia including spits, cooking pots, skillets, bowls, and utensils. To decorate his house he needed furniture, paint, wall coverings, draperies, bed linens, rugs, and wall decorations. And then there was his garden. One can only guess that his was not a simple vegetable garden but one that compared favorably with the most beautifully designed and elaborately ornamented gardens in Annapolis. However, if he did all the work—if he decorated his house, gardened, cooked for himself and the club, and cleaned up after them, including emptying the chamber pot they kept in the dining room so they would not have to go outside to relieve themselves—would he not be entitled to the rewards of that work? Should he not take them? Otherwise, he would have been like a servant or slave who labored constantly with little or no compensation. Furthermore, what about the other members of the club who merely sat at Jole's table and ate his food? It appeared that, like so many of their ancestors, they had succumbed to corruption through gluttony. In this case, it was political corruption because they quickly voted Jole president for all the wrong reasons and kept him in office.

Having first characterized Jole as devilish, Hamilton finally presented him as a sort of savior of the club because he introduced social competition, the very thing to keep all of them within the personal and social golden mean, which was one and the same. No sooner had Jole entertained his fellow members in his lavish fashion than others began to follow suit. No doubt members consumed more but they also worked more. As a result, what threatened to be corruption brought about by excessive consumption in fact ended up a homegrown corollary of Sir Bernard Mandeville's economic theory, expressed in *The Fable of the Bees,* that free-flowing commerce, the circulation of goods, eliminated social and political corruption. In addition to being the social corollary to Hippocrates, Mandeville's theory was also the social corollary of the mechanical theory of the body, in which health and virtue were directly dependent on the rate of circulation of bodily fluids. The club's homegrown corollary was the perfect plan for achieving the personal and social golden mean because one plan worked for both. The club arrived at its solution by focusing on balance and by having neither too little nor too much.

What to Eat

Having successfully established rules concerning their appetites and the healthfulness of social competition, the Tuesday Club went on to tackle the most difficult question. What should they eat? By suggesting that a cheese, the poor man's main course of former times, was equal to a main dish or a ham, club members forced the issue of the qualities of foods and of the people who ate them. Reacting against humoral theory, which insisted on an infinite variety of eaters and appetites, the Tuesday Club went to the opposite extreme when they posited that everyone eat the same thing. Nasifer Jole quickly deduced the weakness in this logic. Faced with this predicament, the club then had to decide how many types of eaters there really were. They came up with two.

Hamilton relayed this belief through a story. In former times, the club had two parties, the Royalists and the Levellers. The Royalists, supporter of "kingly government," were "stout Toapers" who gave the crown of their kingdom to the man who could down a gallon of beer. They feared sudden changes in custom and believed intensely that perseverance produced results.

They put their faith in ancient authorities who told of Persians who ate only once a week and men who "by force of custom" lived exclusively on cable ropes, candle ends, and flint stones, all without being hurt. The Levellers, who could not command such performances among their ranks, protested that men could not design their mouths, throats, or stomachs, and that the kingship should be held in turns by each member. This way, every member could eat and drink as much or as little as he wanted. The Tuesday Club members consisted of both kinds of men. Which type was the better and should exercise power was a moot question. They both should—as long as they kept their appetites in balance.[11]

When the club originally created the one-dish rule, the members followed the trend in which the common foods of former times were now being embraced by higher social classes. This trend was part of a larger Enlightenment movement, which associated luxury with corruption and self-restraint with virtue. The members of the Tuesday Club also, like most human cultures, paired self-restraint with leadership.[12]

Although many members had long since forgotten this idea, a few members had not. One evening the appointed steward, whom Hamilton nicknamed Quirpum Comic Esqr., served only a modest dish of hominy grits, which is made from maize. Immediately after the meal Sir John, Knight and Champion of the Club, objected to the presentation of this Indian dish as substandard fare for their kind of gentleman. A third member, the Orator, jumped to his feet, apologized to the steward for the insult, and pronounced hominy wholesome, simple, and easily digestible. He recalled the ancient days when men lived long, happy, healthy lives because they ate plain food with "no high Spices, no devlish Caustic or Sophisticated Sauces [that] contaminated and Corrupted their Taste." It was before "the monstrous and hellish compositions of moderen Cookery, had contaminated and polluted their kitchens before [the Devil] to[ok] it in his head to send cooks to poison [mankind]." He proclaimed hominy the dish of royalty, Indian royalty who resembled other monarchs around the world except in their distaste for luxury, ambition, and good food. Furthermore, the word *hominy* (spelled "homony" by Hamilton) derived from Latin words meaning "man" and "the only," which indicated that it was the only food for man. Finally, the Orator stressed that simplicity of diet had long been believed by antediluvians to be the key to longevity. He urged his fellow members to have more respect for hominy, to eat it and live to be nine hundred or one thousand years old.[13] The majority of club members either slept through this passionate defense of hominy or forgot it, along with the passing effects of their large meal and generous drink, because they did not vote to add hominy to the now ignored law requiring a gammon or one "meat dish."

Although the Orator's conclusion overstated the case, Anglo-Americans of all social levels in the mid-eighteenth-century Chesapeake did eat the highly processed maize dish. It required time-consuming preparation that greatly changed the taste and character of the Indian corn from which it was made. Hominy was not simply a cornmeal mush. Cooks shelled the corn and scalded it in water and wood ashes or lye to separate the hulls and remove the germ (the live part of the kernel). They dried the kernels and boiled them a second time. Before serving the final dish, they ground the dried kernels, if they wanted hominy grits, and cooked them a third time. The end product resembled an English pottage. Chesapeake colonists did not refer to it as corn, Indian corn, or cornmeal mush, but only as hominy, suggesting that they considered it a different product. Of course, having been hulled, degerminated, twice dried, and boiled, it was. As they began to create their own American identity during the mid-eighteenth century, British Americans adopted hominy as their own. Nothing states this better than the "ode" of the Homony Club, an Annapolis successor to the Tuesday Club, which pronounced hominy the ruler over luxury, gluttony, and Epicureanism.[14]

By the end of the century, maize had come into its own as proper American food. The first recipe calling for maize was printed in the first cookery book authored by an American woman, Amelia Simmons, at the end of the eighteenth century. Furthermore, the political radical Joel Barlow had written and published what by now is a classic poem, *The Hasty Pudding*. Barlow dedicated his poem to Martha Washington and pressed her to encourage all Americans to eat hasty pudding and enjoy its regenerating properties. Simplicity of diet, he believed, was "of more consequence than we are apt to imagine." Barlow's intent in writing the poem was to change the "vicious habits" of Americans and to institute the eating of plain dishes. Barlow described his hasty pudding, although a plain dish, as being one of the most sensuous and pleasurable foods one could eat.[15]

Over the century, the idea that human nature consisted of the royalist Stout Toapers and the Levellers thrived. What and how much a person ate still signaled his degree of virtue. However, determining who was the more virtuous of the Toapers and the Levellers was as difficult as it had always been. Virtue, it seems, was in the mind of the eater and his commensal companions. For some, this explained the need for two political parties. At the end of the century when John Adams was president of the United States, for example, Vermont newspaper publisher Matthew Lyon printed his belief that the president was pompous, greedy, and grasping for power. In addition, Lyon published an essay written by Joel Barlow. In the essay Barlow accused Adams of being a corrupt aristocrat. The U.S. government filed suit against Lyon for treason. At the circuit court trial, Lyon chose to defend himself. He did so by pointedly asking Supreme Court Justice William Patterson (whose circuit riding duties required him to hear circuit court cases) one pointed question. Had he ever eaten with the president? If he had, said Lyon, he would know that Barlow's essay was true. Patterson did not agree with Lyon on this point, and Lyon lost his case.[16]

Distinction

Another question addressed by the Tuesday Club was that of identity. Under the humoral system, identity was plastic and could be shaped consciously by the eater. Renaissance health texts used this idea when they encouraged readers to strive for the golden mean. Because of the requirements, only a relative few were able to achieve this mean, and therefore it was a mark of distinction. Virtue in the mechanical age, on the other hand, was a presumption for the entire middling segment of early American society. While virtue signified many positive things, it was no longer the mark of distinction it once was. This change of events raised the question: How then could men distinguish themselves?

In the Tuesday Club, Nasifer Jole showed members one way to do it. He prodigiously consumed material goods other than food and used them to create his own distinctive image. He designed his own clothes with extravagant yardage and created unforgettable ensembles such as the "flaming Suit of Scarlet" he wore shortly after being elected president. With this suit he paired "white Silk Stockings rolld" and shoes that shone "like a looking glass" and were adorned with "large Shining Silver Shoe buckles." He had edged his coat and vest "round with gold twist," the buttons were of "gold & gilt spangles, [and] the button holes trimmed with gold." On his fingers he had "several brilliant rings." He wore this outfit with a "magnificent hat, bound round with massy Scolloped Silver lace, a fine large and full fair wig, [and] white kid Gloves." He carried "a gold headed cane." So amazed by Jole's appearance was Hamilton that he could not "be certain whether or not he had a Silver hilted Sword, with a beautiful Sword knot of Ribbons."[17]

When it came to food and virtue, distinction dropped out of the mix. If someone wanted to be virtuous in the mechanical age, he did not want to distinguish himself with his eating habits. To do so would require either gluttonous behavior or to eat as the poor did. Neither would lead to virtue.

CONCLUSION

The trials of the Tuesday Club show how far Anglo-Americans had traveled from the late sixteenth-century England of William Harrison, when the humors that combined in an uncountable number of ratios created unique individuals, some of whom possessed virtue because of the high quality of their diet and the ability to control their lifestyle. In the world of the Tuesday Club, the social hierarchy had flattened down to just two types of men, the Toapers and the Levellers, neither of whom controlled their biology. Rather, their biology controlled them, even to the point of determining political beliefs.

After a great deal of experimentation and argumentation, the Tuesday Club discovered a few important rules of their new mechanical age. The first was that food security required food intake to be in balance with the activity level of the eaters' lives. This rule of Hippocrates remained as true in 1745 as it had been in 450 B.C. The human appetite had not changed over all those millennia. Personal and social security required the same balance. To achieve the golden mean in an age of abundance, an increased activity level would have to balance the increased consumption. The club's other rules, however, were new. Men in the mechanical age were of two natures. Each had his own style of eating, appetite, and outlook on the world. Neither was wrong. But then again, keeping within the golden mean philosophy, neither was right. And finally, whereas the humoral philosophy had great utility for men wishing to distinguish or even reinvent themselves, the mechanical philosophy with its pipes and juices had little. The elaborate dinner preparations of Nasifer Jole show that Americans had to use other aspects of their material culture to serve that purpose.

CHAPTER

NINE

O

n 23 May 1759, the thirty-six-year-old bachelor Charles Carroll of Annapolis, Maryland, sent a shopping list to his agent in London, William Anderson. Carroll, known as the Barrister to distinguish him from several other men of the same name living in the same area, specified several items for dining. The set of tea and coffee cups, he wrote, should include the teapot, slop basin, and accessories and should cost about six guineas. The coffeepot was to be silver and of a three-pint capacity. Other desired silver items included castors, salvers, butter boats, candlesticks, one-pint drinking cans, and salt cellars. His dozen sets of matching silver-handled knives, forks, and spoons were to be sent in a black shagreen case. All were to be "of the neat Plain Fashion" with his coat of arms "as suitable to the Fashion Engraved thereon." The plates, soup plates, dishes, and two pickle boats were to be of "burnt china." The second set of plates, soup plates, water plates, and variously sized dishes were to be of the "best hard mettle." He wanted four quart and four pint decanters, two dozen wineglasses, and a half-dozen water glasses. Finally, he ordered six blue-and-white china deep dishes of different sizes, a dozen custard cups of the same make, and twelve coarse blue-and-white "patte pans." Carroll knew, when he wrote the letter, that he would have to wait up to twelve months for the goods to arrive. He paid for everything with pig iron.[1]

Charles Carroll, Barrister, had the year before started to build a new house on his plantation on the banks of the Patapsco River on property he inherited from his father, Dr. Charles Carroll of Annapolis, who had known and worked with members of the Tuesday Club. The Barrister named his plantation Mount Clare, after his sister Mary Clare and his grandmother Clare Dunn Carroll. By 1756 his mansion-building activities were commonplace in all the British American colonies. Although the Barrister had inherited a fortune, making him one of the wealthiest men in Maryland, his house was neither unique nor novel. The plan was in the popular *Select Architecture,* published by Robert Morris, in London in 1755 and in *Twelve Designs,* published by John Payne, in Dublin in 1757. Furthermore, the same design house had already been built in Maryland. The Barrister, however, did not treat his house as ordinary. He paid careful attention to many of the features and details of his new home, including, as the above list indicates, the style of the butter boats and the plain fashion of the engraved silver that would sit upon the grand table, which he had ordered the previous year. Actually, he ordered two. They were "suitable" mahogany tables, made to fit into each other and measuring, together, five feet by ten feet. They came (or at least they were ordered) with twelve matching mahogany chairs, "with Black Leather seats of the Neat Plain Fashion and strong at about £2 per chair."[2]

The mid-eighteenth century witnessed the material embellishment of colonial wealth the likes of which had not been seen in America before. This increase in consumption actually began around 1690 and reached its full flower after 1720. It was the beginning of a trend in American history toward material refinement, in which colonists hoped that their refined material lives were "in truth but outward signs of what the inhabitants hoped would be an inward grace. They wished to transform themselves along with their environments." The appetite for material goods, particularly among the wealthy, seemed to have high limits, as the orders of the Carrolls demonstrate. One has to wonder why.[3]

The members of this generation did use material goods to display an inner grace, but this was not a novel practice. The consumption of one particular material good—food—had been used by the English for centuries to achieve that very goal. In seeking to establish and display inner grace, men and women also sought to distinguish themselves from others. Until the eighteenth century and the change in worldview brought about by the Scientific Revolution, food was the most effective tool to distinguish oneself from others. Afterward, particularly in America, food continued to be the best way to achieve inner grace. However, it did so for the bulk of Americans, binding them together and thereby losing much of its former flexibility for ordering, ranking, and distinguishing people within the group. Just at the time this happened, the English Industrial Revolution provided other material goods, which served that very purpose.

The Barrister provides an excellent example of how early American elites used food to maintain their common identity as middling Americans, and the material culture surrounding food to establish their superiority. He had a tricky task because, unlike the elite of previous generations, he had to remain a yeoman and be a member of the elite at the same time. To stay within the golden mean of food security, he had to control the quality and quantity of the foods he ate and balance them with the right amount of activity. This is how he did it.

INSIDE THE HOUSE

His house was distinctive, but not unique. Similar if not exactly the same type of houses could be seen throughout the colonies. The same was true of the interior furnishings. By September 1760, Carroll was living in his new house and found he needed more items from England. His list that year specified fine damask tablecloths of three different sizes, a "substantial copper cooler to contain about a dozen bottles and a smaller one to set on a table and cool a bottle and glasses," pewter candle molds, and more silver: a stand for the middle of the table, a silver punch ladle light in the handle so as not to chip the punch bowl, a silver soup or tureen ladle, and a "Shagreen or other Fashionable Tea Chest with silver furniture with two silver Tea Canisters and a sugar canister or Dish neatly Chased or Carved [for] about thirteen pounds." This last piece he wished his young female cousins living in London to select, as a favor to a bachelor such as he, because he believed it was "a piece of Peculiarly Lady's Furniture." The one he received was not in the neat plain fashion, as so many of the other items he ordered over the years. In addition, he wanted one "Large Neat Pouty Poul Tea Waiter" costing about one and a half guineas. "Pouty Poul" refers to Pontypool, Wales, where tin-plate factories existed that produced culinary equipment.[4]

When the Barrister married his twenty-one-year-old cousin, the prominent and wealthy Margaret Tilghman, in June 1763, his shopping lists became longer. On 2 September 1763, he requested a five-quart skillet and cover, a copper fish kettle, two dozen wineglasses, six wine- and water glasses, numerous decanters, three glass stands of different sizes for the middle of their table, and matching glasses for syllabubs, sweetmeats, and other foods. This list also included an order for bohea, green, and best hyssop teas, numerous loaves of single- and double-refined sugar, along with cinnamon, mace, nutmeg, cloves, and ginger spices. At the end of a sizable order for clothes, jewelry, shoes, stomachers, ribbons, and a hat, the Barrister placed a request for "The Best Book of Cooking Published." This may very well have been the mainstream and popular *British Housewife* by Elizabeth Bradley.[5]

During the following year, 1764, more iron crossed the ocean and more cooking and eating paraphernalia arrived. They were not quite the tools of the yeoman farmer. The Carrolls received a silver bread server "in the fashion of Fruit Baskets or Sea Shells," silver-handled table and dessert knives, forks, and spoons, a three-pint chocolate pot, a cream pot, and a waiter, again engraved, this time with his crest or his wife's. On 2 October, he ordered William Anderson to purchase more spices, two wicker picnic baskets, an array of enameled china plates and soup, salad, pudding, and pickle dishes, "nankeen" breakfast plates, napkins, and tablecloths. Four days later he requested merchants in Bristol to send him six strong frying pans with "Good Long Handles," two dozen large stone butter pots, and four dozen strong, gallon-sized pewter basins. A month later he wrote to William Anderson again, this time asking for a china terrine and sauceboats to match the china he had ordered previously, six china shells for escalloped oysters, and a dozen each of table and dessert knives and forks with stained ivory handles.[6]

The Carrolls continued ordering food items in 1768. Early in the year they requested tea (usually green, hyssop, and "Blue fig"), a small number of spices, sugar, and some coffee. On 21 July, in addition to the tea, sugar, and cinnamon, the Barrister asked for a quarter-hundred of the best ship's biscuit, a half-hundred of Spanish whiting, a firkin of the best split peas, two quart bottles of capers, two of anchovies, one of olives, and one of the best salad oil. Listed along with these foodstuffs were yet more dishes, a dozen "enamelled thick old China Cawdle [caudle] or Chocolate Basins with Saucers," two pint-sized coffeepots of the best burnt or enameled china, and two china pint cans. To match glasses they had previously received, he asked for three dozen more wineglasses, two wine- and water glasses, two quart and two pint decanters, and four mustard glasses. They also needed another salver "or something Proper to Raise a Middle Dish on [a] Table of Either Glass or China, Rather China." Along with this lengthy list, the Barrister sent a more unusual request. He wanted a "Sober orderly woman of a Good Character that understands Cooking Pickling [and] Preserving." Like many of his other requests, the Barrister was quite careful about detail, stating that if she were elderly, they would both like her better and if she were above the ordinary rank of servants his wife would like her better. Furthermore, he cautioned, "she must not be of the flirting kind or one that will give herself airs." He proposed to pay her ten or twelve pounds sterling a year.[7]

The Carrolls' culinary and gastronomic material goods belied their status as ordinary yeomen, who might have had a silver item or two, probably a teapot or a tankard. No yeoman family would have had the types of sets owned and used by the Carrolls, or the large quantity of china and crystal. The Barrister's letters to William Anderson carefully ordered "the best," a request that would distinguish him not only from the middling sort but from all other gentry men and women without his wealth. In case the quality should be missed, the engraved crests served to make the point, as did the large table and the fine tablecloths. While intensely desiring the highest quality in all their purchases, the Carrolls were careful not to appear ostentatious, a symbol of the (to them) outmoded aristocratic lifestyle. They accomplished this goal by being careful about style. Silver knives, forks, and spoons, the dining table, the black leather seats of its accompanying chairs, and numerous other items were all to be "of the Neat Plain Fashion." Even the English cook—a status symbol in a world where slaves, maidservants, or housewives did the cooking—had to be of the neat plain style, as the Barrister phrased it, sober and orderly.[8]

The Carrolls used simplicity of style to carve lines around themselves and the middling sort who, too, embraced a plain neat style in the eighteenth century, as is demonstrated by the illustration of Paul Revere. A silversmith by trade, at least in this painting, Revere exhibits the essence of simplicity. Once the Carrolls demonstrated their affinity with other colonists, they employed quality and variety to separate themselves from the crowd. Generations of English men and women before them had used the quality and variety of food for the same purpose. However, had the Carrolls started eating the elaborate meals of their sixteenth-century ancestors, they would have undermined their food security with a grossly exaggerated quality of food. Overconsumption in mid-eighteenth-century America could be in quantity or quality, but this mistake would have placed them outside the individual and social golden mean as people lacking in virtue.

The influence of Margaret Carroll on the bachelor's quarters into which she moved can be seen in their transatlantic order three months after their marriage. They asked for three glass stands of different sizes for the middle of their table and matching glasses for syllabubs, sweetmeats, and other such dishes, often considered the jewels of women's cookery. A syllabub is a drink, of which the common variety involves putting wine, sugar, and nutmeg into a punch bowl, then taking it to the dairy barn, placing it under a cow, and milking the cow to get the desired amount of milk. To this was added rich cream. Should one not wish to take the punch bowl to the barn, an alternative method directed the cook to warm milk over the fire to the temperature it would be if it had just come from the cow, to put it into a large teapot, then, holding the teapot high above the bowl, to pour the milk into the punch bowl.[9] Desserts like syllabub were meant for entertaining, as pleasurable treats, not as everyday fare. When presented on fine china or silver stands, these desserts demonstrated a way that wealthy Americans could, and did, positively distinguish themselves from Americans of a lower status. As such, these desserts played an important role in the continual task of ordering people and their world.

The kitchen at Mount Clare was an outbuilding connected to the main house by a short wall. The rectangular building was set back from and perpendicular to the front of the house, making it a long walk from the kitchen to the dining room, which was at the front of the house. One room, measuring about eighteen feet wide and more than twenty feet long, the kitchen had a scullery next to it in the same building. Storage would have been in movable cupboards, chests, and shelves. There was also a huge fireplace for cooking and more than likely an oven for baking. Judging by his request for a "Copper that will Hold forty Gallons to be set in Brick work Strong and Substantially made," the kitchen may also have had a sort of brick stove made to fit the kettle. On 17 November 1765, the Barrister ordered a jack for the fireplace that was to have all of the necessary weights, ropes, pulleys, and chains. He requested two iron dripping pans and a brass kettle and cover to hang on a hook. In addition, he wanted an eighteen-gallon beer kettle and a two-and-a-half-gallon brass kettle, both to hang on hooks. A year later, he wanted a copper Dutch oven ("Pretty Large"), six large long-handled frying pans, bellows, a hearth broom, and numerous sifters. In 1766 he ordered a quart skillet and cover, a three-and-a-half-gallon brass kettle with a cover, and two iron teakettles. Two years later, he needed a twenty-six-inch-long tin fish kettle with an interior fish plate, six larding pins, a set of tagging irons for cutting and marking paste, an egg slicer, and two jack spits (a large one for roasting sizable joints of meat and a smaller one for fowls).[10]

Who cooked in this kitchen? And what did they cook? This last order and others for equipment as well as condiments such as anchovies and capers suggest that the Carrolls got their English cook, or at least someone who was well versed in English cookery. It is impossible to ascertain exactly what she cooked, but a safe guess would include boils and roasts, at the very least, the basics of Anglo-American cookery. Not long after Margaret married the Barrister, a five-quart skillet, a copper fish kettle, and the best English cookbook published arrived at the Carroll wharf on the Patapsco River.

"THE FARM"

In addition to furnishing the kitchen and dining room, the Barrister had ambitious plans for the grounds surrounding his house. In 1760 he asked William Anderson to find a man who understood "Common Gardening as laying of Turf Kitchen and Flower Gardening." In a subsequent letter he asked for the latest edition of "Miller's Gardening Dictionary." In 1765 the Barrister began ordering seeds and rootstock, specifying "the best" broccoli, celery, and beet seeds. In October 1766 his order was much larger. Again, broccoli seeds top the list, but along with them are asparagus "enough for 3 or 4 beds thirty feet long and six feet wide," turnips, cauliflower, peas, and white, red, and purple cabbages. The seeds, he said, came from the latest edition of *The Compleat Body of Husbandry* by Matthew Hale.[11]

By 1767 he and his wife were ready for nursery stock for an orchard. His wife, he said, took pleasure in gardening. Of the two cherry trees, one was to be "the Hertfordshire heart" and the other "Carnation Cherry." He wanted three young plum trees of any kind, and one each "Early black damask," "violet Predigron," and "St. Catherine." Of the sixteen pear trees he ordered, eight were to be grafted on "good free stocks." He wanted one each of Red Muscadelle, Early Ruselet, Bergamot, Iargonelle, Royal Pear, Dry Martin, Black Pear of Worcester, and Easter St. Germain. Peaches he planted by the stone. He ordered one or two dozen of six clingless peaches, Early White Nutmeg, Early Red Nutmeg, Bell Cherruse, Early Magdalen, Bell Grade, Early Purple, and two cling varieties, Old Newington and Monstrous Pavia of Pompone. In April 1768 the Carrolls ordered vines "of your best and Largest Eating Grape Black and White" and "a bearing lemon tree or two" from a merchant in

Madeira. Later that year, in addition to cantaloupe seeds, he ordered more plum and cherry trees of the same varieties he had previously ordered, four kinds of apricots (orange, "Turkey," "Brida," and "Roman"), and more pear trees, all of them to be more than three years old from the graft. In addition to an extensive orchard, Mount Clare also had an orangery in which the Carrolls grew oranges and lemons. In 1770 they began to build the pinery, in which they would grow pineapples.[12]

In the mid-eighteenth century the planting of so many fruit trees was not extravagant, as it might seem from a twenty-first-century perspective. Most farms and plantations at that time had orchards. Even for tenants renting the land on which they lived, the lease agreement usually specified that they plant and maintain fruit trees. This practice began in the seventeenth century. For example, when Francis Barnes of Maryland agreed to rent 250 acres in 1652, he also agreed to plant within twelve months twenty apple, twenty peach, twenty cherry, and ten pear trees. He also agreed to fence the trees to prevent damage from foraging livestock and to practice good husbandry. Other leases required the planting of two hundred to four hundred trees of different kinds.[13]

Whether the tenant actually complied with the lease was another matter, though. For example, one historian has found that only about half the tenants living on the lower western shore of Maryland planted all the trees they agreed to plant. As one might suspect, the number of trees on any particular farm or plantation varied according to the size of the farm and the needs of the owners or occupants. Large plantations could have thousands of trees in their orchards. Zachariah Manor, a plantation in Charles County, Maryland, for example, had 4,200 apple and peach trees in 1767. On the whole, however, historians have concluded that the middling-size farm, at least in the Chesapeake region, had about 250 or 300 fruit trees. Apple and peach were the most common species. Landholders and tenants planted numerous varieties of each. Colonists practiced fruit cultivation so extensively that seeds and grafts could be acquired from neighbors, friends, correspondents, and by mid-century, a number of commercial suppliers. This context puts the Carrolls' London tree orders in perspective. They certainly were not unusual in their request for stock and seeds. Perhaps they were more unusual in that they requested their stock and seeds from England rather than planting what by the time were common American varieties.[14]

The vegetable seeds ordered by the Carrolls show a mix of the common and the exotic. Beets, turnips, peas, and cabbages were all traditional English garden produce and foods. They grew well and widely in early America, and their seeds were easily available. The other vegetable seeds desired by the Carrolls proved a different matter. Broccoli, celery, asparagus, and cauliflower, considered exotic because they were not easily available, did not appear regularly in gentry gardens until mid-century and even then not widely. As the letters of many colonists show, ordering seeds from England did not mean that if and when the seeds arrived they would be viable. Colonists often complained of old, rotted, or heat-damaged seeds that had to be thrown away. The exotic vegetables required more time and attention from the gardener than other vegetables such as turnips and beets. Of the three exotic vegetables ordered by the Carrolls, they more than likely grew celery the most easily, although the vegetables may have had an adjustment period. However, by the end of the century, cultivators claimed that celery grew exceedingly well in the Chesapeake region. Asparagus and cauliflower did too.[15]

Outside the house, the Carrolls performed the very same skillful acts of inclusion and exclusion as they used inside with food-related items. A yeoman farmer actively involved himself in the production of his own food. The combination of activity and the quality of homegrown fresh foods were two aspects of his lifestyle that gave him virtue. The Carrolls did the same. Margaret liked to garden. She made up the list of fruit trees to be ordered and probably the list of vegetables as well, using *Miller's Gardening Dictionary*, one of the most popular English-language dictionaries of the time. The Barrister continued the conversion of his plantations from tobacco to wheat, a task started by his father. He built a mill, and at the time he ordered the ship's biscuits, he planned to start a bakery to bake them for sale. He experimented with grasses for his meadows and forage for his herd of dairy cattle. At one point he raised sheep. What could be a better sign of a yeoman farmer than one who produced wheat, the grain of life and health within English culture, and went further to produce the common cracker? But he did not perform the work himself. Nor is it likely that Margaret took up her English hoe and pruners (ordered from London) to labor in her garden and orchard. Those acts would have perhaps been too inclusive. As they did with house furnishings, they excluded themselves from others within the yeoman group by the quality and variety of their horticultural output. If they planted commonly available varieties of fruit and vegetable seeds, they did not plant only those varieties. They ordered the best kinds from England.[16]

CONCLUSION

Even though the philosophical lines of food security shifted to include the mean of society, colonial Americans still had to place themselves carefully within its limits. For many this meant working hard not to appear excessive. Charles Carroll, Barrister, spent a great deal of time, money, and effort to establish his lines of demarcation. First, he was and wanted to seem to be an Englishman. The eating paraphernalia, the foods, and the cook he ordered from England were to achieve this goal. Although we do not know what foods Margaret Carroll actually served her husband, family, and friends, it is safe to say that they were solidly English. Many of those foods would have bound the Carrolls tightly with other British Americans, and indeed with other British people all over the world. The foods established the limitations of the group. Any British person sitting at the Carrolls' mahogany tables would have known what to do with a roast, a boil, a pudding, and a trifle. Pickled oysters would not have intrigued the guests as something foreign. The Carrolls' guests would have recognized the smell of and had a taste for wheat bread; indeed they would have been offended if they were not given it, as was the boatwright who left the table before finishing breakfast when William Byrd served him corn pone instead of wheat bread.[17] Their guests would have understood pottage as a basic part of their culinary heritage, but they also would have bristled if the Carrolls had served it to them as a central dish of their mid-afternoon main meal. Breakfast or supper would have been different matters.

Working from this basis, the Barrister also wanted to distinguish himself from the group. Distinction provides structure because it sorts and separates the members of a society, but any type of distinction must be finely crafted because too much would put one outside the group. Hence the need for style and control. When the Barrister specified an English cook, he wanted the best English food—not French, Chinese, or any other type of food. When he wrote many times in his letters to London that he wanted the best in the neat plain style, he was trying carefully to walk that line between distinction and exclusion. Had he ordered ostentatious clothes, or an older style prevalent in Shakespearean times, he would have put himself outside the borders of his group. When he ordered his several varieties of apples, he wanted distinctive English-approved fruits. He did not order kumquats.[18]

Scholars of material culture and consumption often label behavior such as the Carrolls' behavior as social display, and it is indeed just that, but it plays a far more important role than merely showing the world that you have more than others, or better quality material possessions than others. Of course this behavior distinguishes you from others who do not have what you have. It also groups you with those people who do. Both distinction and inclusion are extremely important because misjudgment of either will put you on the outside of your group. In order to stay within the golden mean of food security Charles Carroll, Barrister, could not be extravagant or exotic in the foods he ate, nor could he live an idle life. This would label him a man without virtue. But eating the same foods as most of his neighbors did not give him distinction either. Eating on mahogany tables, with china and silver of the best, plain, and latest style did.

So did the clothes he wore. On 23 September 1761, the Barrister wrote to William Anderson to complain about a suit he had ordered and received. The lace his tailor had put on the coat was too large. The Barrister felt it was too "Broad and Glaring being full two Inches wide and weight 25 ounces to the Coat and waistcoat." He must have that lace taken off and replaced with lace he wanted Anderson to send him. "Send me in a Fashionable Double Gold Lace not above two thirds of the width of the former and I suppose about Sixteen or Seventeen ounces Weight with vellum or what is necessary to make about 18 Gold Holes and Buttons Suitable for the Coat." Whether the Barrister got his new lace is not known, though we can know that the suit on which he wished to put the new lace would have been in the latest plain fashion. The long coats that men wore displayed numerous buttons, most of which were not used to keep the coat closed. In fact, the very cut of the coat would have prevented it from closing. This coat style, as well as the way it was worn, drew the eye to the most important bodily feature—the stomach. The prominence of the stomach and, in some portraits, the large size of the stomach in comparison to the subject's head, all suggest not a fat stomach so much as a capacious one fully efficient in properly digesting food to promote physical, moral, and spiritual virtue. It is a pity that there does not exist a portrait of the Barrister sitting down to his English meal at his English table wearing his English suit eating English foods and being thoroughly and virtuously the American yeoman.[19]

Conclusion

At the same time that Charles Carroll, Barrister, was sending requests for the numerous items he and his wife needed or wanted for themselves and their home, they also sent orders for goods to be sent to the Baltimore Iron Works. As part-owner he contributed a portion of goods to the workers at the forge. In addition, a store existed at the works, and many of the items the Barrister ordered from London may have been resold there. Either workers or neighbors could buy from the store.[1]

From the information available we can glean a little about the diets of the slaves at the ironworks. They all had access to beef and pork, though whether it was salted or fresh is unknown. When the Barrister's father acted as general manager of the operation in 1736, the company had 3,238 pounds of pork and 3,696 pounds of beef on hand. They did have a company farm and had beef delivered on the hoof, so workers may have eaten fresh meat as well. Items the Barrister ordered indicate some of the foods that were consumed by workers, managers, and neighbors. Direct references to food include tea and sugar. From 1755 to 1764, the Barrister ordered bohea, fig blue, and green teas. He asked for the same variety for his own household. Orders for sugar also appear, although the ironworks received single-refined only, not the double-refined he purchased for his own use. Spices ordered include ginger and pepper, not the classic English foursome of cinnamon, nutmeg, mace, and cloves. The Barrister ordered tableware and cooking equipment more regularly than foodstuffs. Dishes made of pewter along with plates, mugs, jugs, and bowls of white stoneware went to the works, as did, in August 1758, two dozen painted punch bowls. No china or silver went there. By 1764 the Barrister requested delft plates and bowls along with stoneware. Over the decade, William Anderson shipped many dozen frying pans to the works (the only kind of cooking pan ordered). Also frequently ordered were fish hooks and fishing line.[2]

The combination of frying pans and fish hooks and the fact that the iron-works was located near the Patapsco River suggest that some ironworkers ate fish as a part of their diet, and this inference is consistent with what is known about the traditional African diet. West Africans, who constituted a large per-centage of slaves in early America, by and large ate a predominantly vegetar-ian diet. Roots, herbs, and cereals composed the bulk of their diet, which they accented with small amounts of beef, goat, mutton, fish, and fowl. Gen-erally only the elite ate measurable quantities of meat. The primary food for many of the poor was the yam. They cooked it with bits of fish, spices, partic-ularly pepper, and some palm oil. It was—to put it into the framework of this study—pottage. In addition to domestic foodstuffs, Africans gathered and hunted from the wild. Snakes, monkeys, pelicans, alligators, hippopotamuses, eagles, and turtles all provided at least occasional variety. After Portuguese traders engaged Africans in trade in the fifteenth century, new food items such as maize, cassava, peanuts, tomatoes, sweet potatoes, hot chili peppers, the French bean, and Muscovy ducks entered their culinary repertoire.[3]

When African slaves first came to the North American colonies in the early seventeenth century, they ate generally the same foods as the white servants. This makes perfect sense, because both groups came from a tradition in which pottage served as the dietary mainstay for many if not most of the members of their society. Around the 1730s, servants demanded and received wheat instead of maize, and more meat. At this point the diets of Africans and Englishmen diverged. The Africans continued to eat maize. Historians have generally assumed this divergence to be due to parsimoniousness on the part of the slaveholders. However, given the fact that changes to basic diet, particu-larly in folk cultures, occur very slowly and that the most difficult change oc-curs with the staple grain, this may not entirely be the case. William Byrd II told naturalist Mark Catesby that, when he switched the rations of his slaves from maize to wheat, they protested and begged him to give them maize again. George Washington reported a similar response many years later.[4]

Studies of the North American slave diet in general support the conclusion that most masters supplied their slaves with pork and maize. Sometimes, de-pending on the time, place, and management philosophy of the plantation owner, they rationed beef, dried fish, vegetables, and wheat. In addition, many slaves raised animals and vegetables for their own consumption and sale. Ar-chaeological evidence unearthed from coastal plantations in Georgia, South Carolina, Virginia, and Louisiana show that slaves ate many more wild and do-mestic plants and animals than had previously been revealed in the documen-tary evidence. Despite these studies, some historians have concluded that slaves were poorly fed and that they ate a monotonous diet. These conclusions seem to be based on protein analyses and a modern view of a diet based on starch, in this case maize.[5]

Over the eighteenth century, Southern agricultural slavery developed in two ways. The Upper South, consisting of the Chesapeake region, with its large tobacco and grain plantations, had sizable slave populations who performed intensive agricultural labor all day long. The slaves had minimal leisure time and depended greatly on their rations. South Carolina and Georgia agriculturalists and some industrialists who used slaves employed what was known as the task system. Slaves working within this system had daily tasks, and when they had completed those tasks, they were able to pursue personal interests. Many used this time to supplement their rationed diet by gardening, raising chickens, hunting, and fishing. Although this fact has prompted one historian to conclude that the slaves were forced to garden because of the scantiness of their rations, they may also have been motivated by the ability to eat their traditional foods. They grew African root crops such as tania, and grains such as millet, sorghum, and sesame. They planted okra and African peppers. They also grew yams. Mark Catesby commented on slaves' reactions to a new yam. They were "delighted with all their African food, particularly this which a great part of Africa subsists on."[6]

THE LARGER PICTURE

How do slaves and their diets fit into the larger picture of food security in Anglo-American colonial thought? The response to this question must be that they fit quite nicely. In fact, it could be said that they were the missing piece of the puzzle. Even 165 years before the Barrister sent his orders for English tables, dishes, foods, and a cook, certain eating habits united English men and women into a common group. However, other eating habits divided members within that group. The most distinctive dividers were the categories of refined and crass. Refined people ate high quality foods that differed significantly from the gross foods eaten by crass people. As a result refined people (who were also the wealthy) differed from crass people in many ways, the most important of which for this study was that only they could be truly virtuous. In early modern England, those people who were virtuous could be rulers. Therefore, the refined eaters were the rulers and the gross eaters were the ruled. When applied in England, this tidy philosophy enforced a social system in which only the wealthy were entitled to rule.

The philosophy and its application in North America took a different turn. In the beginning of colonization, the refined eaters could not get their refined foods, a fact that significantly disturbed the line between the two groups. Over time this situation changed, in large part because of the change in the philosophy of the body and what it should eat, brought about by mechanism, the fertility of America's soil, and the industry of the immigrants. The new philosophy of the body as a mechanism rather than an organism seriously shrank the range of physiological distinctions that could exist between people. Basically, a body could be overfed, underfed, or well fed or, to put it another way, oversecure, undersecure, or secure. The virtuous person was still the food-secure person, but the foods required for that security had changed. In the mechanical age, the food-secure person ate a middling diet, one of fresh and wholesome foods cooked into dishes that were honest and uncomplicated. The amount of food that a virtuous person ate still had to match his or her activity level, which was considered to be somewhere between sedentary and laborious. The lifestyle of the yeoman farmer, or the urban artisan, was considered ideal. British Americans believed that their lifestyle matched the yeoman ideal closely. Their improved diet and lifestyle moved much of the society over the line between virtuous and unvirtuous that the English had drawn so carefully and boldly for centuries with the foods they ate.

It is important to underscore the fact that people were reclassified. The line was not erased, or even smudged. The categories of virtuous leaders and unvirtuous followers were not changed or eliminated. The movement of farmers, laborers, and other middling types left a significantly smaller number of people who could not, according to the philosophy, be virtuous. They were those pottage eaters—the slaves and the poor. The objection could be made that, by the 1760s, early Americans of all classes also ate pottage made of maize. They called it hominy or hasty pudding, which was on the way to becoming the national dish. While hominy or hasty pudding united all Americans, the details of its preparation and consumption divided them. Africans and most likely the poor probably ate two pottage meals a day. Middling and upper Americans did not; they ate pottage for the less significant meals of the day, breakfast or supper. Furthermore, the slaves and the poor, when they ate meat, consumed the lesser cuts of pork and beef; the middling and upper Americans ate fuller cuts. Although the poor and slaves ate of many of the same food groups as members of the middling and upper segments of society, the quality and quantity of their dishes differed significantly.

Throughout the eighteenth century, the philosophy of food security remained an active force in American thought. Some might say it became an even more powerful force, as evidenced in Thomas Jefferson's *Notes on the State of Virginia,* a methodical endeavor published in 1787 that merged nicely into what had already become a two-century-old genre of descriptions and analyses of Virginia's people, natural assets, and projected or realized potential as a colony or state. Jefferson's chapter on animal, vegetable, and mineral productions gives a succinct description of the flora and fauna native to Virginia as well as those cultivated by its inhabitants. His work differs greatly from prior descriptions of Virginia or other parts of the British American colonies in that it merely lists the flora and fauna and gives little indication of what the indigenous and European inhabitants ate. Earlier authors often proffered lengthy descriptions of this subject, in one case over a hundred pages that equated British North America to gastronomic paradise. Jefferson chose instead to inform the reader using clean spare lists and charts denoting common names and Linnaean classifications. He chronicled only native plants for their usefulness as food and wrote nothing about the edibility of indigenous mammals, fish, or birds. Four short paragraphs on current farm, garden, and orchard produce and a short explanation of the non-indigenous plants cultivated by the Indians at the time of European contact were the only mention of human food–related activities.[7]

Even though he gave such cursory treatment to foodstuffs, Jefferson relied on the philosophy of food security. The importance of food to virtue runs through the text. He had more in mind than simply to describe what people ate. Rather, he used scientific data he had collected to refute the hypothesis made by the world-renowned French naturalist Georges Louis Leclerc, comte de Buffon, that New World species and inhabitants were inferior to those of Europe. As Jefferson relayed it, Buffon believed nature to be less active and less energetic in the New World than in the Old World, in large part because of the decreased heat and increased moisture of the climate of the New World as compared to that of Europe. As a result, of the animal species common to both Europe and America, those living in America were smaller and fewer. Furthermore, Buffon contended that animals peculiar to the New World grew to a generally smaller size than similar species in Europe. Finally, he claimed that domesticated European animals taken to the New World degenerated there.[8]

Buffon extended his argument to New World humans. While he was content to discuss only the bulk and quality of animals, he included physical, moral, and intellectual characteristics when he referred to humankind. For proof, Buffon turned to the Indians and listed numerous examples of their degenerate state. The natives, he wrote, were "feeble," "less strong in body," and "less sensitive" than Europeans and "yet more timid and cowardly." If they had plenty of food and drink, they were lazy. Holding little love for their families, they treated their women harshly and had "icy" hearts and a "cold society." Physical love constituted their only morality. Buffon linked most of these defects to what he believed to be the Indians' chief deficit, their lack of ardor for their females and their consequent lack of love for their fellow men. Although Buffon stopped short of making the point that Europeans living in the New World had also degenerated, the implication was clear. Most Western peoples living in the eighteenth century believed in the connectedness of nature. To state that the New World climate affected all of mammalian nature except humans from Europe would have opposed current cultural axioms. In any event, what Buffon did not explicate, others did, and Jefferson's refutation answered them as well.[9]

Jefferson responded eloquently but carefully in defense of the equality of the Europeans and Indians living in the New World and the inhabitants of Europe. He clearly did not believe that the local climate was the deterministic force Buffon claimed it to be, although he did think it was important. He first addressed the general statements about the animal kingdom, doubting that the bulk and faculties of animals "depend[ed] on the side of the Atlantic on which their food happen[ed] to grow, or which furnishe[d] the elements of which they [we]re compounded." Both New and Old Worlds, he wrote, were warmed by the same sun and had soils of the same chemical composition. They could not, therefore, be less sustaining for one group than another. Small variations among organic creatures may have been due to soil, climate, and food, but they would not turn a mouse into a mammoth. Furthermore, he asserted that differences of size depended on "circumstances unsearchable to beings with our capacities" and as such provided the floor and ceiling to the growth of any species. He supported his position with several charts showing that in fact New World animals, whether native or transplanted from Europe, actually surpassed comparable European species in size.[10]

As for humans, Jefferson believed that the Indians of North America had probably been formed in mind as well as in body "on the same module with the *Homo sapiens Europaeus*." Their difference from the English or any other Europeans lay in their diet, activity level, and degree of civilization. The Indians ate wild foods straight from the forest in addition to their staple grain, maize. As nature's yearly bounty varied, they experienced famine. They lived hard lives of hunting, fishing, and constant exposure to the elements, so nature restrained them and kept them, like wild animals, in bounds. If Europeans were "reduced to the same diet and exercise" as the indigenous Americans, Jefferson wrote, they would behave and look similar to them.[11]

When Jefferson wrote *Notes on the State of Virginia* he believed that he lived in a world where all people could excel and achieve their highest goals regardless of their temperament—if they were given a "middling" diet and the proper acculturation. Contemporary scientific and medical theories support his conclusion, one that would have refuted scientific learning at the beginning of the colonial period. Furthermore, most people living in the Anglo-American society of his Virginia and in the rest of the United States possessed those requirements because of the agrarian character of their society and the abundance of food America produced. Under these criteria, the tools for virtue were available to most.

Even so, two groups within that society failed to attain the high level of achievement already so noticeable among Americans. The comte de Buffon selected one, the Indians, to illustrate his theory about the negative effect of the New World climate. Jefferson easily explained their low level of "achievement" with their uncivilized diet. The other group, the African slaves, presented a more difficult challenge to Jefferson's position. He believed that they had adapted to the Anglo-American diet and culture decades before and that they should have exhibited physical, mental, and moral "improvement," meaning they should have begun to mirror Anglo-Americans in mind, spirit, and virtue. Jefferson saw none of this. Although he conceded that, as slaves, most of them had been confined to hard labor and their "own society," he felt that enough individuals had had exposure to Anglo-American society and had received education for it to have made some difference.

It is surprising that his observation did not undermine his faith in the philosophy of food security. Instead he sought the reason elsewhere, and he found it in taxonomy. Jefferson cautiously suggested that, rather than being a separate race of the species "*Homo sapiens Europaeus*" like the Indians, the Africans were a species unto their own. He posited that nature had "fixed" the differences between the two groups and cited as indicators other than the Africans' skin color, their sparsity of facial and body hair, differing bodily secretions, possible differences in lung structure, requirement for less sleep, and tendency to experience sensationally rather than reflectively.

Thomas Jefferson juggled with a tough philosophical problem when he thought about the slaves in his Virginia. His statement that Indians and Euro-Americans would look and behave the same if they ate the same foods shows his strong belief in the transformative ability of foods. By his way of thinking, the slaves ate British fare. Indeed no person of English descent could believe pottage to be anything but that. So it was possible for Jefferson to include the slaves within the group bound together by the similarity of the foods they ate. However, when Jefferson followed the British tradition (anthropologists would say the human tradition) of embodying social relationships with food, he, a man with a voracious mind for detail, overlooked the intricacies of pottage eating. He concluded that, because the slaves ate the same foods and lived in the same environment, they should have behaved and acted like British Americans. In his eyes they did not.

What this tells us, then, is that in the eighteenth century when Americans started to believe that most members of their society enjoyed food security, fell within its golden mean, and were entitled to the rewards of virtue, they were not doing anything radical or revolutionary. In fact, their beliefs were profoundly conservative, because they fell squarely within a philosophy that had been extant for millennia. When British Americans acted on those beliefs, they maintained a major social divider that was as ancient. Their actions were far from radical. They simply had realized that, because of their life in America and the changed requirements for food security and consequently virtue, many of them were now food secure and entitled to the concomitant social and political benefits.

The early American table, when studied over the period of colonization, tells the story of the formation of American culture differently than other artifacts and documents have done. In the beginning of colonization, relatively few people had elegant tables off which they ate the rich, refined foods of sixteenth- and seventeenth-century England. Their diet signified their virtue; their dinner companions their social status. By far, more colonists had simple or crude tables. A trunk or bench served that function instead—if it was even needed to eat pottage on a bread or wooden trencher. The diet of these eaters told plainly of their lack of virtue and the insufficient quality and quantity of the foods they ate. Their fellow eaters reiterated that fact to early modern observers.

As the colonial period progressed, the diets of most British Americans changed. Tables proliferated (as did the chairs that accompanied them) to accommodate eaters who were now enjoying an expanded diet of various dishes that could not be presented on a bench or held in one's lap, and which required more time to eat. New colonists and European visitors were often astonished at the diet and lifestyle North America offered and frequently commented that the bulk of the colonists ate like the well-to-do of England. The emphasis should be on the numbers of eaters as well as the quality and quantity of the foods they ate. The gap between secure and insecure eaters so visible in the seventeenth century had closed. Colonists of middling and wealthy status could and did sit comfortably at similar tables and ate similar foods. There were differences, of course, but they were minor compared to the differences of a century before.

As the quantity and quality of foods available to colonists changed, so did their understanding of the human body and the foods it required. Those changes were, though, only in the details. The importance of one's diet to virtue remained as strong as ever, as did the importance of virtue to social and political status. In 1785, when Thomas Jefferson published *Notes on the State of Virginia*, a glance at the table, the foods that were on it, the eaters sitting around it, and the portions served them told any contemporary observer what he or she needed to know.

ℳotes

INTRODUCTION

1. John Smith, *The Complete Works of Captain John Smith*, ed. Philip Barbour (Chapel Hill: University of North Carolina Press, 1986), 1: 264–65.

CHAPTER ONE—THE HUMORAL BODY

1. Henry Norwood, "A Voyage to Virginia," in *Tracts and Other Papers*, ed. Peter Force (New York: Peter Smith, 1947), 3.1: 24.

2. Ibid., 20–23.

3. Ibid., 24.

4. Edmund S. Morgan, *American Slavery, American Freedom* (New York: W. W. Norton, 1975), 73; Daniel Cottom, *Cannibals and Philosophers: Bodies of Enlightenment* (Baltimore: Johns Hopkins University Press, 2001), 133–79.

5. *Regimen Sanitatis Salerni,* ann. Thom Paynell (London, 1597); Wyndham Blanton, *Medicine in Virginia in the Seventeenth Century* (Richmond: William Byrd, 1930), 95, 194; Kenneth Albala, *Eating Right in the Renaissance* (Berkeley and Los Angeles: University of California Press, 2002), 30–36; Heikki Mikkeli, "Hygiene in the Early Modern Medical Tradition," *Humaniora* 305 (1999), 54–68.

6. Robert Fludd, *Utriusque cosmi maioris scilicet et minoris metaphysica, physica atque technica historia* (Oppenheim, 1617–1621).

7. Joscelyn Godwin, *Robert Fludd: Hermetic Philosopher and Surveyor of Two Worlds* (Boulder, Colo.: Shambala, 1979), 68–69. For Aristotle, see Thomas S. Hall, *History of General Physiology,* vol. 1, *600 B.C. to A.D. 1900* (Chicago: University of Chicago Press, 1975), 8, 141, 178, 182–83.

8. Chester Burns, "The Non-naturals: A Paradox in the Western Concept of Health," *Journal of Medicine and Philosophy* 1 (1976): 202–11; Albala, *Eating Right,* 115–43; Mikkeli, "Hygiene," 54–68.

9. Paynell, *Regimen Sanitatis,* 141; Elaine O'Hara-May, *Elizabethan Dyetary of Health* (Lawrence, Kans.: Coronado Press, 1977), 52–58; Albala, *Eating Right,* 48–52; Thomas Walkington, *Optick Glasse of Humors* (London, 1664), 76; R. Klibansky, E. Panofsky, and F. Saxl, *Saturn and Melancholy* (London: Nelson, 1961), 3–15; Nancy Siraisi, *Medieval and Early Renaissance Medicine, an Introduction* (Chicago: University of Chicago Press, 1990), 101–4; Thomas Elyot, *Castel of Helth* (London, 1541), 8–9.

10. Paynell, *Regimen Sanitatis,* 145; Walkington, *Optick Glasse,* 125–33 (125); Lemnius, *The Touchstone of the Complexions* (London, 1576), 97 (quote), 135–57; Elyot, *Castel of Helth,* 3; Klibansky, Panofsky, and Saxl, *Saturn,* 97–123.

11. Paynell, *Regimen Sanitatis,* 144; Lemnius, *Touchstone,* 127–35; Elyot, *Castel of Helth,* 2; Walkington, *Optick Glasse,* 109.

12. Paynell, *Regimen Sanitatis,* 143; Elyot, *Castel of Helth,* 2; Lemnius, *Touchstone,* 108–19; Walkington, *Optick Glasse,* 118–24.

13. Walkington, *Optick Glasse,* 110–18 (117); Paynell, *Regimen Sanitatis,* 141–45 (141); Elyot, *Castel of Helth,* 2–3; Lemnius, *Touchstone,* 33–49.

14. Elyot, *Castel of Helth,* 3–8.

15. John Precope, *Hippocrates on Diet and Hygiene* (London: "ZENO," 1952), 14

("humors"); Hippocrates, *Hippocrates* trans. W. H. S. Jones (Cambridge: Harvard University Press, 1962), 1: 325 ("regimen"); Precope, *Hippocrates on Diet*, 53 ("engender stupidity"). It is necessary now to make a note of an important difference in convention between the times we are considering here and the twenty-first century. In those days, the masculine term *Man* and the third-person singular pronoun *he* were commonly used to refer to both men and women. In discussing the original texts, I find myself constrained to follow the same usage in order to avoid undesirable circumlocutions.

16. Galen, *Selected Works*, trans. P. N. Singer (Oxford: Oxford University Press, 1997), 150–53, 161, 167; Robert Montraville Green, *De Sanitate Tuenda: A Translation of Galen's Hygiene* (Springfield, Ill.: Charles C. Thomas, 1951), 15, 17, 26.

17. Green, *Galen's Hygiene*, 14, 16, 17, 20, 75; Galen, *Selected Works*, 85, 202–13, 225, 228–29, 246, 292–94, 349, 362 (248, 233, 233). See also Mikkeli, "Hygiene," 54–56.

18. Burns, "Non-Naturals"; Albala, *Eating Right*, 115–43; Mikkeli, "Hygiene," 54–68.

19. Hippocrates, *Hippocrates*, 225–31.

20. O'Hara-May, *Dyetary*, 102–5; Albala, *Eating Right*, 66; Oswei Temkin, "Nutrition from Classical Antiquity to the Baroque," in *Human Nutrition, Historic, Scientific*, ed. Iago Galdston (New York: International University Press, 1960), 87; Siraisi, *Renaissance Medicine*, 122; Elyot, *Castel of Helth*, 12.

21. O'Hara-May, *Dyetary*, 99–101; Albala, *Eating Right*, 82–84; Thomas Moffett, *Healths Improvement: of Rules Comprizing and Discovering the Nature, and Manner of Preparing all sorts of Foods* (London, 1655), 38–41.

22. O'Hara-May, *Dyetary*, 109–10; Albala, *Eating Right*, 91–99; Elyot, *Castel of Helth*, 14.

23. Precope, *Hippocrates on Diet*, 36, 72. For Galen, see Green, *Galen's Hygiene*, 51; for early modern Europeans, see Elyot, *Castel of Helth*.

24. Albala, *Eating Right*, 54–62.

25. Galen, *Selected Works*, 271.

26. Ibid., xxix, 13, 35–37, 271, 280; Hippocrates, *Hippocrates*, 343, 345, 349, 355; Aristotle, *The Complete Works of Aristotle*, ed. Jonathan Barnes (Princeton: Princeton University Press, 1984), 662. See also Albala, *Eating Right*, 91; O'Hara-May, *Dyetary*, 99–102.

27. Green, *Galen's Hygiene*, 7; Galen, *Selected Works*, 169, 251, 307; Aristotle, *Complete Works*, 526. See also Hippocrates, *Hippocrates*, 343–45, 347, 355, 357; Aristotle, *Complete Works*, 659, 661–63.

28. Galen, *Selected Works*, 169, 280, 195 (280).

29. Albala, *Eating Right*, 69; Thomas Laqueur, *Making Sex: Body and Sex from the Greeks to Freud* (Cambridge: Harvard University Press, 1990), 25–29; Lorraine Daston and Katharine Park, "Hermaphroditism in Renaissance France," *Critical Matrix* 1 (1985), 5.

30. Jane Fajans, "The Transformative Value of Food: A Review Essay," *Food and Foodways* 3 (1998): 143–65.

CHAPTER TWO—THE HUMORAL SOCIETY

1. William Harrison, *The Description of England*, ed. Georges Edelen (Ithaca: Folger Shakespeare Library by Cornell University Press, 1968), 123–25, 444–45 (444–45, 123).

2. C. Anne Wilson, *Food and Drink in Britain* (Chicago: Academy Chicago, 1991), 255–61; Anne Paston-Williams, *The Art of Dining* (London: National Trust, 1995), 85–86; Joan Thirsk, "Food in Shakespeare's England," in *Fooles and Fricassees: Food in Shakespeare's England*, ed. Mary Anne Caton (Washington, D.C.: Folger Shakespeare Library, 1999), 16.

3. Peter Brears, *Food and Cooking in Sixteenth-Century Britain* (London: English Heritage, 2001), 6.

4. Thirsk, "Food in Shakespeare's England," 13–14; Wilson, *Food and Drink*, 210–11, 216.

5. Gervase Markham, *The English House-Wife* (London, 1631), 78–79.

6. Ibid., 79–80.

7. Colin Spencer, *British Food: An Extraordinary Thousand Years of History* (New York:

Columbia University Press, 2003), 123. See also Paston-Williams, *Dining,* 90–94.

8. Joan Thirsk, "Food History and Food Theories, 1500–1700" (Folger Institute Seminar, Washington, D.C., June 1997).

9. Information for this section on dairy products is taken from Wilson, *Food and Drink,* 164–80; Paston-Williams, *Dining,* 86–88; Spencer, *British Food,* 123, 125; Thirsk, "Food in Shakespeare's England," 21–22.

10. Elyot, *Castel of Helth,* 14; Paston-Williams, *Dining,* 88; O'Hara-May, *Dyetary,* 109–10; Albala, *Eating Right,* 91–99.

11. Wilson, *Food and Drink,* 168–70.

12. Thirsk, "Food in Shakespeare's England," 21–22; Wilson, *Food and Drink,* 340–64; Paston-Williams, *Dining,* 95–102; Spencer, *British Food,* 112–13.

13. Wilson, *Food and Drink,* 340–64.

14. Stephen Mennell, *All Manners of Food,* 2nd edition (Urbana: University of Illinois Press, 1996).

15. Harrison, *Description of England,* 126–128, 134, 144 (126, 127, 127).

16. Wilson, *Food and Drink,* 79.

17. Spencer, *British Foods,* 131; Albala, *Eating Right,* 66; O'Hara-May, *Dyetary,* 106, 108; C. Anne Wilson, "The Evolution of the Banquet Course: Some Medicinal, Culinary, and Social Aspects," in *"Banquetting Stuffe,"* ed. C. Anne Wilson (Edinburgh: Edinburgh University Press, 1991), 14–16.

18. Harrison, *Description of England,* 129–30, 133.

19. Ibid., 131–32, 134; J. C. Drummond and Anne Wilbraham, *The Englishman's Food* (London: Jonathan Cape, 1958), 49–57, 99, 102, 465.

20. Harrison, *Description of England,* 131–32, 134 (132).

21. Wilson, *Food and Drink,* 340–64; Paston-Williams, *Dining,* 86–88; Spencer, *British Food,* 123, 125; Thirsk, "Food in Shakespeare's England," 21–22.

22. Drummond and Wilbraham, *Englishman's Food,* 49–57, 99, 102, 465 (56).

23. Harrison, *Description of England,* 113; Smith quoted from Peter Laslett, *The World We Have Lost Further Explored* (New York: Charles Scribner's Sons, 1984), 31. See also Keith Wrightson, *English Society 1580–1680* (New Brunswick: Rutgers University, 1982), 17–38.

24. Laslett, *World We Have Lost,* 31.

CHAPTER THREE—SECURE PEOPLE AND SOCIETIES

1. Susan Bruce, ed., *Three Early Modern Utopias* (Oxford: Oxford University Press, 1999), 21–22.

2. Ibid., 22–24, 216, 217 (22).

3. Ibid., 63 (quote), 51, 54.

4. Frank Manuel and Fritzi Manuel, *Utopian Thought in the Western World* (Cambridge: Belknap Press of Harvard University Press, 1979), 129–30.

5. Bruce, *Early Modern Utopias,* 63–65 (64).

6. Ibid., 65. See also Galen, *Selected Works,* 85, 233, 292, 349.

7. Ibid., 64, 65, 89, 122. See also Manuel and Manuel, *Utopian Thought,* 65, 88–89, 126.

8. Charles L. Sanford, *The Quest for Paradise* (Urbana: University of Illinois Press, 1961), 10.

9. Andrew Appleby, *Famine in Tudor and Stuart England* (Stanford: Stanford University Press, 1978).

10. Thomas Hariot, *A Briefe and True Report of the New Found Land of Virginia* (Frankfurt: Theodore de Bry, 1590; reprint, New York: Readex Microprint Corporation), 14–15.

11. Ibid., 15.

12. Smith, *Complete Works,* 1: 157; Everett Emerson, ed., *Letters from New England: The Massachusetts Bay Colony, 1629–1638* (Amherst, Mass.: University of Massachusetts Press, 1976), 25 ("sixtie"); Francis Higginson, *New England's Plantation, or A Short and True Description*

of the Commodities and Discommodities of that Countrey (London, 1630), B2 (yields).

13. Francis Higginson, "New England's Plantation, or A Short and True Description of the Commodities and Discommodities of that Countrey" (London, 1630), 15, B2; Hariot, *True Report,* 14–15.

14. His Maiestie's Counseil for Virginia, "A Declaration of the State of the Colonie and Affaires in Virginia (1620)," in Force, *Tracts,* 3.5: 12 ("usurie"); Alexander Whitaker, "Virginia's Natural Bounty," in *The Elizabethans' America,* ed. Louis B. Wright (Cambridge: Harvard University Press, 1965), 223 (figs.); Higginson, *Plantation,* 109; William Wood, *New England's Prospect,* ed. Alden T. Vaughan (Amherst, Mass.: University of Massachusetts Press, 1977), 33–36 (36).

15. Thomas Yong, "Extract from a Letter" in *Narratives of Early Maryland 1633–1684,* ed. Clayton Colman Hall (New York: Charles Scribner's Sons, 1910), 60 ("aboundeth"); James Axtell, ed., *America Perceived: A View from Abroad in the Seventeenth Century* (West Haven, Conn.: Pendulum Press, 1974), 15 (colonist), 224 (Ashe), 179 (Swedish settler). See also His Maiestie's Counseil, "Declaration," 12–13; Whitaker, "Virginia's Natural Bounty," 219–24; *Virginia Magazine of History and Biography* 1 (1894): 447; Higginson, *Plantation,* 15; Drummond and Wilbraham, *Englishman's Food,* 101–2.

16. Hariot, *True Report,* 18, 19; Smith, *Complete Works,* 1: 151–53; Nathaniel Shrigley, "A True Relation of Virginia and Mary-Land," in Force, *Tracts,* 3.6: 5; Edward Williams, "Virginia: More Especially the South Part Thereof, Richly and Truly Valued," in Force, *Tracts,* 3.11: 11.

17. His Maiestie's Counseil, "Declaration," 18–19; Smith, *Complete Works,* 1: 151–53; Shrigley, "True Relation," 5; Hariot, *True Report,* 19; Axtell, *America Perceived . . . Seventeenth Century,* 16, 22, 36–37, 135, 171–72, 219; Williams, "Virginia," 11.

18. Hariot, *True Report,* 19–20; Smith, *Complete Works,* 1: 154–55; Williams, "Virginia," 12 (another source); Axtell, *America Perceived . . . Seventeenth Century,* 138–39 ("infinite herds"), 225. See also Wood, *New England's Prospect,* 43.

19. Hariot, *True Report,* 20–21; Smith, *Complete Works,* 1: 156–57; Williams, "Virginia," 21; Smith, *Complete Works,* 1: 156.

20. Emerson, *Letters,* 27, 110–11, 116 (Higginson's note). See also Hariot, *True Report,* 20–21; Smith, *Complete Works,* 1: 156, 347; Shrigley, "True Relation," 4; Williams, "Virginia," 21–23; His Maiestie's Counseil, "Declaration," 22; Whitaker, "Virginia's Natural Bounty," 219–24.

21. Emerson, *Letters,* 110 (Hammond); Shrigley, "True Relation," 4 (one writer); Williams, "Virginia," 12 (earlier author); Hariot, *True Report,* 20; Smith, *Complete Works,* 1: 155–56; Williams, "Virginia," 21 (promotional piece); His Maiestie's Counseil, "Declaration," 13. See also Emerson, *Letters,* 110; Father Andrew White, "An Account of the Colony of the Lord Baron Baltamore, 1633," in Hall, *Narratives,* 5–10.

22. Axtell, *America Perceived . . . Seventeenth Century,* 23.

23. "A cheiff Lorde of Roanoac," Hariot, *True Report,* n.p.

24. Emerson, *Letters,* 37, 64; *Journal of the English Plantation at Plimoth* (London, 1622), 32; Smith, *Complete Works,* 2: 114–15. See also Karen Ordahl Kupperman, *Indians and English: Facing Off in Early America* (Ithaca: Cornell University Press, 2000), 41–76.

25. Thomas Morton, *New English Canaan,* ed. Jack Dempsey (Scituate, Mass., Digital Scanning, 2000), 8.

26. Ibid., 8–10 (9).

27. Ibid., 8–13 (11, 9).

28. Ibid., 49, 27, 37, 40.

29. Ibid., 1, 14, 22, 24, 26, 37, 40, 48, 49 (quote), 50.

30. Ibid., 103–14.

CHAPTER FOUR—INSECURITY AND THE COMMON KETTLE

1. Susan Myra Kingsbury, ed., *The Records of the Virginia Company of London* (Washington, D.C.: U.S. Government Printing Office, 1933), 3: 299.

2. Whitaker, "Virginia's Natural Bounty," 222; Walter Todkill and Russell Anas, "Occurrents in Virginia," in *Purchas His Pilgrimes,* ed. Samuel Purchas (New York: Macmillan, 1906), 480–87; Morgan, *American Slavery, American Freedom,* 70–91; Edmund S. Morgan, "The Labor Problem at Jamestown," *American Historical Review* 76 (1971): 595–611; Carl Bridenbaugh, *Jamestown, 1544–1699* (New York: Oxford University Press, 1980), 45–60; Carville V. Earle, "Environment, Disease, and Mortality in Early Virginia," in *The Chesapeake in the Seventeenth Century: Essays on Anglo-American Society,* ed. Thad W. Tate and David L. Ammerman (Williamsburg: Institute of Early American Culture and History, 1979), 96–125; Wyndham B. Blanton, "Epidemics, Real and Imaginary, and Other Factors Influencing Seventeenth-Century Virginia's Population," *Bulletin of the History of Medicine* 31 (1957): 54–62; Karen Ordahl Kupperman, "Apathy and Death in Early Jamestown," *Journal of American History* 66 (1979): 24–40.

3. Smith, *Complete Works,* 1:xxix, xxxvi, xl, xlii, xliv, xlix.

4. Polly Wiessner and Wulf Schiefenhövel, *Food and the Status Quest* (Providence: Berghahn Books, 1996).

5. Felicity Heal, *Hospitality in Early Modern England* (Oxford: Clarendon Press, 1990), 3.

6. Ibid., 19–20, 24–26 (19, 25).

7. Ibid., 28–32 (31).

8. Ibid., 13–15.

9. Ibid., 19, 110, 110.

10. Percy cited from Edward Wright Haile, ed., *Jamestown Narratives: Eyewitness Accounts of the Virginia Colony* (Champlain, Va.: Roundhouse, 1998), 100.

11. Smith, *Complete Works,* 1: 35, 2: 142–43 (142).

12. Haile, *Jamestown Narratives,* 183–202 (189).

13. Ibid., 192.

14. Heal, *Hospitality,* 113; Moffett, *Healths Improvement,* 80, from Albala, *Eating Right,* 195; Wingfield from Haile, *Jamestown Narratives,* 192.

15. Smith, *Complete Works,* 2: 114, 162–63 (quote), 264–65; Green, *Galen's Hygiene,* 7.

16. Helen C. Rountree, *The Powhatan Indians of Virginia* (Norman: University of Oklahoma Press, 1989), 32–45; James E. McWilliams, *A Revolution in Eating* (New York: Columbia University Press, 2005), 96–99.

17. Smith, *Complete Works,* 1: 203–79.

18. Ibid., 264–65.

19. Paul Rozin et al., "Disgust: The Cultural Evolution of a Food-based Emotion," in *Food Preferences and Taste: Continuity and Change,* ed. Helen Macbeth (Providence: Berghahn Books, 1997), 65–82; Ellen Messer, "Three Centuries of Changing European Tastes for the Potato," in ibid., 101–14.

20. Smith, *Complete Works,* 1: 209–10 (210).

21. John Gerard, *Gerard's Herball* (London, 1636; reprint, London: Gerald Howe, 1927), 25–26; John Parkinson, *Theatrum Botanicum* (London, 1640), quoted in John J. Finan, *Maize in the Great Herbals* (Waltham, Mass.: Chronica Botanica, 1950), 167–68; Brown, *Genesis,* 660, 572; John Hammond, "Leah and Rachel, or The Two Fruitfull Sisters Virginia, and Mary-land," in Force, *Tracts,* 3.14: 10.

22. Sir Thomas Gates, "Articles, Lawes, and Orders, Divine, Politique, and Martiall for the Colony in Virginea," in Force, *Tracts,* 3.2: 14 (quotes), 16; Morgan, *American Slavery, American Freedom,* 80.

23. Joan Thirsk, "Food History and Food Theories, 1500–1700" (seminar, Folger Institute, Washington, D.C., June 1997).

24. Smith, *Complete Works*, 1: 168.

25. Edward D. Neill, *History of the Virginia Company of London* (Albany, N.Y.: Joel Munsell, 1869), 180.

26. Alexander Brown, *The Genesis of the United States* (New York: Russell and Russell, 1964), 83, 166–67; Philip Alexander Bruce, *Economic History of Virginia in the Seventeenth Century* (New York: Macmillan, 1896), 195–96, 198, 202.

27. Brown, *Genesis*, 482; Smith, *Complete Works*, 1: 247.

28. Neill, *Virginia Company*, 180, 237.

29. Kingsbury, *Virginia Company*, 3: 299.

30. Bruce, *Economic History*, 257–59; Neill, *Virginia Company*, 237–38, 275.

31. Neill, *Virginia Company*, 417 (Thorpe); Kingsbury, *Virginia Company*, 3: 455 (Nuce).

32. Morgan, *American Slavery, American Freedom*, 71–91.

33. William Bradford, *Of Plymouth Plantation, 1620–1647*, ed. Samuel Eliot Morison (New York: Modern Library, 1967), 77; *Mourt's Relation* from *Journal of the English Plantation at Plimoth*, March of America Facsimile Series no. 21 (Ann Arbor: University Microfilms, 1966), 5.

34. Bradford, *Of Plymouth Plantation*, 96.

35. Ibid., 109–11 (109, 111).

36. Ibid., 116–18.

37. Ibid., 120–31, 141 (127, 127, 130, 130, 131).

38. Ibid., 130.

39. Ibid., 120.

40. Ibid., 121.

CHAPTER FIVE—THE MECHANICAL BODY

1. Jeremiah Wainewright, *A Mechanicall Account of the Non-Naturals*, 2nd ed. (London, 1708), A2. See also Thomas S. Hall, *History of General Physiology* (Chicago: University of Chicago Press, 1975), 1: 219.

2. Wainewright, *Mechanicall Account*, A2.

3. Ibid., 2–6 (2, 3).

4. Hall, *General Physiology*, 1: 220–24.

5. Ibid., 1: 225–27 (225).

6. Robert Hugh Kargon, *Atomism in England from Hariot to Newton* (Oxford: Clarendon Press, 1966), 1–4; Lester King, *The Road to Medical Enlightenment, 1650–1695* (New York: Science History Publications, 1970), 62–65.

7. Lester King, *The Philosophy of Medicine: The Early Eighteenth Century* (Cambridge, Mass.: Harvard University Press, 1978), 65–68, 99.

8. Ibid., 65–75.

9. Hall, *General Physiology*, 1: 225–29. I am much indebted to this work for the following discussion of changing ideas in the seventeenth century.

10. Ibid., 228, 288.

11. Ibid., 261–62.

12. Ibid., 250–60.

13. Ibid., 228–29.

14. Ibid., 342–348.

15. Ibid., 280–94 (282, 287).

16. King, *Philosophy of Medicine*, 33–36 (33, 35, 35).

17. King, *Medical Enlightenment*, 23–24, 38.

18. King, *Philosophy of Medicine*, 73, 76, 83 (quote).

19. Ibid., 87–91.

20. George Cheyne, *An Essay of Health and Long Life* (London, 1724).

21. Anita Guerrini, *Obesity and Depression in the Enlightenment: The Life and Times of George Cheyne* (Norman: University of Oklahoma Press, 2000), 57, 133.

22. Cheyne, *Essay of Health,* 21.

23. Ibid., 19.

24. Ibid., 231.

25. Steven Shapin, "How to Eat like a Gentleman: Dietetics and Ethics in Early Modern England," in *Right Living: An Anglo-American Tradition of Self-Help Medicine and Hygiene,* ed. Charles E. Rosenberg (Baltimore: Johns Hopkins University Press, 2003), 30–32.

26. Cheyne, *Essay of Health,* 17–18, 87–88, 106–8, 139–43, 170–71.

27. Ibid., xix.

28. Ibid., v, 22–23, 30–31.

29. Ibid., 22–27, 73.

30. Ibid., 29.

31. Ibid., 22, 73.

32. Ibid., 30–34 (30, 33, 34).

33. Ibid., 33–34, 39–40.

34. Ibid., 27.

35. John Arbuthnot, *An Essay Concerning the Nature of Aliments and the Choice of Them, According to the Different Constitutions of Human Bodies* (London, 1731); *A Letter to George Cheyne, M.D., F.R.S., To Shew the Danger of Laying Down General Rules to Those Who Are Not Acquainted with the Animal Oeconomy, &c.* (London, 1724); Pillo-Tisanus, *An Epistle to Ge—ge Ch—ne, M.D., F.R.S. Upon His Essay of Health and Long Life* (London, 1725); Edward Strother, *An Essay on Sickness and Health . . . In Which Dr. Cheyne's Mistaken Opinions in His Late Essay Are Occasionally Taken Notice Of* (London, 1725); George Cheyne, *The English Malady* (London, 1733), ii (quote).

36. Cheyne, *Essay of Health,* xiii, xiv.

CHAPTER SIX—AMERICAN ICONS

1. Trustees of Georgia, "Rules of the Year 1735," quoted in Waverly Root and Richard de Rochemont, *Eating in America: A History* (Hopewell, N.J.: Ecco Press, 1995), 86.

2. Francis Moore, "A Voyage to Georgia, Begun in the year 1735," in Wayne D. Rasmussen, ed., *Agriculture in the United States* (New York: Random House, 1975), 1: 141; James Edward Oglethorpe, "A New and Accurate Account of the Provinces of South Carolina and Georgia" (London, 1733), in ibid., 1: 132–33.

3. McWilliams, *Revolution in Eating;* David Hackett Fischer, *Albion's Seed* (New York: Oxford University Press, 1991).

4. R. W. Fogel et al., "Secular Changes in American and British Stature and Nutrition," *Journal of Interdisciplinary History* 14 (1983): 445–81.

5. Robert Beverley, *The History and Present State of Virginia,* ed. Louis B. Wright (Chapel Hill: University of North Carolina Press, 1947), 129–36.

6. Ibid., 146–47, 153.

7. Richard Croom Beatty and William J. Mulloy, *William Byrd's Natural History of Virginia, or The Newly Discovered Eden* (Richmond, Va.: Dietz Press, 1940), 19, 51–81, 88–92 (89, 19).

8. Beverley, *Present State,* 150.

9. John Lawson, *Lawson's History of North Carolina* (1709; Richmond, 1952), in Rasmussen, *Agriculture,* 1: 153–55 (153).

10. Ibid., 154.

11. Ibid., 154–55.

12. Ibid., 150–51.

13. Ibid., 151.

14. Ibid., 151–52 (152).

15. William Penn, "A Further Account of the Province of Pennsylvania [1685]," in ibid., 122–23 (122).

16. Ibid., 123–26 (123–24).

17. Peter Kalm, *Travels into North America* (London, 1772), in Rasmussen, *Agriculture*, 1: 175–80 (179).

18. *Martha Washington's Booke of Cookery and Booke of Sweetmeats,* transcribed by Karen Hess (New York: Columbia University Press, 1981), 3, 7, 447–48, 456–63.

19. Katherine Harbury, *Colonial Virginia's Cooking Dynasty* (Columbia: University of South Carolina Press, 2004).

20. Gilly Lehmann, *The British Housewife* (London: Prospect Books, 2003), 207, 226–32; *The Whole Duty of a Woman* (London, 1712), 133–34; Jennifer Stead, "Quizzing Glasse: or Hannah Scrutinized, Part I," *Petits Propos Culinaires* 13 (1983): 99–24; Jennifer Stead, "Quizzing Glasse: or Hannah Scrutinized, Part II," *Petits Propos Culinaires* 14 (1983): 17–30; Jane Carson, *Colonial Virginia Cookery: Procedures, Equipment, and Ingredients in Colonial Cooking* (Williamsburg, Va.: Colonial Williamsburg Foundation, 1985), xi–xviii.

21. Spencer, *British Food,* 221.

22. Martha Bradley, *The British Housewife* (London, 1763), 3–6 (5–6).

23. Ibid., 7–31.

24. Ibid., 37, 42.

25. Ibid., 14, 122, 122.

26. Ibid., 15–16.

27. Axtell, *America Perceived . . . Eighteenth Century,* 20–32 (25, 31).

28. Andrew Burnaby, *Travels through the Middle Settlements in North-America* (Ithaca: Cornell University Press, 1960), 4–25 (13, 22, 22, 23).

29. Axtell, *America Perceived . . . Eighteenth Century,* 18 (Schaw), 36–44 (37, 41, 41).

30. William Byrd, "History of the Dividing Line," in William Byrd, *The London Diary (1717–1721) and Other Writings,* ed. Louis B. Wright and Marion Tinling (New York: Oxford University Press, 1958), 533, 533, 554, 557, 544.

31. Ibid., 534, 542–50, 555–61, 565 (548, 555, 558, 560, 548, 556).

32. Ibid., 565.

33. Burnaby, *Travels,* 53–61, 71, 73–74, 85, 89–90, 92, 94, 101, 105, 110 (56, 61, 61, 74, 105).

CHAPTER SEVEN—WHICH GOLDEN MEAN?

1. James Slotkin, *Readings in Early Anthropology* (Chicago, Il.: Aldine, 1965), 80–174; Clarence Glacken, *Traces on the Rhodian Shore* (Berkeley and Los Angeles: University of California Press, 1967), 429–60.

2. Hippocrates, *Hippocrates,* 1: 107–9, 115–17 (115, 117).

3. See the works by Karen Kupperman, Andrew Wear, David R. Connaughey, A. Cash Koeniger, Carole Shammas, Martha Finch, Jorge Canizares Esguerra, and Mark Harrison in Works Cited.

4. Cotton Mather, *Things for a Distress'd People to think upon* (Boston, 1696), in John Canup, "Cotton Mather and 'Criolian Degeneracy,'" *Early American Literature* 24 (1989): 25. See also John Canup, *Out of the Wilderness* (Middletown, Conn.: Wesleyan University Press, 1990), 256–89.

5. Cotton Mather, *Diary of Cotton Mather: Volume 1, 1681–1709* (New York: Frederick Ungar, 1911), 27 February 1696/1697, 2 October, 4 December 1697, 2 April, 20 May 1698, 18 July 1699, 29 November 1698.

6. Ibid., 15 December 1683.

7. Frank H. Ellis, "Four New English Broadsides," *Yale University Library Gazette* 60 (1986): 112–13. See also Mennell, *All Manners of Food.*

8. William Ian Miller, "Gluttony," *Representations* 60 (1997): 97.

9. Dante, *The Inferno of Dante*, trans. Robert Pinsky (New York: Farrar, Strauss and Giroux, 1994), 45–51.

10. Mather, *Diary*, 12 May 1683.

11. Ibid., xxi.

12. Nicholas Bownde, *The Holy Exercise of Fasting* (Cambridge, 1604), 196–210; George Downame, *The Christians Sanctuarie* (London, 1604), 1–6; Henry Mason, *Christian Humiliation* (London, 1625), 6–7, 12; George Buddle, *A Short and Plaine Discourse* (London, 1609), 61–72.

13. Cotton Mather, *The Angel of Bethesda*, ed. Gordon W. Jones (Barre, Mass.: American Antiquarian Society and Barre Publishers, 1972), 30.

14. Ibid., 6 (quotes), 17 (story of king and doctor), 32–38. See also Margaret Humphreys Warner, "Vindicating the Minister's Medical Role: Cotton Mather's Concept of the *Nishmath-Chajim* and the Spiritualization of Medicine," *Journal of the History of Medicine* (July 1981): 278–95.

15. Mather, *Angel of Bethesda*, 6, 33 (33). See also A. Lockhart Gillespie, *The Natural History of Digestion* (London: Walter Scott, 1898), 1–19; Michael Foster, *Lectures on the History of Physiology* (Cambridge: Cambridge University Press, 1901), 121–254; Robert P. Multhauf, "J. B. Van Helmont's Reformation of the Galenic Doctrine of Digestion," *Bulletin of the History of Medicine* 29 (1955): 154–63; Walter Pagel, "J. B. Van Helmont's Reformation of the Galenic Doctrine of Digestion—and Paracelsus," *Bulletin of the History of Medicine* 29 (1955): 563–68; Walter Pagel, "Van Helmont's Ideas on Gastric Digestion and the Gastric Acid," *Bulletin of the History of Medicine* 30 (1956): 524–68; Lester King, "Iatrochemistry," in King, *Philosophy of Medicine*, 64–94; Karl Y. Guggenheim, "Paracelsus and the Science of Nutrition in the Renaissance," *Journal of Nutrition* 123 (1993): 1189–94.

16. Canup, "'Criolian Degeneracy,'" 27; also Canup, *Out of the Wilderness*.

17. For more on William Byrd, see the works by Kenneth Lockridge, Michael Zuckerman, Richmond Croom Beatty, William Byrd, Pierre Marambaud, Ross Pudaloff, Douglas Anderson, Kevin Hayes, and Susan Manning in Works Cited.

18. See William Byrd, *The Secret Diary of William Byrd of Westover, 1709–1712*, ed. Louis Wright and Marion Tinling (Richmond, Va.: Dietz Press, 1941), 30 July 1710, 2 March 1712.

19. Ibid., 22 August, 20, 16 March, 20 May, 10 June, 25 September 1711.

20. Ibid., 22 May 1712 (quotes), 2 February 1710, 18 January 1712, 2 July 1711 (quote).

21. Ibid., 14 May 1711, 13 June, 23 August 1712.

22. Royal Society of London, *Philosophical Transactions* 19 (1695–1697), reprint (New York: Johnson Reprint, 1963), 781–82 (quotes); *Journal of the Royal Society*, 20 July, 10 November 1697. See also Minutes of the Royal Society, 20 July 1697, Sloane Mss., 3341, f. 54, Br. Mus., cited in Maude Woodfin, "William Byrd and the Royal Society," *Virginia Magazine of History and Biography* 40 (1932): 27–29; Byrd, *Secret Diary*, 13 November 1710.

23. Byrd, *Secret Diary*, 24 January 1710.

24. Ibid., 2 June, 5 February, 3 February 1712.

25. Elyot, *Castel of Helth*, 45–46; O'Hara-May, *Dyetary*, 87–89; Albala, *Eating Right*, 136–37; Everard Maynwaringe, *The Method and Means of Enjoying Health, Vigour, and Long Life* (London, 1683), 143–49; Cheyne, *Essay of Health*, 77–87.

26. Byrd, *Secret Diary*, 8 February 1709.

27. Elyot, *Castel of Helth*, 59–62; O'Hara-May, *Dyetary*, 89–95; Maynwaringe, *Method and Means*, 137–43; Cheyne, *Essay of Health*, 89–106.

28. Albala, *Eating Right*, 131–32.

29. Elyot, *Castel of Helth*, 52–53; O'Hara-May, *Dyetary*, 64–73, 97–98; Albala, *Eating Right*, 131–32; Maynwaringe, *Method and Means*, 149–54.

30. Thomas Tryon, *Way to Health, and Long Life and Happiness* (London, 1697); Leonardus Lessius, *Hygiasticon* (Cambridge, 1634); Luigi Cornaro, *A Treatise on Temperance and Sobrietie* (Cambridge, 1634); Albala, *Eating Right*, 57–58.

21. Byrd, *Secret Diary,* 11, 19, 20 February 1709, 13 September, 10 October 1710, 24 March 1711.

32. Ibid., 9 June, 29 July, 30 September, 24 October, 4, 15 November 1709, 10, 12, 17 April, 4 July, 27 September 1710, 9, 16, 21 April 1711, 25 January 1712.

33. Elyot, *Castel of Helth,* 15–16.

34. Ibid, 15–17, 40.

35. Ibid., 42. See also Elyot, *Castel of Helth;* Tryon, *Way to Health;* Paynell, *Regimen Sanitatis.*

36. Byrd, *Secret Diary,* 8 June 1709, 8 May, 17 June 1710, 5 April, 22 March 1711; Elyot, *Castel of Helth,* 74–75. See also O'Hara-May, *Dyetary,* 172.

37. Kenneth Albala, "Milk: Nutritious and Dangerous," in *Proceedings of the Oxford Symposium on Food and Cookery, 1999,* ed. Harlan Walker (Totnes, Devon: Prospect Books, 2000), 19–30; Phyllis Pray Bober, "The Hierarchy of Milk in the Renaissance, and Marsilio Ficino on the Rewards of Old Age," ibid., 93–97.

38. Byrd, *Diary,* 17, 18 November 1709, 11, 25 January, 25 December 1710, 28 April, 13 June 1711; Cheyne, *Essay of Health,* ix; Joseph R. Conlin, "Another Side to William Byrd of Westover: An Explanation of the Food in His Secret Diaries," *Virginia Cavalcade* 26.3 (1977): 124–33; George Cheyne, *The Letters of Doctor George Cheyne to the Countess of Huntingdon,* ed. Charles F. Mullett (San Marion, Calif.: Huntington Library, 1940), v–xxiv.

39. Kenneth Lockridge, *The Diary, and Life, of William Byrd II of Virginia, 1674–1744* (Chapel Hill: University of North Carolina Press, 1987), 104–5; Byrd, *London Diary,* 25–27 July 1718, 6, 7 May 1719.

40. Byrd, *London Diary,* 18, 25, 31 May, 2, 4 September, 26, 27 December 1720.

41. Marion Tinling, ed., *The Correspondence of the Three William Byrds of Westover, Virginia, 1684–1776* (Charlottesville: University Press of Virginia for the Virginia Historical Society, 1977), 1: 370.

CHAPTER EIGHT—A MECHANICAL SOCIETY

1. Dr. Alexander Hamilton, *The History of the Ancient and Honorable Tuesday Club,* ed. Robert Micklus, 2 vols. (Chapel Hill: University of North Carolina Press, 1990), 1: 35.

2. Bernard Bailyn, *Ideological Origins of the American Revolution* (Cambridge: Belknap Press of Harvard University Press, 1992); David Shields, *Civil Tongues and Polite Letters* (Durham: University of North Carolina Press, 1997), xx, 177, 181–82; Robert Micklus, *The Comic Genius of Dr. Alexander Hamilton* (Knoxville: University of Tennessee Press, 1990), 24–25, 34.

3. Hamilton, *History,* 1: 247, 127, 130–31.

4. Ibid., 136–38 (136–37).

5. Ibid., 173.

6. Gilbert Chinard, *Benjamin Franklin on the Art of Eating* (Philadelphia: American Philosophical Society, 1958), 20, 43–45 (20, 43); Benjamin Franklin, *The Autobiography of Benjamin Franklin,* ed. Louis P. Masur (Boston: Bedford/St. Martins, 2003), 94–96.

7. Benjamin Rush, *Sermons to the Rich and Studious on Temperance and Exercise* (London, 1772), iv, 9–20 (iv, 10, 12, 13).

8. Hamilton, *History,* 1: 130.

9. Ibid., 150. See also Dr. Alexander Hamilton, *Records of the Tuesday Club of Annapolis, 1745–1756,* ed. Elaine G. Breslaw (Urbana: University of Illinois Press, 1988), 13.

10. Hamilton, *History,* 1: 54, 171, 212 (171).

11. Hamilton, *History,* 1: 88.

12. Robert Micklus, "'The History of the Tuesday Club': A Mock-Jeremiad of the Colonial South," *William and Mary Quarterly,* 3rd ser., 40 (1983): 42–61; Fajans, "Value of Food," 143–65.

13. Hamilton, *History,* 2: 207–8.

14. John F. Mariani, *The Dictionary of American Food and Drink* (New Haven: Ticknor and Fields, 1983), s.v. "hominy"; Audrey H. Ensminger et al., *Foods and Nutrition Encyclopedia*, 2nd ed. (Boca Raton: CRC Press, 1994), s.v. "corn"; Wilson, *Food and Drink*, 210–15; "Ode to the Homony Club," 23 January 1773, in "Papers of the Homony Club" (Gilmore Papers, Maryland Historical Society MS 387.1, 1773).

15. Joel Barlow, "Hasty Pudding," in *The Literature of the New Republic*, ed. Edwin Cady Harrison (New York: Holt, Rinehardt and Winston, 1969), 224–27.

16. Julius Goebel, *Antecedents and Beginnings to 1801*, vol. 1 of *History of the Supreme Court of the United States*, ed. Paul A. Freund (New York: Macmillan, 1971), 638; George Rosen, "Political Order and Human Health in Jeffersonian Thought," *Bulletin of the History of Medicine* 26 (1952): 32–44.

17. Hamilton, *History*, 1: 190.

CHAPTER NINE—THE YEOMAN FARMER

1. "Letters of Charles Carroll, Barrister," *Maryland Historical Magazine* 32 (1937): 353 (quotes); Michael Trostel, *Mount Clare* (Baltimore: National Society of Colonial Dames of America in the State of Maryland, n.d.), 11–14.

2. "Letters of Charles Carroll, Barrister," *Maryland Historical Magazine* 32 (1937): 187.

3. Richard Bushman, *The Refinement of America* (New York: Vintage Books, 1993), xi–xii (xii). See also Cary Carson, "The Consumer Revolution in Colonial British America: Why Demand?" in *Of Consuming Interests: The Style of Life in the Eighteenth Century*, ed. Cary Carson, Ronald Hoffman, and Peter J. Albert (Charlottesville: University Press of Virginia, for U.S. Capitol Historical Society, 1994), 483–700.

4. *Maryland Historical Magazine* 33 (1938): 188, 188, 189, 187; also Spencer, *British Food*, 213.

5. *Maryland Historical Magazine* 33 (1938): 378–80 (380).

6. Ibid. 34 (1939): 181, 184, 188, 188.

7. Ibid. 37 (1942): 188, 188, 186–87, 187.

8. Ibid. 32 (1937): 353.

9. Ibid. 37 (1942): 198–99.

10. Ibid. 37 (1942): 66; 38 (1943): 189–90.

11. Ibid. 32 (1937): 363; 33 (1938): 188; 35 (1940): 202; 36 (1941): 339.

12. Ibid. 37 (1942): 67–68 (for 1767); 38 (1943): 184–85 (for 1768). See also Trostel, *Mount Clare*, 47–48.

13. Elizabeth B. Pryor, "Orchard Fruits in the Colonial Chesapeake," *National Colonial Farm Research Report No. 14* (Accokeek, Md.: Accokeek Foundation, 1983), 5.

14. Ibid., 4–8.

15. Elizabeth B. Pryor, "Exotic Vegetables in the Colonial Chesapeake," *National Colonial Farm Research Report No. 18* (Accokeek, Md.: Accokeek Foundation, 1983), 2–10, 17–27.

16. Trostel, *Mount Clare*, 57–60.

17. Byrd, *Secret Diary*, 2 March 1711.

18. For the dynamics of distinction, see Pierre Bourdieu, *Distinction: A Social Critique of the Judgment of Taste* (Cambridge: Harvard University Press, 1984), 226–317.

19. *Maryland Historical Magazine* 33 (1938): 199.

CONCLUSION

1. Ronald L. Lewis, "Slave Families at Early Chesapeake Ironworks," *Virginia Magazine of History and Biography* 86.2 (1978): 169–79.

2. Keach Johnson, "The Genesis of the Baltimore Ironworks," *Journal of Southern History* 19.2 (1953): 175–76; "Baltimore Company Accounts" (Carroll-Maccubbin Papers, Maryland Historical Society). *Maryland Historical Magazine* 31 (1936): 306 (for 1755); 32

(1937): 348 (for August 1758); 33 (1938): 192, 383–84; 34 (1939): 186–87 (for 1764).

3. Anne Yentsch, "Hot, Nourishing, and Culturally Potent: The Transfer of West African Cooking Traditions to the Chesapeake," *Sage* 9 (1995): 15–29.

4. Lorena S. Walsh, *From Calabar to Carter's Grove* (Charlottesville: University of Virginia Press, 1997), 75–79, 101–2, 290; Philip D. Morgan, *Slave Counterpoint* (Chapel Hill: Omohundro Institute for Early American History and Culture, 1998), 134; McWilliams, *Revolution in Eating*, 114–18, particularly 115 for both Byrd and Washington on maize.

5. Lewis C. Gray, *History of Agriculture in the Southern United States to 1860* (Washington, D.C.: Carnegie Institute, 1933), 1: 563–65; Kenneth Stampp, *The Peculiar Institution: Slavery in the Ante-Bellum South* (New York: Knopf, 1956), 282; Leslie Howard Owens, *This Species of Property* (New York: Oxford University Press, 1976), 50–69; Richard S. Dunn, *Sugar and Slaves* (Chapel Hill: University of North Carolina Press, 1973), 278–79; Richard Sutch, "The Care and Feeding of Slaves," in *Reckoning with Slavery*, ed. Paul A. David et al. (New York: Oxford University Press, 1976), 231–301; Eugene Genovese, *Roll, Jordan, Roll: The World the Slaves Made* (New York: Vintage Books, 1976), 62–63, 603–4, 638–39; Ronald L. Lewis, *Coal, Iron, and Slaves* (Westport, Conn.: Greenwood Press, 1979), 153–54, 160–62; Gloria Main, *Tobacco Colony* (Princeton, N.J.: Princeton University Press, 1982), 136; Philip D. Morgan, "Work and Culture: The Task System and the World of Low Country Blacks, 1700–1880," *William and Mary Quarterly*, 3rd ser., 39 (1982): 569–75; Stacy Moore Gibbons, "'Established and Well-Cultivated' Afro-American Foodways in Early Virginia," *Virginia Cavalcade* 39 (1989): 70–83; Elizabeth J. Reitz, Tyson Gibbs, and Ted. A. Rathbun, "Archaeological Evidence for Subsistence on Coastal Plantations," in *The Archaeology of Slavery and Plantation Life*, ed. Teresa A. Singleton (Orlando: Academic Press, 1985), 163–91; Diana C. Crader, "Slave Diet at Monticello," *American Antiquity* 55.4 (1990): 690–717; Patricia Samford, "The Archaeology of African-American Slavery and Material Culture," *William and Mary Quarterly*, 3rd ser., 53 (1996): 95–97; Eric Klingelhofer, "Aspects of Early Afro-American Material Culture: Artifacts from the Slave Quarters at Garrison Plantation, Maryland," *Historical Archaeology* 21 (1987): 112–19; Walsh, *Carter's Grove*, 86, 89, 194–200, 293; Yentsch, "Hot, Nourishing, and Culturally Potent," 23.

6. Morgan, *Counterpoint*, 134–41 (141).

7. Beatty and Mulloy. *Byrd's Natural History*, 51–81, for the hundred pages on gastronomic paradise; Thomas Jefferson, *Notes on the State of Virginia*, ed. William Peden (Chapel Hill: University of North Carolina Press for the Institute of Early American History and Culture, 1982), 38–43, 65–72.

8. Jefferson, *Notes*, 47. All references to Buffon are taken from Jefferson's text, which synthesized numerous sections of the multivolume Georges Louis Leclerc, comte de Buffon, *Histoire Naturelle, Générale et Particulière* (Paris, 1749–1804).

9. Jefferson, *Notes*, 58–59. See also Gilbert Chinard, "Eighteenth-Century Theories on America as a Human Habitat," *Proceedings of the American Philosophical Society* 91 (1947): 28–38; Kupperman, "Fear of Hot Climates."

10. Jefferson, *Notes*, 47, 50–52, 63 (47, 63).

11. Ibid., 58, 62. See also Chinard, "Eighteenth-Century Theories," 30.

Works Cited

Albala, Kenneth. *Eating Right in the Renaissance*. Berkeley and Los Angeles: University of California Press, 2002.

———. "Milk: Nutritious and Dangerous." In *Proceedings of the Oxford Symposium on Food and Cookery, 1999*, ed. Harlan Walker, 19–30. Totnes, Devon: Prospect Books, 2000.

Anderson, Douglas. "Plotting William Byrd." *William and Mary Quarterly*, 3rd ser., 55 (1999): 701–22.

Appleby, Andrew. *Famine in Tudor and Stuart England*. Stanford: Stanford University Press, 1978.

Arbuthnot, John. *An Essay Concerning the Nature of Aliments and the Choice of Them, According to the Different Constitutions of Human Bodies*. London, 1731.

Aristotle. *The Complete Works of Aristotle*. Edited by Jonathan Barnes. Princeton: Princeton University Press, 1984.

The Art of Cookery Refin'd and Augmented. London, 1654.

Axtell, James, ed. *America Perceived: A View from Abroad in the Seventeenth Century*. West Haven, Conn.: Pendulum Press, 1974.

———. *America Perceived: A View from Abroad in the Eighteenth Century*. West Haven, Conn.: Pendulum Press, 1974.

Bailyn, Bernard. *Ideological Origins of the American Revolution*. Cambridge: Belknap Press of Harvard University Press, 1992.

"Baltimore Company Accounts." Carroll-Macubbin Papers. Maryland Historical Society.

Barlow, Joel. "Hasty Pudding." In *The Literature of the New Republic*, ed. Edwin Cady Harrison. 2nd ed. New York: Holt, Rinehardt and Winston, 1969.

Beatty, Richmond Croom. *William Byrd of Westover*. Boston: Houghton Mifflin, 1932.

Beatty, Richmond Croom, and William J. Mulloy. *William Byrd's Natural History of Virginia, or The Newly Discovered Eden*. Richmond, Va.: Dietz Press, 1940.

Beverley, Robert. *The History and Present State of Virginia*. Edited by Louis B. Wright. Chapel Hill: University of North Carolina Press, 1947.

Blanton, Wyndham B. "Epidemics, Real and Imaginary, and Other Factors Influencing Seventeenth-Century Virginia's Population." *Bulletin of the History of Medicine* 31 (1957): 54–62.

———. *Medicine in Virginia in the Seventeenth Century*. Richmond: William Byrd, 1930.

Boulton, Alexander O. "The American Paradox: Jeffersonian Equality and Racial Science." *American Quarterly* 47 (1995): 467–92.

Bourdieu, Pierre. *Distinction: A Social Critique of the Judgment of Taste*. Cambridge: Harvard University Press, 1984.

Bownde, Nicholas. *The Holy Exercise of Fasting*. Cambridge, 1604.

Bradford, William. *Of Plymouth Plantation, 1620–1647*. Edited by Samuel Eliot Morison. New York: Modern Library, 1967.

Bradley, Martha. *The British Housewife*. London, 1763.

Brears, Peter. *Food and Cooking in Sixteenth-Century Britain*. London: English Heritage, 2001.

Breen, Timothy. *The Marketplace of Revolution*. New York: Oxford University Press, 2004.

Bridenbaugh, Carl. *Jamestown, 1544–1699*. New York: Oxford University Press, 1980.

Brown, Alexander. *The Genesis of the United States*. New York: Russell and Russell, 1964.

Bruce, Philip Alexander. *Economic History of Virginia in the Seventeenth Century*. New York: Macmillan, 1896.

Bruce, Susan, ed. *Three Early Modern Utopias*. Oxford: Oxford University Press, 1999.

Buddle, George. *A Short and Plaine Discourse*. London, 1609.

Burnaby, Andrew. *Travels through the Middle Settlements in North-America*. Ithaca: Cornell University Press, 1960.

Burns, Chester. "The Non-naturals: A Paradox in the Western Concept of Health." *Journal of Medicine and Philosophy* 1 (1976): 202–11.

Bushman, Richard. *The Refinement of America*. New York: Vintage Books, 1993.

Byrd, William. *Another Secret Diary of William Byrd of Westover for the Years 1739–1741*. Edited by Maude H. Woodfin, translated by Marion Tinling. Richmond, Va.: Dietz Press, 1942.

———. *The London Diary (1717–1721) and Other Writings*. Edited by Louis B. Wright and Marion Tinling. New York: Oxford University Press, 1958.

———. *The Secret Diary of William Byrd of Westover, 1709–1712*. Edited by Louis Wright and Marion Tinling. Richmond, Va.: Dietz Press, 1941.

———. *William Byrd's Natural History of Virginia, or The Newly Discovered Eden*. Edited by Richmond Croom Beatty and William J. Mulloy. Richmond, Va.: The Dietz Press, 1940.

Canizares Esguerra, Jorge. "New World, New Stars: Patriotic Astrology and the Invention of Indian and Creole Bodies in Colonial Spanish America, 1600–1650." *American Historical Review* 104 (1999): 33–68.

Canup, John. "Cotton Mather and 'Criolian Degeneracy.'" *Early American Literature* 24 (1989): 25.

———. *Out of the Wilderness*. Middletown, Conn.: Wesleyan University Press, 1990.

Carroll, Charles. "Letters of Charles Carroll, Barrister." *Maryland Historical Magazine* 31 (1936): 298–332; 32 (1937): 35–46, 174–90, 348–65; 33 (1938): 187–202, 374–88; 34 (1939): 180–89; 35 (1940): 200–207; 36 (1941): 70–73, 336–44; 37 (1942): 57–68, 414–19; 38 (1943): 181–91, 362–69.

Carson, Barbara. *Ambitious Appetites: Dining Behavior and Patterns of Consumption in Federal Washington*. Washington, D.C.: American Institute of Architects, 1990.

Carson, Cary. "The Consumer Revolution in Colonial British America: Why Demand?" In *Of Consuming Interests: The Style of Life in the Eighteenth Century*, ed. Cary Carson, Ronald Hoffman, and Peter J. Albert, 483–700. Charlottesville: University Press of Virginia, for U.S. Capitol Historical Society, 1994.

Carson, Jane. *Colonial Virginia Cookery: Procedures, Equipment, and Ingredients in Colonial Cooking*. Williamsburg, Va.: Colonial Williamsburg Foundation, 1985.

Catesby, Mark. *The Natural History of Carolina, Florida, and the Bahama Islands. . . .* 2 vols. London, 1731–1743.

Cheyne, George. *The English Malady*. London, 1733.

———. *An Essay of Health and Long Life*. London, 1724.

———. *An Essay on Regimen*. London, 1740.

———. *The Letters of Doctor George Cheyne to the Countess of Huntingdon*. Edited by Charles F. Mullett. San Marino Calif.: Huntington Library, 1940.

Chinard, Gilbert. *Benjamin Franklin on the Art of Eating*. Philadelphia: American Philosophical Society, 1958.

———. "Eighteenth-Century Theories on America as a Human Habitat." *Proceedings of the American Philosophical Society* 91 (1947): 27–57.

Cogan, Thomas. *The Haven of Health*. London, 1584.

Cohen, I. Bernard. *Science and the Founding Fathers: Science in the Political Thought of Jefferson, Franklin, Adams, and Madison*. New York: W. W. Norton, 1997.

Conlin, Joseph R. "Another Side to William Byrd of Westover: An Explanation of the Food in His Secret Diaries." *Virginia Cavalcade* 26.3 (1977): 124–33.

Connaughey, David R. "Medical Landscapes: The Perceived Links between Environment, Health, and Disease in Pre-twentieth-century North America." Ph.D. diss., University of North Carolina, 1986.

Cornaro, Luigi. *A Treatise on Temperance and Sobrietie.* Cambridge, 1634.

Cottom, Daniel. *Cannibals and Philosophers: Bodies of Enlightenment.* Baltimore: Johns Hopkins University Press, 2001.

Crader, Diana C. "Slave Diet at Monticello." *American Antiquity* 55.4 (1990): 690–717.

Dante [Alighieri]. *The Inferno of Dante.* Translated by Robert Pinsky. New York: Farrar, Strauss and Giroux, 1994.

Daston, Lorraine, and Katharine Park. "Hermaphroditism in Renaissance France." *Critical Matrix* 1 (1985): 1–19.

Downame, George. *The Christians Sanctuarie.* London, 1604.

Drummond, J. C., and Anne Wilbraham. *The Englishman's Food.* London: Jonathan Cape, 1958.

Dunn, Richard S. *Sugar and Slaves.* Chapel Hill: University of North Carolina Press, 1973.

Earle, Carville V. "Environment, Disease, and Mortality in Early Virginia." In *The Chesapeake in the Seventeenth Century: Essays on Anglo-American Society,* ed. Thad W. Tate and David L. Ammerman, 96–125. Williamsburg: Institute of Early American Culture and History, 1979.

Ellis, Frank H. "Four New English Broadsides." *Yale University Library Gazette* 60 (1986): 111–18.

Elyot, Thomas. *Castel of Helth.* London, 1541.

Emerson, Everett, ed. *Letters from New England: The Massachusetts Bay Colony, 1629–1638.* Amherst, Mass.: University of Massachusetts Press, 1976.

Ensminger, Audrey H., et al. *Foods and Nutrition Encyclopedia.* 2nd ed. Boca Raton: CRC Press, 1994.

Fajans, Jane. "The Transformative Value of Food: A Review Essay" *Food and Foodways* 3 (1998): 143–65.

Finan, John J. *Maize in the Great Herbals.* Waltham, Mass.: Chronica Botanica, 1950.

Finch, Martha. "'Civilized' Bodies and the 'Savage' Environment of Early New Plymouth." In *"A Centre of Wonders": The Body in Early America,* ed. Janet Moore Lindman and Michele Lise Tarter, 43–60. Ithaca: Cornell University Press, 2001.

Fischer, David Hackett. *Albion's Seed.* New York: Oxford University Press, 1991.

Fludd, Robert. *Utriusque cosmi maioris scilicet et minoris metaphysica, physica atque technica historia.* Oppenheim, 1617–1621.

Force, Peter. *Tracts and Other Papers.* 4 vols. Washington, D.C.: William Q. Force, 1844; reprint, New York: Peter Smith, 1947.

Foster, Michael. *Lectures on the History of Physiology.* Cambridge: Cambridge University Press, 1901.

Franklin, Benjamin. *The Autobiography of Benjamin Franklin.* Edited by Louis P. Masur. Boston: Bedford/St. Martins, 2003.

Galen. *Selected Works.* Translated by P. N. Singer. Oxford: Oxford University Press, 1997.

Gates, Sir Thomas. "Articles, Lawes, and Orders, Divine, Politique, and Martiall for the Colony in Virginea." In Force, *Tracts,* 3(2).

Genovese, Eugene. *Roll, Jordan, Roll: The World the Slaves Made.* New York: Vintage Books, 1976.

Gerard, John. *Gerard's Herball.* London, 1636. Reprint, London: Gerald Howe, 1927.

Gibbons, Stacy Moore. "'Established and Well-Cultivated' Afro-American Foodways in Early Virginia." *Virginia Cavalcade* 39 (1989): 70–83.

Gillespie, A. Lockhart. *The Natural History of Digestion.* London: Walter Scott, 1898.

Glacken, Clarence. *Traces on the Rhodian Shore.* Berkeley and Los Angeles: University of California Press, 1967.

Glasse, Hannah. *The Art of Cookery Made Plain and Easy.* London, 1747.

Godwin, Joscelyn. *Robert Fludd: Hermetic Philosopher and Surveyor of Two Worlds*. Boulder, Colo.: Shambala, 1979.

Goebel, Julius. *Antecedents and Beginnings to 1801*. Vol. 1, *History of the Supreme Court of the United States*, ed. Paul A. Freund. New York: Macmillan, 1971.

Gray, Lewis C. *History of Agriculture in the Southern United States to 1860*. Washington, D.C.: Carnegie Institute, 1933.

Green, Robert Montraville. *De Sanitate Tuenda: A Translation of Galen's Hygiene*. Springfield, Ill.: Charles C. Thomas, 1951.

Greene, John C. *American Science in the Age of Jefferson*. Ames, Ia.: The Iowa State University Press, 1984.

Guerrini, Anita. *Obesity and Depression in the Enlightenment: The Life and Times of George Cheyne*. Norman: University of Oklahoma Press, 2000.

Guggenheim, Karl Y. "Paracelsus and the Science of Nutrition in the Renaissance." *Journal of Nutrition* 123 (1993): 1189–94.

Haile, Edward Wright, ed. *Jamestown Narratives: Eyewitness Accounts of the Virginia Colony*. Champlain, Va.: Roundhouse, 1998.

Hall, Clayton Colman, ed. *Narratives of Early Maryland, 1633–1684*. New York: Charles Scribner's Sons, 1910.

Hall, Thomas S. *History of General Physiology*. 2 vols. Chicago: University of Chicago Press, 1975.

———. *Ideas of Life and Matter*. Chicago: University of Chicago Press, 1969.

Hamilton, Dr. Alexander. *The History of the Ancient and Honorable Tuesday Club*. Edited by Robert Micklus. 2 vols. Chapel Hill: University of North Carolina Press, 1990.

———. *Records of the Tuesday Club of Annapolis, 1745–1756*. Edited by Elaine G. Breslaw. Urbana: University of Illinois Press, 1988.

Hammond, John. "Leah and Rachel, or The Two Fruitfull Sisters Virginia, and Maryland." In Force, *Tracts*, 3(14).

Harbury, Katherine. *Colonial Virginia's Cooking Dynasty*. Columbia: University of South Carolina Press, 2004.

Hariot, Thomas. *A Briefe and True Report of the New Found Land of Virginia*. Frankfurt: Theodore de Bry, 1590. Reprint, New York: Readex Microprint Corporation, 1966.

Harrison, Mark. *Climates and Constitutions*. New York: Oxford University Press, 1999.

Harrison, William. *The Description of England*. Edited by Georges Edelen. Ithaca: Folger Shakespeare Library by Cornell University Press, 1968.

Hayes, Kevin. *The Library of William Byrd of Westover*. Madison, Wis.: Madison House, 1997.

Heal, Felicity. *Hospitality in Early Modern England*. Oxford: Clarendon Press, 1990.

Higginson, Francis. *New England's Plantation, or A Short and True Description of the Commodities and Discommodities of that Countrey*. London, 1630.

Hippocrates. *Hippocrates*. Translated by W. H. S. Jones. Vol. 1. Cambridge: Harvard University Press, 1962.

His Maiestie's Counseil for Virginia. "A Declaration of the State of the Colonie and Affaires in Virginia (1620)." In Force, *Tracts*, 3(5).

Jefferson, Thomas. *Notes on the State of Virginia*. Edited by William Peden. Chapel Hill: University of North Carolina Press for the Institute of Early American History and Culture, 1982.

Johnson, Keach. "The Genesis of the Baltimore Ironworks." *Journal of Southern History* 19.2 (1953): 157–79.

Jones, Hugh. *The Present State of Virginia*. Edited by Richard L. Morton. Chapel Hill: The University of North Carolina Press, 1956.

Jordan, Winthrop. *White over Black*. Chapel Hill: The University of North Carolina Press, 1968.

Journal of the English Plantation at Plimoth. London, 1622. March of America Facsimile Series no. 21. Ann Arbor: University Microfilms, 1966.

Kalm, Peter. *Travels into North America*. London, 1772. In Rasmussen, *Agriculture*, 1: 175–80.

Kargon, Robert Hugh. *Atomism in England from Hariot to Newton*. Oxford: Clarendon Press, 1966.

King, Lester. "Iatrochemistry." In King, *Philosophy of Medicine*, 64–94.

———. *The Philosophy of Medicine: The Early Eighteenth Century*. Cambridge, Mass.: Harvard University Press, 1978.

———. *The Road to Medical Enlightenment, 1650–1695*. New York: Science History Publications, 1970.

Kingsbury, Susan Myra, ed. *The Records of the Virginia Company of London*. 4 vols. Washington: U.S. Government Printing Office, 1933.

Klibansky, R., E. Panofsky, and F. Saxl. *Saturn and Melancholy*. London: Nelson, 1961.

Klingelhofer, Eric. "Aspects of Early Afro-American Material Culture: Artifacts from the Slave Quarters at Garrison Plantation, Maryland." *Historical Archaeology* 21 (1987): 112–19.

Koeniger, A. Cash. "Climate and Southern Distinctiveness." *Journal of Southern History* 54 (1988): 21–44.

Kupperman, Ordahl Karen. "Apathy and Death in Early Jamestown." *Journal of American History* 66 (1979): 24–40.

———. "Climate and Mastery of the Wilderness in Seventeenth-Century New England." In *Seventeenth-Century New England*, ed. David D. Hall and David Grayson Allen, 3–37. Boston: Colonial Society of Massachusetts (distributed by University Press of Virginia), 1984.

———. "Fear of Hot Climates in the Anglo-American Colonial Experience." *William and Mary Quarterly*, 3rd ser., 41 (1984): 213–40.

———. *Indians and English: Facing Off in Early America*. Ithaca: Cornell University Press, 2000.

———. "The Puzzle of the American Climate in the Early Colonial Period." *American Historical Review* 87 (1982): 1266–67.

Laqueur, Thomas. *Making Sex: Body and Sex from the Greeks to Freud*. Cambridge: Harvard University Press, 1990.

Laslett, Peter. *The World We Have Lost Further Explored*. New York: Charles Scribner's Sons, 1984.

Lawson, John. *Lawson's History of North Carolina*. 1709. Richmond, 1952. In Rasmussen, *Agriculture*, 1: 150–55.

Lehmann, Gilly. *The British Housewife*. London: Prospect Books, 2003.

Lemnius, Levinus. *The Touchstone of the Complexions*. London, 1576.

Lessius, Leonardus. *Hygiasticon*. Cambridge, 1634.

A Letter to George Cheyne, M.D., F.R.S., To Shew the Danger of Laying Down General Rules to Those Who Are Not Acquainted with the Animal Oeconomy, &c. London, 1724.

Lewis, Ronald L. *Coal, Iron, and Slaves*. Westport, Conn.: Greenwood Press, 1979.

———. "Slave Families at Early Chesapeake Ironworks." *Virginia Magazine of History and Biography* 86.2 (1978): 169–79.

Lockridge, Kenneth. "Colonial Self-Fashioning: Paradoxes and Pathologies in the Construction of Genteel Identity in Eighteenth-Century America." In *Through a Glass Darkly: Reflections on Personal Identity in Early America*, ed. Ronald Hoffman, Mechal Sobel, and Fredrika J. Teute, 274–342. Chapel Hill: University of North Carolina Press, 1997.

———. "The Commonplace Book of a Colonial Gentleman in Crisis: An Essay." In *The Commonplace Book of William Byrd of Westover*, ed. Kevin Berland, Jan Kirsten Gilliam, and Kenneth A. Lockridge, 90–115. Chapel Hill: University of North Carolina Press, 2001.

————. *The Diary, and Life, of William Byrd II of Virginia, 1674–1744*. Chapel Hill: University of North Carolina Press, 1987.

————. *On the Sources of Patriarchal Rage: The Commonplace Books of William Byrd and Thomas Jefferson and the Gendering of Power in the Eighteenth Century*. New York: New York University Press, 1992.

Main, Gloria. *Tobacco Colony*. Princeton, N.J.: Princeton University Press, 1982.

Malone, Dumas, ed. *Dictionary of American Biography*. New York: Charles Scribner's Sons, 1933.

Manning, Susan. "Industry and Idleness in Colonial Virginia: A New Approach to William Byrd II." *Journal of American Studies* 28 (1994): 169–90.

Manuel, Frank, and Fritzi Manuel. *Utopian Thought in the Western World*. Cambridge: Belknap Press of Harvard University Press, 1979.

Marambaud, Pierre. *William Byrd of Westover, 1674–1744*. Charlottesville: University Press of Virginia, 1971.

Mariani, John F. *The Dictionary of American Food and Drink*. New Haven: Ticknor and Fields, 1983.

Markham, Gervase. *The English House-Wife*. London, 1631.

Martha Washington's Booke of Cookery. Transcribed by Karen Hess. New York: Columbia University Press, 1981.

Martin, Edwin T. *Thomas Jefferson: Scientist*. New York: Henry Schuman, 1952.

Mason, Henry. *Christian Humiliation*. London, 1625.

Mather, Cotton. *The Angel of Bethesda*. Edited by Gordon W. Jones. Barre, Mass.: American Antiquarian Society and Barre Publishers, 1972.

————. *Diary of Cotton Mather: Volume 1, 1681–1709*. New York: Frederick Ungar, 1911.

————. *Things for a Distress'd People to think upon*. Boston, 1696.

Maynwaringe, Everard. *The Method and Means of Enjoying Health, Vigour and Long Life*. London, 1683.

McWilliams, James E. *A Revolution in Eating*. New York: Columbia University Press, 2005.

Mennell, Stephen. *All Manners of Food*. 2nd edition. Urbana: University of Illinois Press, 1996.

————. "On the Civilizing of Appetite." In *The Body: Social Progress and Cultural Theory*, ed. Mike Featherstone, Mike Hepworth, and Bryan S. Turner, 126–56. London: Sage Publications, 1991.

Messer, Ellen. "Three Centuries of Changing European Tastes for the Potato." In *Food Preferences and Taste: Continuity and Change*, ed. Helen Macbeth, 101–14. Providence: Berghahn Books, 1997.

Micklus, Robert. *The Comic Genius of Dr. Alexander Hamilton*. Knoxville: University of Tennessee Press, 1990.

————. "'The History of the Tuesday Club': A Mock-Jeremiad of the Colonial South." *William and Mary Quarterly*, 3rd ser., 40 (1983): 42–61.

Mikkeli, Heikki. "Hygiene in the Early Modern Medical Tradition." *Humaniora* 305 (1999): 1–177.

Miller, William Ian. "Gluttony." *Representations* 60 (1997): 92–112.

Moffett, Thomas. *Healths Improvement: of Rules Comprizing and Discovering the Nature, and Manner of Preparing all sorts of Foods*. London, 1655.

Morgan, Edmund S. *American Slavery, American Freedom*. New York: W. W. Norton, 1975.

————. "The Labor Problem at Jamestown." *American Historical Review* 76 (1971): 595–611.

Morgan, Philip D. *Slave Counterpoint*. Chapel Hill: Omohundro Institute for Early American History and Culture, 1998.

————. "Work and Culture: The Task System and the World of Low Country Blacks, 1700–1880." *William and Mary Quarterly*, 3rd ser., 39 (1982): 569–75.

Morton, Thomas. *New English Canaan*. Edited by Jack Dempsey. Scituate, Mass.: Digital Scanning, 2000.

Multhauf, Robert P. "J. B. Van Helmont's Reformation of the Galenic Doctrine of Digestion." *Bulletin of the History of Medicine* 29 (1955): 154–63.

Neill, Edward D. *History of the Virginia Company of London.* Albany, N.Y.: Joel Munsell, 1869.

Norwood, Henry. "A Voyage to Virginia." In Force, *Tracts,* 3: 1–24.

"Ode to the Homony Club." 23 January 1773. "Papers of the Homony Club." Glimore Papers, MS 381.1, Maryland Historical Society.

Oglethorpe, James Edward. "A New and Accurate Account of the Provinces of South Carolina and Georgia." London, 1733. In Rasmussen, *Agriculture,* 1: 132–33.

O'Hara-May, Elaine. *Elizabethan Dyetary of Health.* Lawrence, Kans.: Coronado Press, 1977.

Owens, Leslie Howard. *This Species of Property.* New York: Oxford University Press, 1976.

Pagel, Walter. "J. B. Van Helmont's Reformation of the Galenic Doctrine of Digestion—and Paracelsus." *Bulletin of the History of Medicine* 29 (1955): 563–68.

———. "Van Helmont's Ideas on Gastric Digestion and the Gastric Acid." *Bulletin of the History of Medicine* 30 (1956): 524–36.

Parkinson, John. *Theatrum Botanicum.* London, 1640.

Paston-Williams, Anne. *The Art of Dining.* London: National Trust, 1995.

Paynell, Thom, ann. *Regimen Sanitatis Salerni.* London, 1597.

Penn, William. "A Further Account of the Province of Pennsylvania [1685]. In Rasmussen, *Agriculture,* 1: 122–25.

Pillo-Tisanus. *An Epistle to Ge—ge Ch—ne, M.D., F.R.S. Upon His Essay of Health and Long Life.* London, 1725.

Precope, John. *Hippocrates on Diet and Hygiene.* London: "ZENO." 1952.

Pryor, Elizabeth B. "Exotic Vegetables in the Colonial Chesapeake." *National Colonial Farm Research Report No. 18.* Accokeek, Md.: Accokeek Foundation, 1983.

———. "Orchard Fruits in the Colonial Chesapeake." *National Colonial Farm Research Report No. 14.* Accokeek, Md.: The Accokeek Foundation, 1983.

Pudaloff, Ross. "'A Certain Amount of Excellent English': The Secret Diaries of William Byrd." *Southern Literary Journal* 15 (1982): 101–19.

Rasmussen, Wayne D., ed. *Agriculture in the United States.* 4 vols. New York: Random House, 1975.

Reitz, Elizabeth J., Tyson Gibbs, and Ted. A. Rathbun. "Archaeological Evidence for Subsistence on Coastal Plantations." In *The Archaeology of Slavery and Plantation Life,* ed. Teresa A. Singleton, 163–91. Orlando: Academic Press, 1985.

Rosen, George. "Political Order and Human Health in Jeffersonian Thought." *Bulletin of the History of Medicine* 26 (1952): 32–44.

Rountree, Helen C. *The Powhatan Indians of Virginia.* Norman: University of Oklahoma Press, 1989.

Royal Society of London. *Philosophical Transactions* 19 (1695–1697). Reprint, New York: Johnson Reprint, 1963.

Rozin, Paul, et al. "Disgust: The Cultural Evolution of a Food-based Emotion." In *Food Preferences and Taste: Continuity and Change,* ed. Helen Macbeth, 65–82. Providence: Berghahn Books, 1997.

Rush, Benjamin. *Sermons to the Rich and Studious on Temperance and Exercise.* London, 1772.

Samford, Patricia. "The Archaeology of African-American Slavery and Material Culture." *William and Mary Quarterly,* 3rd ser., 53 (1996): 95–97.

Sanford, Charles L. *The Quest for Paradise.* Urbana: University of Illinois Press, 1961.

Shammas, Carole. "English-born and Creole Elites in Turn-of-the-Century Virginia." In *The Chesapeake in the Seventeenth Century,* ed. Thad W. Tate and David L. Ammerman, 274–96. Chapel Hill: University of North Carolina Press, 1979.

Shapin, Steven. "How to Eat like a Gentleman: Dietetics and Ethics in Early Modern England." In *Right Living: An Anglo-American Tradition of Self- Help Medicine and Hygiene,* ed. Charles E. Rosenberg, 21–58. Baltimore: Johns Hopkins University Press, 2003.

Shields, David. *Civil Tongues and Polite Letters.* Durham: University of North Carolina Press, 1997.

Shrigley, Nathaniel. "A True Relation of Virginia and Mary-Land." In Force, *Tracts,* 3(6).

Siraisi, Nancy. *Medieval and Early Renaissance Medicine, an Introduction.* Chicago: University of Chicago Press, 1990.

Smith, John. *The Complete Works of Captain John Smith.* Edited by Philip Barbour. 4 vols. Chapel Hill: University of North Carolina Press, 1986.

Spencer, Colin. *British Food: An Extraordinary Thousand Years of History.* New York: Columbia University Press, 2003.

Stampp, Kenneth. *The Peculiar Institution: Slavery in the Ante-Bellum South.* New York: Knopf, 1956.

Stead, Jennifer. "Quizzing Glasse: or Hannah Scrutinized, Part I." *Petits Propos Culinaires* 13 (1983): 9–24.

———. "Quizzing Glasse: or Hannah Scrutinized, Part II." *Petits Propos Culinaires* 14 (1983): 17–30.

Strother, Edward. *An Essay on Sickness and Health . . . In Which Dr. Cheyne's Mistaken Opinions in His Late Essay Are Occasionally Taken Notice Of.* London, 1725.

Sutch, Richard. "The Care and Feeding of Slaves." In *Reckoning with Slavery,* ed. Paul A. David et al., 231–301. New York: Oxford University Press, 1976.

Temkin, Oswei. "Nutrition from Classical Antiquity to the Baroque." In *Human Nutrition: Historic and Scientific,* ed. Iago Galdston, 78–97. New York: International University Press, 1960.

Thirsk, Joan. "Food History and Food Theories, 1500–1700." Folger Institute Seminar, Washington D.C., June 1997.

———. "Food in Shakespeare's England" In *Fooles and Fricassees: Food in Shakespeare's England,* ed. Mary Anne Caton, 13–26. Washington, D.C.: Folger Shakespeare Library, 1999.

Tinling, Marion, ed. *The Correspondence of the Three William Byrds of Westover, Virginia, 1684–1776.* Vol. 1. Charlottesville: University Press of Virginia for the Virginia Historical Society, 1977.

Todkill, Walter, and Russell Anas. "Occurrents in Virginia." In *Purchas His Pilgrimes,* ed. Samuel Purchas, 480–87. New York: Macmillan, 1906.

Trostel, Michael. *Mount Clare.* Baltimore: National Society of Colonial Dames of America in the State of Maryland, n.d.

Trustees of Georgia. "Rules of the Year 1735." As quoted in Waverly Root and Richard de Rochemont, *Eating in America: A History.* Hopewell, N.J.: Ecco Press, 1995.

Tryon, Thomas. *Way to Health, and Long Life and Happiness.* London, 1697.

Turner, Bryan S. *The Body and Society: Explorations in Social Theory.* Oxford: Basil Blackwell, 1984.

———. "The Discourse of Diet." In *The Body: Social Process and Cultural Theory,* ed. Mike Featherstone, Mike Hepworth, and Bryan S. Turner, 157–69. London: Sage Publications, 1991.

———. "The Government of the Body: Medical Regimens and the Rationalization of Diet." *The British Journal of Sociology* 33 (1982): 254–69.

Virginia Magazine of History and Biography 1 (1894): 447.

Wainewright, Jeremiah. *A Mechanicall Account of the Non-Naturals.* 2nd ed. London, 1708.

Walkington, Thomas. *Optick Glasse of Humors.* London, 1664.

Walsh, Lorena S. *From Calabar to Carter's Grove.* Charlottesville: University of Virginia Press, 1997.

Warner, Margaret Humphreys. "Vindicating the Minister's Medical Role: Cotton Mather's Concept of the *Nishmath-Chajim* and the Spiritualization of Medicine." *Journal of the History of Medicine* (July 1981): 278–95.

Wear, Andrew. "Perceptions of Health and the Environment of North America in the Early Seventeenth Century." *Society for the Social History of Medicine Bulletin* 35 (1984): 11–13.

Whitaker, Alexander. "Virginia's Natural Bounty." In *The Elizabethans' America*, ed. Louis B. Wright. Cambridge: Harvard University Press, 1965.

White, Father Andrew. "An Account of the Colony of the Lord Baron Baltamore, 1633." In Hall, *Narratives of Early Maryland*, 5–10.

Wiessner, Polly, and Wulf Schiefenhövel. *Food and the Status Quest*. Providence: Berghahn Books, 1996.

Williams, Edward. "Virginia: More Especially the South Part Thereof, Richly and Truly Valued." In Force, *Tracts*, 3(11).

Wilson, C. Anne. *Food and Drink in Britain*. Chicago: Academy Chicago Publishers, 1991.

———. "Ideal Meals and Their Menus from the Middle Ages to the Georgian Era." In *"The Appetite and the Eye,"* ed. C. Anne Wilson, 98–122. Edinburgh: Edinburgh University Press, 1991.

Wood, William. *New England's Prospect*. Edited by Alden T. Vaughan. Amherst, Mass.: University of Massachusetts Press, 1977.

Woodfin, Maude. "William Byrd and the Royal Society." *Virginia Magazine of History and Biography* 40 (1932): 27–29.

Wrightson, Keith. *English Society 1580–1680*. New Brunswick: Rutgers University Press, 1982.

Yentsch, Anne. "Hot, Nourishing, and Culturally Potent: The Transfer of West African Cooking Traditions to the Chesapeake." *Sage* 9 (1995): 15–29.

Yong, Thomas. "Extract from a Letter." In Hall, *Narratives of Early Maryland*, 60.

Zuckerman, Michael. "Fate, Flux, and Good Fellowship: An Early Virginia Design for the Dilemma of American Business." In *Business and Its Environment: Essays for Thomas C. Cochran*, ed. Harold Issadore Sharlin, 161–84. Westport, Conn.: Greenwood Press, 1983.

———. "William Byrd's Family." *Perspectives in American History* 12 (1979): 253–311.

Index